28 August 1975

For Roy and Sally:

I hope this brings
back thoughts of good
times together and
visions of a lot more
to come.

The Best,

Chuck

Cromwell and the New Model
Foreign Policy

CROMWELL AND THE NEW MODEL FOREIGN POLICY

England's Policy Toward France, 1649-1658

Charles P. Korr

UNIVERSITY OF CALIFORNIA PRESS

Berkeley, Los Angeles, London

University of California Press
Berkeley and Los Angeles, California

University of California Press, Ltd.
London, England

ISBN: 0-520-02281-5
Library of Congress Catalog Card Number: 72-82231
Copyright © 1975 by The Regents of the University of California

Printed in the United States of America

To L. M. K. and H. K.

My deepest wish is that they could have read this together.

Contents

Acknowledgments

When I began the research on the doctoral dissertation which is the basis for this book, I assumed it would be a lonely period of consulting sources and thinking my way through their implications. To my happy surprise, the effort involved in both the dissertation and the book has been anything but a period of solitary isolation. The most memorable and happiest times involved in this book have been the talks I have had with other scholars and friends. Sometimes I almost felt that I was writing the book aloud.

I have been very fortunate to have had the assistance and encouragement of many generous friends. I am sure that they know the gratitude I feel, but I think it is fitting to state it publicly. It is difficult to generalize about the ways in which I have been helped, but I can state, with no fear of contradiction, that each of the persons mentioned below has made a contribution to me that goes far beyond what appears in the pages that follow.

I want to thank the graduate division of the University of California, Los Angeles (and most particularly, Dean Horace Magoun) and the Folger Shakespeare Library for grants that enabled me to do much of the research.

When I first began the dissertation, Philip Knachel and Earl Miner helped me "feel" my way back into the seventeenth century. Later, the many conversations I had with Paul Seaver and William Maltby helped me to understand the implications of my work and gave me important insights into what was involved in the transition from a dissertation to a book. Six years after I began the research, the book still would not have seen the light of day without the help of Doreen Buerck, who deciphered and typed the manuscript and Alain Hénon of the University of California Press.

One of the most rewarding aspects of doing research on Cromwell is the opportunity to have close contacts with English academic life and British scholars. I appreciate the help of the staff of the Institute of Historical Research and especially the then-Secretary, A. Taylor Milne. It was at the Institute that I was fortunate to meet Robert Latham and Ian Roy, whose knowledge of the seventeenth century is matched by their willingness to share it with wandering American graduate students and scholars.

Professor Ragnhild Hatton welcomed me into her seminar and gave me the first opportunity I had to set out my ideas on the "New Model Foreign Policy" and to defend them in the discussion that followed. I spent many pleasant afternoons talking about my work, and a wide range of other subjects, with Professor R. B. Wernham. Because of him, I looked forward to my visits to Oxford as something more important and enjoyable than the chance to work in the Bodleian or the Worcester College Library.

There are five persons to whom I feel a special sense of gratitude. Roy Schreiber guided me through some of the early problems in research and also read much of the original manuscript. William Lamont read both drafts of the complete manuscript. He was a virtual arsenal of ideas, many of which spurred me to rethinking my concept of Cromwell and the situation he faced. Anne Storer Korr kept asking me the prodding, sometimes almost embarrassing, questions about my work which never allowed me to become either complacent or slipshod about it. Andrew Lossky was the perfect mentor for a dissertation—searching and imaginative in his questions, but never stifling or overbearing in his advice. S. T. Bindoff guided me through most of the research in London. It is impossible to think of my favorite city without thinking of him and a multitude of kindnesses. No one can really understand my feelings about Professors Lossky and Bindoff who has not been fortunate enough to know them as both teachers and friends.

I hope that my friends, who have helped me so much, will think that this book is worth the time and effort they put into it.

Introduction

"The Wogs start at Calais" was a crude, but direct, nine-teenth-century statement of Englishmen's ignorance and distrust of their cross-Channel neighbors. This feeling was also strong in the seventeenth century, and it was reasonable to expect that during the middle decades of the century, while England was split by factionalism and the Civil Wars, the tendency toward isolation and political ethnocentrism should have been reinforced. The commission of the un-thinkable act, the execution of the king, should have pushed the Commonwealth and its leaders into further international isolation. Added to these elements for a foreign policy of withdrawal and negativism was the personality of Oliver Cromwell. In many ways, he represented the stereotype of the "backwoods" squire who had neither knowledge of nor interest in international politics and its power structure.[1]

Remarkable as it may seem in the face of these conditions, Cromwellian England became a new and positive force in the European state system.[2] From 30 January 1649 to 3 September 1658 Cromwell dominated the political scene in England.* He had risen from the secondary ranks of the Commons to become the man who led the attack on the person of the King. Most of his actions during the Interre-gunum have been subjected to close scrutiny, but the opera-tion of one important area, the conduct of foreign policy, has received scant attention. For the most part, historians have chosen to comment on the success or failure of Crom-well's foreign policy without analyzing the motives underly-ing the policy. Success is attributed to his diplomacy because the navy made England respected and feared. Some attention has been paid to the active role that Cromwell played in

1

Continental affairs, and the seizure of Dunkirk and involvement with the Vaudois have been viewed as triumphs for the Protectorate. The "success" of Cromwell's diplomacy usually rests on a feeling that he raised the prestige of England and brought it back to a position of parity with other European powers. The critics of Cromwell's foreign policy have been more precise than his supporters. It has been asserted that his foreign policy failed because he was wedded to a combination of Elizabethan myths and Puritan bigotry—that he was incapable of understanding the new balance of power between France and Spain because of his inplacable, unthinking hatred of the home of the Inquisition and the Armada. This blindness supposedly led to the disastrous attack on Spanish possessions in the West Indies. The attack on Hispaniola and Jamaica had enough of the aura of an Elizabethan buccaneering raid about it to lead some historians to picture it as a sign of Cromwell's desire to return to past glories that no longer fit the realities of his age.

Cromwell's contemporaries appeared more interested in the role he played in the world than have later historians. The most incisive analayses of Cromwell's foreign policies have been made by Michael Roberts and Christopher Hill. Roberts reminds us that we must understand Cromwell's actions in the context of what was politically possible and desirable at the time when Cromwell had to make his decisions. We must also keep in mind that Cromwell's perceptions were shaped by his understanding of the possibility of a Catholic conspiracy at work in the outside world—a conspiracy that was inimical to the overthrow of monarchy as well as to the reformed religion. Hill presents a unique understanding of the scope of Cromwell's foreign policy and offers an explanation for its motivation, the growth of English trade and imperial power. One need not agree with Hill's analysis of causation to recognize that he has succeeded in showing that Cromwell did not compartmentalize foreign and domestic politics in the way that the Stuart monarchs had and which other Cromwellian scholars had assumed the Protector had done. One purpose of this study is to build upon the framework established by Roberts and Hill and to show how Cromwell's perceptions of events caused him to construct a foreign policy that represented the priorities he had established for his rule in England.

Cromwell's critics and supporters—contemporaries as well as later-day observers—have generally agreed that the series of treaties with Cardinal Mazarin of France were the most far-reaching diplomatic steps taken by Cromwell. Despite the importance of the arrangements with France, the process by which the alliance was forged has been overshadowed by the Western Design. The attack on the Indies was certainly more dramatic than the negotiations between Cromwell and Mazarin, but the war with Spain can be understood only within the broader context of Cromwell's view of his position in international politics. It has been widely accepted that the Western Design was an unplanned disaster that catapulted Cromwell into a war with Spain and an alliance with France. The chronology of the events do not make this interpretation tenable. The planning stages for the Western Design gave long consideration to its possible ramifications and the impact it would have on England's position in the broader world context. Cromwell may have miscalculated the effect of his actions (although I do not believe this was the case with the Western Design), but he did not act in haste or without thought. A close analysis of the manner in which Cromwell conducted foreign policy makes unacceptable the notion that he stumbled into war or an international commitment. Cromwell did everything possible to retain his freedom of action and to keep the broadest range of options open to him. Cromwell understood the value placed upon him by foreign statesmen, and did nothing to diminish or call it into question.

During the Civil Wars, politically aware Englishmen became absorbed in the problems of domestic politics. Thus, when Cromwell assumed control of the government, he had broader discretion to exercise his power in the realm of foreign affairs than in most other areas. Many options were open to him, and his decisions indicated the priorities he established for the Protectorate. These options are the key to this study of foreign policy. By determining what they were, as well as how they were perceived by Cromwell, important conclusions can be made about the policies that he finally chose. To identify these options, I have relied not only upon official English correspondence but also upon the views of English and foreign observers, the views of diplomats who dealt with England, and the opinions (sometimes informed, sometimes only guesses) that appeared in personal correspondence, newsletters, and pamphlets. There was a great deal of conjecture throughout Europe about what Cromwell intended to do. Supposedly informed opinions, which appeared at the same time and were often based on the same sources, contradicted one another with an intriguing regularity.

The objective of this study is to ascertain the reasons underlying Cromwell's policies toward France. I regard it as an inquiry into the foreign policy of England, not as a work of diplomatic history or of the even broader subject of international politics. The focal point of the study is the evolution of Cromwell's policy toward France. I have placed other foreign considerations within the framework of how they affected England's relationship with France. In turn, an explanation of the policy toward France helps to explain Cromwell's actions toward the United Provinces, Spain, and other states. I have used non-English sources as a means of establishing the situation in which Cromwell and his advisers operated, not of analyzing the policies of foreign states. I have centered my work on the perceptions held by the men who directed the policies of England, and I have attempted to explain the actions of one state and its leaders. The analysis of foreign policy is, in part, a study of how policy was formulated and implemented. However, that aspect is certainly not the most important consideration I have had in mind. I think that if foreign policy is viewed as an integral part of Cromwell's attempt to govern England, it can provide another way to explain his conception of the purpose of the Revolution and the Protectorate. I am not studying foreign policy in isolation. I am using that aspect of Cromwell's activities as a technique by which to determine his perceptions of his role during the Interregnum. It is difficult to speak of a "Cromwellian" policy until after the expulsion of the Rump, although many of his attitudes were certainly formed before then. The major part of the analysis deals with the Protectorate, during which time Cromwell had greater freedom to enforce his will upon the course of English foreign politics.

Cromwell recognized that the Stuart monarchs had weakened their position in England by not understanding that foreign affairs played a role in domestic politics and could be used to bolster the government. Cromwell did not make the same mistake. The measures he took toward the outside world were not divorced from his feelings on religion, his views on the role of the state, or other vital questions that arose during the turbulent decades of the 1640s and 1650s. I intend to present another way of looking at the real—as opposed to the idealized or articulated—priorities that Cromwell established for his government. Once he realized that foreign policy gave him a means by which he could assert aggressive leadership toward accomplishing the important goals of his rule, he devoted much of his energy toward a diplomatic structure whose overriding purpose was to insure his position as the political leader of England.

Special mention must be made of the most important set of sources for his study, the letters of intelligence received by John Thurloe, Cromwell's close confidant and the man through whom almost all correspondence from abroad passed. Although Thurloe's intelligence sources usually performed at a high level of competence, some reports were marred by a lack of precise information. Another problem was an occasional attempt by a correspondent to present circumstances in a form that he thought would satisfy Thurloe. Cromwell and Thurloe read these letters in a critical manner and tried to integrate them into the world of events that they already knew to be true. We must realize that the letters of intelligence cannot be treated as definitive comments on the events they described, but they are an invaluable source when attempting to determine how Cromwell viewed his position in the world and why he chose a particular line of policy. When the Protector and his advisers analyzed the effects of their policies and possible consequences of future actions, they were largely dependent on the letters of intelligence.

Despite his comparative freedom in foreign policy, Cromwell's designs were often affected by factors over which he had no control. The escape of Cardinal de Retz from a French prison, the "massacre" of the Vaudois in the Piedmont, or Henrietta Maria's attempts to bring her youngest son into the Church of Rome could not be predicted or controlled by either Cromwell or Mazarin. If the unpredictable did not complicate negotiations enough, there was also the unique position of the leaders of the Commonwealth and Protectorate as "men of blood," the murderers of their rightful sovereign.

In addition to traditional political considerations, the respective personal situations of Cromwell and Mazarin played a large role in the negotiations. Both of them had achieved power as a result of a brutal internal struggle; both realized not only the value of power but also its cost. Mazarin and Cromwell made it clear that power was not something to be gathered for its own sake but must be used. Their experiences enabled them to realize the predicament in which the other might find himself. Despite the apparent chasm between a prince of the Church and the Puritan Lord Protector, they were linked through their common interest and the respect they each held for the ability of the other to recognize his own interests and to judge the sincerity and usefulness of a possible ally.

Inevitably, the personality of Cromwell looms large in any analysis of the Interregnum. This study, in part, becomes an explanation of the idiosyncratic nature—as opposed to what might be described as traditional diplomacy—of his policies. A discussion of Cromwell suffers from a combination of too little and too much evidence. Despite the vast number of his speeches and letters to which we have access, there is little documentary material dealing with his views on the outside world and his policies toward it. The extensive comments he made concerning foreign relations were ex post facto statements meant to gain support for policies that had been decided and in some cases already implemented. There is even less evidence regarding the mechanics by which Cromwell formulated his policy. There is, for instance, no way to be sure whom Cromwell consulted about various aspects of his policy or whose suggestions were incorporated into his decisions. The evidence does appear overwhelming that, whatever the decision-making process, the final word was that of the Protector.

I do not think that Cromwell's foreign policy represents one enormous coherent design other than it was directed toward insuring the survival of the regime. There is, however, a pattern that emerged in both objectives and techniques, to the point where the two became inseparable at times. Foreign policy was calculated to operate in the same fashion as had his rise to power at the head of the New Model Army. He intended to go from victory to victory, and not to take the chance of endangering his reputation for success. Cromwell also showed a capacity to bring his idealism into focus with reality. He was able to manipulate situations or delay action until he found a way to avoid making a clear-cut distinction between pragmatic considerations and ideals rather than sacrificing either of them. Cromwell made a virtue out of delaying tactics, using them to boost the price of his support. He was a seller in a seller's market of military and naval power, and he knew it. Important decisions were postponed to the last possible minute as a means of maintaining his freedom of action.

Obviously, this study has one underlying assumption: that Cromwell was a rational political being. By this I mean that he thought he knew what actions were in his interest and that he tried to work toward those ends. It does not presuppose that Cromwell was correct in attempts to identify his interests or in the best way to implement them. Cromwell tried—and rather successfully—to use foreign policy to create a new sense of national interest or identity. This was to act as a substitute for the dynastic or personal loyalty that he could never command from his countrymen. In the final analysis, this idea of national interest was supposed to protect the preeminence of the man who fostered the ideal— Oliver Cromwell. This poses the additional question of whether Cromwell's interest coincided with that of England. Unless one credits him with a huge capacity for hypocrisy and self-deceit, it must be concluded that he saw the two interests as being identical, viewing himself as part of God's higher plan for England.

1

The Establishment of the Commonwealth: Its International Setting

The first two Stuart monarchs refused to allow England to play an important role in international politics. While rival camps in Europe were preparing for war, James I was trying to act as a mediator and peacemaker. His actions succeeded merely in demonstrating the international unimportance of England and in giving his recalcitrant subjects more about which to complain. Charles I, with the aid of Buckingham, did involve England more directly on the Continent, participating in an ill-conceived war that had unclear objectives and even more obscure strategy. The mark of Charles's diplomacy was that he set England at war with both France and Spain, themselves implacable foes and the leaders of the two great forces dividing Europe.

Charles's unfortunate involvement in foreign affairs might have convinced him that isolation was a better policy. In any case, the troubles of the Continent were relegated to a minor position by the King's inability to deal with Parliament. While the Thirty Years' War reached an important new stage with the death of Gustavus Adolphus and the French declaration of war against Spain, Charles I's attention was directed to his attempts to rule without recourse to Parliament.

The efforts at "personal rule" by the King were brought to an abrupt conclusion by the invasion by the Scots and the rebellion in Ireland. Shortly after the King abandoned his capital, he looked to his fellow monarchs for assistance. However, England's Civil Wars were fought with litle outside interference, although the Stuart cause had an emotional, as well as a practical, appeal to other monarchs; the success of rebellion in England might raise serious questions about the efficacy and legitimacy of monarchy in other states.[1]

The natural source of support for the Stuarts should have been France, ruled, in turn, by the brother-in-law of Charles I and the nephew of his queen. In 1644, Henrietta Maria arrived in Paris to raise support for the flagging efforts of her husband, but she received little besides sympathy. While Parliament and the Crown were carrying on their struggle for power, a series of important changes had occurred in France and Spain which not only affected the course of the war between them but determined their responses to England's Civil Wars.

England had far from a monopoly on civil disorders in the 1640s. At the start of the decade, Spain was rocked by revolutions in Catalonia and Portugal, which caused political and financial panic and brought an end to the government of Olivares. As J. H. Elliott has described it, "At the time of his [Olivares's] fall from power, the Spanish monarchy seemed to have no future—only a past."[2] France used the revolt in Catalonia to insinuate itself into the homeland of its enemy, and Spain appeared unable to salvage the situation.

On 19 May 1643, Spanish troops suffered their first major defeat in memory, at the Battle of Rocroi. Despite the military disaster, Spain had good reason to believe that the future was favorable for its cause. A few days before the news of Rocroi reached Paris, Louis XIII died. His death followed by less than a year that of his adviser, the implacable foe of Spain, Cardinal Richelieu.

After Rocroi, Spain continued to wage a war of delay against France, with the hope that a minority reign would disable France even more than the revolts of 1640 had crippled Spain. During the middle years of the decade, the combatants bore a greater resemblance to punch-drunk fighters battling from force of habit than to finely tuned

military machines. One important advantage remained with
Spain—the presence of an adult king.

Philip IV was neither an innovator nor an administrator
of great talent, but he did provide stability. His willingness
to support the policies of his ministers enabled Don Luis
de Haro to assume power gradually and to bring some order
out of the chaos that existed in 1643. By 1647, the successor
to Olivares had obtained most of the powers held by the
former first minister. De Haro's first priority was to cut back
on Spain's worldwide commitments. In attempting this, he
ran afoul of Philip's stubborn ideas of legal rights. The King
was reluctant to come to terms with the Dutch or the French
if that meant compromising his legitimate claims. Don Luis
finally convinced his master that peace with the Dutch was
essential if Spain hoped to do anything more than fight
France to an inconclusive and expensive standstill.[3] De Haro
was to use the same pragmatic arguments when faced with
the equally difficult task of convincing Philip to grant recognition to the regicide government of the English Commonwealth and to enter into personal dealings with Oliver Cromwell.

It had been an impressive feat for Spain merely to survive
the mid-1640s intact. The recognition of the independence
of the United Provinces had only formalized a situation that
already existed. De Haro separated the Dutch from their
French ally by playing on the Provinces' fear of a strong
state on its borders. He had disclosed Mazarin's secret offer
to exchange Catalonia for Flanders. Then de Haro had used
the internal dissensions of Catalonia to win back the rebel-
lious province.[4] By the end of the decade, Spain appeared
to have developed a new sense of stability and to have made
its priorities clear. The bargain struck at Münster, combined
with the end of the war in Germany, allowed the restructured
Spanish monarchy to concentrate its resources on the war
with France.

The government of Philip IV stabilized itself just as the
Stuarts and the Bourbons were undergoing their greatest
trials. Charles I's defeat in the first Civil War demonstrated
the power of the New Model Army, but did not settle the
political relationship between Crown and Parliament. The

King tried to play competing elements in the opposition off against one another. He waited expectantly for the differences between Independents and Presbyterians, Levellers and Parliamentarians, moderates and radicals to tear apart the fragile fabric of the victorious coalition. Charles expected to emerge from the disorder with new power, as the symbol of reconciliation and unity.

Charles's duplicity, and the resultant second Civil War, sealed his fate as well as the immediate future of the monarchy in England. Cromwell and the army were convinced that the King could not be trusted, and that he was "guilty of high treasons, and of the murders, rapines, burnings . . . and mischief to this nation. . . ." He was sentenced to death "as a tyrant, traitor, murderer, and public enemy to the good people of this nation."[5]

The execution of Charles I plunged England into a great experiment in government. It also severed the ties between England and the "civilized" states of Europe. Foreign reaction to Parliament's victory in the war had been unfavorable, but there had been few open expressions of hostility. Charles's death destroyed any goodwill that might have existed toward the cause of Parliament and the rebels. The leaders of the new state were "men of Blood," capable of any crime. They could not be trusted, and something should be done to make them pay for their crimes. The murder of Dr. Dorislaus, three days after his arrival at The Hague, and the expulsion of English merchants by the Russian Tsar were only two examples of the hostility toward the Commonwealth. There appeared to be little, however, that foreign states could do to right the wrong committed against the house of Stuart.[6]

The heir to the Stuart throne looked to the French monarchy for assistance. The restoration of the Stuarts was a minor concern to Cardinal Mazarin; the pressing problem was the maintenance of the royal government's power to govern in France and the successful conclusion of the war against Spain. The victory at Rocroi had been the legacy of Richelieu's efforts to reconstruct the armies of France. He had also left a legacy of discontent and financial problems which served to neutralize the importance of Rocroi. Even before the death of Louis XIII, opposition to the financial exactions of the war had led prominent subjects to question Richelieu's foreign policy. The peace faction drew into its ranks those men dissatisfied with other aspects of Richelieu's policies—policies that were continued by Cardinal Mazarin, his handpicked successor.

Internal stability for France was crucial to carrying on the war, but it was threatened by minority rule and a long regency. At first, the transition to the new monarchy appeared to go smoothly. Most observers expected the policies of the regent, Anne of Austria, to be a reaction against those of Richelieu, a man whom she blamed for driving a wedge between herself and her husband. Experienced men at court thought Mazarin was a political lightweight who would be replaced as soon as Anne felt comfortable in her new role.

It soon became clear that Anne intended to support Mazarin's policies and that the Cardinal was going to continue the course established by Richelieu. However, the prestige and goodwill the Queen regent possessed were not enough to overcome the widespread dislike for Mazarin and the desire to strike at a dead man through his successor.

Before the government of Anne and Mazarin was faced with open rebellion, it had taken its first measures against the Commonwealth. In August, 1649, it issued an edict prohibiting trade with England. The edict echoed customary charges against the new government: its leaders had "bathed their hands in the blood of their King" and enslaved the people of England and Ireland. However, there were further, uniquely French, accusations made. The English were accused of "enriching themselves in the ruin of his illustrious Queen and inforcibly withholding from her that Dowry . . . allotted for her maintenance." The Commonwealth was also charged with breaking the ancient bonds of friendship between the two states and with dispatching "their incendiaries, like Locusts, in all parts of Christianity" to stir up rebellion. According to the edict, the King of France felt himself "bound both as a Christian and a King, by the bonds of Religion and Nature, and the long continued League [sic] between the Kingdoms . . . to restore King Charles the Second our Cosin, to the Throne of his Kingdomes." To do this,

Louis was prepared to pay the costs of raising "eight regiments of horse and twelve of foot in hopes that France would set an example for other princes to follow."[7]

The sentiments expressed in Louis's edict were exactly what the Royalists expected from an anointed king, the nephew of the widow of Charles I. At the same time, the edict must have rekindled Parliament's old fears that France was going to assist the Stuarts and that Catholicism was going to be introduced into England.[8] The appeal to "all the kings and princes of Christendom" reinforced the Commonwealth's feelings of isolation. Parliament's fear of intervention was not realized. France was in no position, financially or militarily, to aid the Stuarts, and its situation was deteriorating rather than improving.

The immediate danger posed by the edict was its effect on English trade. Parliament retaliated by banning the importation of any wines, wool, or silk from France into any of the dominions controlled by the Commonwealth. The ban left no doubt that it was an answer to Louis's edict and that Parliament felt that France had acted in bad faith by seizing English goods while trade treaties were still in effect between the two states. Nevertheless, the tone of the Parliament's reply was conciliatory while at the same time it asserted forcefully its claim to be the successor to the government that had contracted the treaty with France.[9]

Despite its bold front, the Commonwealth was unsure of its position. Its claim to legitimacy was based on the tenuous foundation of being the lawful successor to the king it had executed. It was uncertain whether it could command the support of its own people in times of stress. Aside from other domestic questions, the Commonwealth was faced with a dissident, unpacified Scotland, Continental states that had condemned the murder of Charles, and vocal Royalists who were calling for an international crusade to restore legitimate government. Any activities that hinted of foreign support for Charles Stuart aroused deep concern in London, and rumors of such activities were investigated as thoroughly as possible.

In the course of investigating the possibilities of an alliance between France and Scotland, one of Cromwell's advisers,

Walter Strickland, formulated a plan for closer ties between the Commonwealth and France. Strickland's activities during the Civil Wars made him particularly well qualified to analyze possible threats to the Commonwealth from abroad. Since 1642, he had represented Parliament in the United Provinces. Much of his time had been spent trying to insure that the Dutch would not assist the King or the Royalists. Strickland was certainly more aware than most officials in the new government of the hostilities that existed toward the rebels and of the revulsion that had been caused by the execution of the King. He recognized that there was a real danger of a foreign coalition against the Commonwealth and the crucial importance of France to any anti-English alliance.

On 14 January 1650, Strickland wrote to Cromwell stating that England did not have to fear French cooperation with the Scots, because Mazarin did not respect the Scots and "judgeth them the worst and meanest of men." The opinion was based on Strickland's reading of the dispatches of Montreul, Mazarin's agent in Scotland, in which Montreul had warned that even if France supported Charles by sending arms and troops into Scotland, nothing could be accomplished because the Scots would keep the supplies for themselves and abandon the King, as they had his father.

Strickland thought that England should have more than a mere reliance on France's distrust of the Scots: "It will be in our interest to be fast friends with them [France] thires to be so with us; and that being, noe forraign enemies could doe you harm." He did not think that France could approach England, and therefore suggested to Cromwell that he exert pressure on Parliament to send a representative to France with some proposal for closer relations. Strickland stressed the need for quick action, because he feared drastic changes in the political situation in France. He warned that England might lose the opportunity of "the harvest for us to gather in our friends, which will never be soe conveniently done again, whilst the French will soe wilst we sleep." Realizing that his ideas were not in accord with the prevailing sentiment in Parliament, Strickland justified them by stating, "I am sure it is honourable to do our business . . . and shut the door of the Scots King for all forraign troops: which I am assured . . . may now be done."[10]

Strickland's views were to be extremely important. He was the first of Cromwell's advisers to discuss the advantages of coming to an agreement with France. He also recognized, unlike other English observers, the troubled, shifting nature of politics in France. His view of France was developed as part of a much more important design—a plan to isolate Charles Stuart and to strengthen the position of the Commonwealth. These proposals were made not to Parliament but directly to Cromwell, and they gave Cromwell an introduction to the problems of Anglo-French relations.

On 18 January 1650, the situation that Strickland described was radically changed. The princes, who had led the opposition to Mazarin, were imprisoned, and the Cardinal's position was strengthened for the moment. He made no hostile moves toward the Commonwealth, but some of his advisers were sure he was preparing to aid the Stuarts.[11] Mazarin was certainly not willing to endanger his own situation or the position of France in the war with the Habsburgs just to restore Charles, but if a scheme could be devised that would aid both the Cardinal and the Stuarts, he would certainly be interested. Such a plan was begun in September, 1650, by William II, Prince of Orange, and d'Estrades, the French ambassador to the United Provinces.

The Prince had initiated the discussion by stating that he wanted closer ties with France.[12] Mazarin responded to d'Estrades that these ties should take the form of a break between the United Provinces and Spain.[13] The Prince and d'Estrades agreed on a treaty that included plans for a joint invasion of the Spanish Netherlands and spelled out the military obligations of both parties. Article 3 stated that by 1 May 1651, the King of France and the Prince of Orange would take steps against Cromwell and do all they could to reestablish the King in England. Secret articles appended to the treaty bound William to supply a fleet that was to be stationed in the Channel to act against either Spain or the English rebels.[14]

The effects of this proposed treaty must be relegated to

the "what if" category of historical study. In November, 1650, the Prince of Orange died, leaving an infant as his heir. His death was a crushing blow to any plans he had made to improve the position of his house and to Mazarin's hopes for an alliance against Spain. The men who took control in the United Provinces were part of the faction that had forged the peace with Spain in 1648. The new government in England was the immediate beneficiary of William's death.

Mazarin did not have much leisure time in which to reflect upon the consequences of the Prince of Orange's death. Anne of Austria tried to silence the Parlement of Paris, which had expressed its grievances against Mazarin, the war, and the resultant fiscal policies. The outcry against her actions demonstrated the discontent that existed toward the regency. The outgrowth of this discontent, the first stage of the Fronde, threatened to paralyze the government.

During the parlementary Fronde, the government also had to be wary of an invasion from Spain. The greatest fear was, however, that the government would not be able to exercise its will within the borders of France. The take-over of the Fronde by the aristrocracy brought the crisis to a head. The arrest of the princes and their prompt release showed the inability of the monarchy to cope with the first direct challenge of its authority.

The Fronde enjoyed momentary successes. In February, 1651, Mazarin went into exile, in an attempt to rob the Frondeurs of their most obvious target. The exile gave the Frondeurs a chance to substitute their policies, and their failure showed the almost wholly negative nature of the movement. Even though there were disruptions in almost all parts of France, there was little coordination between them. The Frondeurs—Catholics and Huguenots, jurists and aristocrats—had contradictory goals and no plans for the future.[15]

While the Fronde was threatening to destroy the central government in France, and to render it incapable of continuing the war with Spain, the new government in England was consolidating its grip on the state. The inability of foreign powers to intervene in England gave the Commonwealth a much-needed respite.[16] Cromwell, as the prime mover of

Charles's execution and the leader of the army, moved quickly to neutralize the threats to the Commonwealth. His campaign in Ireland was marked by excesses that led to years of bitterness, but it did succeed in its aim—to slam shut the door for possible invasion of England. As the internal situation of the Commonwealth became more stable, its attractiveness as an ally rose sharply.

Another threat endangering the Commonwealth was the gathering Royalist forces in Scotland. Once again, it was Cromwell to whom the Rump Parliament turned. His expedition to Scotland was preceded by the same type of careful preparations that had marked the invasion of Ireland.

His position in the government mirrored the stresses operating on the Commonwealth. He was the leading personage in the government and a servant of Parliament, but his reputation and power rested on the army. As the political divisions within England became increasingly clear, Cromwell made some effort to bridge the gaps between factions. His efforts had some success, but the real test of his work would not come until—and if—the invading armies were defeated.

Cromwell's victory at Dunbar was not decisive, but it set back the Royalist plans and gave the Rump new triumphs to herald. The campaign reinforced the growing view on the Continent that Cromwell and the Rump exercised a virtual monopoly of power in the British Isles. Many Continental diplomats moved from their awe of Cromwell's military successes to conclude that he represented the strength and solidity of the new English government. Issues dividing the army from the Rump, among them toleration and legal reforms, were part of a more fundamental problem—the definition of why the revolution had been fought and who should benefit from its triumphs. The necessity to protect the Commonwealth against external threats stopped the crisis of the new regime from coming to the surface. England had the outward appearance of an entrenched government, a striking comparison with France which was being ripped apart by the Fronde.

At the beginning of 1651, the position of the Commonwealth in the world was marked by a series of paradoxes,

and showed the importance of appearances as opposed to
reality. The Rump had acquired respect and a degree of
acceptance because it appeared to be in control of a state
with military power. However, the army and Cromwell, the
instruments that raised the Rump to a position of international importance, were the same forces that acted against
the stability that would be necessary for the new government
to exert any long-term influence in iternational politics.
Despite its inherent weaknesses, the government of the
Rump played a more direct and forceful role in the outside
world than any government had since the accession of the
Stuarts.

It might be true that the leaders of the Rump asserted
themselves with such arrogance in the outside world to
compensate for a growing sense of insecurity at home, but
this explanation assumes both a cunning and a lack of
self-confidence that its leaders had not shown in other areas.
The Rump, although often not through its own efforts, had
gone from success to success. There was little reason for its
leaders to expect these successes to end, and no reason not
to use them to build a foreign policy determined to reflect
their ideas of why they now controlled the destinies of
England.

2

The Commonwealth Viewed
from the Outside

While Mazarin and Anne were battling the Fronde, relations between England and France were deteriorating. Constant reports appeared about raids made upon merchantmen by vessels from the other state. Morosini, the Venetian ambassador in France, was convinced that England would declare war on France as soon as the disturbance in Scotland was quieted, and that France would declare war on England if a Bourbon-Habsburg peace could be concluded.[1] He was not alone in the belief that hostilities between England and France were prevented only by their preoccupation with other matters. Apprehension in France about war with England increased when ships of the Commonwealth scored a major victory over the fleet of Prince Rupert. According to Mazarin's intelligence reports, the Commonwealth intended to find immediate use for its large fleet. It was thought that the fleet probably would be sent to the Mediterranean, "where they will reduce France to the necessity of doing the same thing as Portugal."[2]

Sir Richard Browne, the long-time Stuart representative at the French court, thought Mazarin was willing to make concessions in order to gain the support of the Commonwealth. Browne was convinced, however, that England would receive no communication or representative from France until the latter formally recognized Parliament as the legal government of England. Unlike Strickland, Browne did not think that recognition by France was improbable. Therefore, Browne tried to convince some of Mazarin's advisers that France could not pacify the Commonwealth, "but that [it is] inevitable (if Cromwell's forces receive no considerable cheque in Scotland or Ireland) they will make warre upon France the next summer . . . and that they plainly find they have a wolfe by the eare and know not well which way to turn themselves."[3] Browne hoped to show Mazarin that fear of English action could be removed only by one action—the restoration of Charles Stuart.

Compared with other European states, France was at a disadvantage in attempts to come to terms with England. Circumstances forced Mazarin to accept the presence of the leading Royalists, since he had little choice but to shelter the "daughter of France" after her husband's "murder."

A series of events involving Admiral Blake demonstrated how Spain, having more freedon of action than France, decided to mend its differences with the Commonwealth. In November, 1650, a fleet under the command of Blake presented itself before the Spanish port of Cartagena. He informed the governor of the castle that the fleet had come to seize some of Prince Rupert's ships, that were sheltered in the port. Blake stated that he had received cooperation elsewhere in Spain, and assumed that "pirates" would not be protected at Cartagena. In any case, he said he intended to seize Rupert's prizes before "they join themselves unto the French which is likely to be their last refuge."[4]

After receiving no satisfaction from the Governor of Cartegena, Blake wrote to the King of Spain. The Admiral stated that he had been told at Cádiz that the King has ordered Spanish ports not to admit Rupert's ships. Blake demanded that this prohibition be enforced at Cartagena.[5] Within a week, the King instructed the Governor to give Blake the ships he requested, because Spain wanted good relations with the Commonwealth.[6] The King offered to compensate Blake for any damage caused to his ships by the guns at Cartagena, and told Blake that no orders had been sent to any Spanish garrison to receive Rupert's fleet. Blake thanked the King for his expressions of goodwill to Parliament and "his real demonstration of the same,"[7] but also urged that proceedings concerning Rupert's other prizes should be hurried.

At Cartagena, Blake demonstrated the Commonwealth's determination to use force to support its rights. He accomplished more, in a shorter time, than could have been done through diplomatic channels. Observers in France were disturbed by the situation at Cartagena, because it appeared that cooperation already existed between Spain and England. That cooperation might lead to closer ties, which could endanger France.

Anglo-Spanish relations took a sharp turn for the worse (or the better, from France's standpoint) when the parliamentary representative Ascham was killed in the streets of Madrid in December, 1650. The Spanish court expressed its regrets and promised that the murderers would be punished.[8] Parliament's reply acknowledged the King of Spain's statement, but demanded action and stated that there was little chance for friendship between the two states until the murderers paid for their crime.[9]

Despite some difficulties, Spain had established better relations with the Commonwealth than had any other state. She had been the first major power to recognize the Commonwealth, and Spain's representative, Alonso de Cardenas, had made valuable contacts in England. A formal method had been established by which the two states could exchange views and proposals, and they had discovered concrete issues about which they could talk.

The "regicides" who ruled England made themselves acceptable, not by changing their philosophy but by demonstrating their power. Spain was no longer dealing in vague generalities of morality and ideology when talking with the Commonwealth, a posture to which France still found itself confined.

Many observers were convinced that England and Spain would become allies by the middle of 1651. That arrangement might enable Spain to secure the aid of the English fleet in the war against France, and allow Spanish forces to be used against targets such as Dunkirk and Bordeaux. Assistance from England might also aid Spain in ending the

rebellion in Portugal.[10] Despite the expectations of the Spanish government, as well as of others, the Commonwealth
made no positive replies to de Haro's offers of closer ties.

The Venetian ambassador in Spain summarized the frustration of Spain's position toward England. Spain had been
the first state to recognize Parliament, and "they [Spain]
considered they bought it and could dictate the course of
its foreign policy."[11] If this estimate was correct, Spain's
hopes were rudely jolted. Rather than attacking Portugal,
the Commonwealth received a representative from the house
of Braganza,[12] and showed an arrogant disregard for Spain's
interests.

The rhetoric of the Commonwealth toward other states
was extremely abrasive. In the summer of 1651, Cromwell
declared that since England had quieted its internal disorders, it should start thinking of aiding other states to throw
off the tyranny under which they were ruled.[13] This statement was widely interpreted as another sign of England's
belligerence toward all other states, but Cardenas refused
to be carried away by the emotion-packed idea of "establishing republican governments throughout Europe." He
thought that the important part of Cromwell's speech had
been its assertion that England should begin an active foreign
policy, with the prime consideration of strengthening the
security of the new government.[14] Cardenas defined his
mission as convincing the Commonwealth that cooperation
with Spain would help achieve stability in England.

The Commonwealth seemingly reacted in a casual manner
to diplomatic approaches. Even as late as mid-1652, its
leaders had probably not adjusted their attitude to fit their
new importance in international affairs. Once more the
Venetian ambassador in Spain accurately summarized the
Commonwealth's attitude toward other states, saying that
Englishmen asserted with "arrogance, rather than boast-
fulness, that all princes sought the friendship of England,
and because of its military power and commercial prosperity
[England rendered itself] necessary to the whole world."[15]

Although France lagged behind most states in trying to
establish amicable relations with the Commonwealth, this
did not mean that the question had not been subjected to

close scrutiny. In January, 1651, one of Mazarin's close advisers in foreign policy matters, Servien, drew up a lengthy memorandum concerning relations with the Commonwealth. He began with the proposition that nothing could be more prejudicial to the reputation of the King of France than to recognize the Commonwealth.[16] To do this would mean abandoning his cousin and giving sanction to the regicides, a policy that not only seemed dishonorable but might set a bad example for other monarchies. Servien also suspected that the government in England might try to reproduce its revolutions in other countries, regardless of diplomatic arrangements.

Like most Frenchmen, Servien could present a watertight case, in moral terms, for not recognizing the Commonwealth. However, he proceeded to show that, as a minister of state, he could not afford the luxury of considering only morality and Louis's reputation. Servien had to deal with power, and when he got down to the mundane activity of counting ships, he admitted, "England is now the master of the seas." Actions taken by England could harm the war effort of France. There was even the possibility that England would join with various factions within France, and this would "lead to extreme peril." Servien's central theme was that nothing must be done to antagonize England at the present time. At a more favorable juncture, France could act against the Commonwealth. His proposed solution to France's diplomatic dilemma, in contrast to his opening assumptions, was to enter into negotiations with England immediately and "give them the title they desire."[17]

Some diplomats like Sir Richard Browne were convinced that France would continue to spurn the Commonwealth, for honor's sake.[18] Servien noted that France had placed itself in a dangerous position by its outspoken and open protection of the Stuarts. From his point of view, it appeared that France and Mazarin had received nothing in return for its commitment to the Stuarts except the animosity of the Commonwealth and the constant carping of the Royalists. The Cardinal could overlook the latter, but the former was not easily ignored.[19]

Servien's suggestions might have served as the basis for

a change in France's policies if the Cardinal had not left Paris the next month to go into self-imposed exile. His departure added a new uncertainty about any changes in Anglo-French relations. No one in England could predict French policy until there was a clear idea about who would be making the decisions.

Despite Mazarin's exile, a new representative, a Huguenot, the Sieur de Gentillot, was sent to England. His instructions stated that France was willing to recognize the Commonwealth, but only if prior agreements were reached concerning trade embargoes and maritime raiding.[20] His real mission was to insure that Parliament did not sign an alliance with Spain, and to "augment the desire of the English to treat with France."[21] Gentillot hoped to convince the English that problems between themselves and France were only misunderstandings and could be solved easily. He was instructed to propose that all letters of marque granted against one another be withdrawn, that trade be restored on a normal basis, and that the relationship between the two states be regularized as soon as possible. He was also given the power to make suggestions concerning the restoration of prizes and the rights of warships to use ports in England and France, and to propose that both states pledge not to aid the enemies of the other.[22]

At first glance, it appeared that the policies set forth in Gentillot's instructions and Strickland's memorandum to Cromwell were heading toward the same point. However, Gentillot's instructions were based on two misleading assumptions. The first was that England wanted to "regularize relations" with France and to conclude an alliance against Spain. There was no indication that policy makers in the Commonwealth had accepted, or even considered, this. The second assumption was a more serious error, because it viewed England out of context. Gentillot was supposed to deal with the Commonwealth as though it was a member of community of states even though France had not formally recognized the Commonwealth as the de jure government of England.

Strickland's concentration on France and his failure to consider the reactions of any third parties to an Anglo-French agreement led him to ignore the broader effects of closer ties between England and France. His desire for an agreement with France was based on one consideration: maintaining the governmental integrity of the new regime in England. Strickland intended to insure that "noe forraign enemies could do you harm:" and to "shut the door of the King of Scots for all forraign troops,"[23] but he did not consider that those ends might be endangered by bringing Spain into open hostility against England.

Strickland and Gentillot based their observations on a narrow concept of the interests of their respective states. In England's case, this meant recognition and security for the new government; in France's, aid in the war against Spain. Gentillot's offer of a pledge by both sides to refuse aid to enemies of either of them could have been a quid pro quo that was acceptable to Strickland, but not when it was viewed in the context of France's actions toward the Commonwealth. France still asserted that Charles Stuart was the lawful ruler of England. Was it possible, therefore, for France to consider him an enemy of England? Until France changed its attitudes toward the Stuarts, the two states could not even reach agreement on who their respective "enemies" were.

Neither Gentillot's instructions nor Strickland's memorandum represented the positions of their governments. Gentillot was only a temporary representative, and his instructions were subject to immediate revision. Strickland's views carried even less official weight. The papers of Gentillot and Strickland demonstrated another barrier to closer cooperation between England and France—neither state considered the possibility that the other side might be working from a different frame of reference.

Officials from the Commonwealth refused to talk with Gentillot until France granted recognition. This treatment should have been expected, in light of the Commonwealth's treatment of diplomats who had offered it more than Gentillot. He proposed nothing that Parliament felt was valuable or that could not be obtained on its own terms. Even if he had offered more, Parliament still would have to be wary about the instability of the French kingdom.

Gentillot did not stay long in England and after his departure, relations between the two states became moribund. Officials in France were unsure how to interpret Gentillot's mission, and the Commonwealth seemed blithely unconcerned with the whole matter. This is not to say that the Commonwealth ignored France. In February, 1651, the Council of State sent Colonel Edward Sexby, a former Leveller agitator, to France "to give an account of the state of the country and the affections of the people."[24] Sexby's mission and the Council's choice of agents could only reinforce Servien's fears that the Commonwealth was contemplating a role in France's domestic controversies.[25]

Only the Royalists derived any satisfaction from the situation. They assumed that the tenuous links between France and the Commonwealth had been shattered, and that negotiations would not be resumed. Nicholas, with the Royalists' gift for seeing the best in any situation, assumed that Gentillot did not return to England because France had received information from agents in London "about the King's [Charles's] good condition and the great distraction among the rebels."[26]

Nicholas's optimism about a break between England and France was not shared by Sir Richard Browne. He learned that despite Gentillot's reception, France was continuing to sound out the possibilities of an agreement with the Commonwealth. Browne saw no insurmountable political or ideological gap between the two states and warned his fellow Royalists that the Commonwealth's diplomatic position would improve greatly if the government became more secure in England and Cromwell gained more victories in Scotland.[27]

Browne had set out the crucial question facing all the diplomats who dealt with the Commonwealth: could it maintain effective control over its own people? No state could afford to commit itself too deeply to either the Commonwealth or the Royalists until there were clear signs of who would rule England. In emotional terms, the Stuarts represented the true government of England, but diplomatic considerations had to be based on more than emotion.

Many important Royalists did not deceive themselves into thinking that the overthrow of the Commonwealth would be an easy task. As early as March, 1650, Thomas Elyott admitted that "the notorious people in England now have the power and sway in the realm of England."[28] Foreign support was essential for the proposed invasion of England, but most of the King's advisers were convinced that foreign leaders would make no commitments to Charles until they saw the outcome of his treaty with the Scots.[29]

Charles was driven to the expedient of a proposed alliance with the Duke of Lorraine. The Duke had been frustrated in his attempts to gain power in France and Germany and saw a new opportunity in England. Lorraine possessed two important qualifications as far as the Royalists were concerned: an army, and the proper lineage. He recognized his value to Charles, and the proposed price for his services was high. Lorraine said that he would pay for the armies he used to support Charles. In return, he wanted coastal towns in counties Galway and Limerick placed under his control and complete power over the associates of the Duke of York. His interest in the Duke became obvious when Lorraine told Lord Taafe (Charles's representative in the negotiations) that he expected the pope to confirm his divorce. The children of Lorraine's second marriage would then have the rights of legitimacy, and a marriage between York and Lorraine's daughter could be discussed more fully.[30]

The Commonwealth had isolated the Royalists from effective support and forced Charles to fall back on an adventurer like Lorraine. To gain Lorraine's support, Charles was being asked to bargain away part of the little freedom of action that he still possessed and to give up valuable territory and an important diplomatic weapon, the Duke of York's marriage prospects. Even though negotiations with Lorraine collapsed, Charles's involvement in them was a propaganda victory for the Commonwealth.[31] He had called on a foreign prince to help restore the Stuarts, a man who had represented the Catholic forces in the religious wars. This proposed alliance recalled the charge that had been leveled, but never proved against Charles I.[32]

3

The Commonwealth Asserts Itself

By late summer, 1651, many foreign diplomats were convinced that Charles's diplomatic position would be almost hopeless if he did not quickly do something to counter the armed strength of the Commonwealth. The roles to be played by the Stuarts and the "regicides" in the international scene could be resolved only by an open clash between them for control of England.

In August, 1651, the Royalists mustered their resources behind an army that was operating in Scotland. It made some progress, but the problem of supplying it was complicated because many Royalist ships had been impounded by admiralty courts in the Spanish Netherlands. Attempts were made to bring diplomatic pressure to bear on the Habsburg officials, but the prospect for the release of the ships looked dim because "except [if] his Majesty [Charles Stuart] should possibly defeat Cromwell nothing will be ordered for us [the Royalists.]"[1] The best alternative port for the Royalists was Dunkirk, where they thought they could count on the friendship of the governor, d'Estrades. This hope was also tempered by the need for military successes against the Commonwealth, a need that was most clearly enunciated by the Duke of Ormonde when he heard the rumor (which proved to be false) of the defeat of Charles's forces.

I fear that this rub will be enough to carry the business [support from Dunkirk and favorable judgements in French prize courts] against us, if nothing but Cromwell's being defeated, could carry it for us, and if the King be defeated not only our ships, but d'Estrades friendship will be in danger.[2]

There is no need to retell the story of Charles's march toward the Battle of Worcester and the defeat he suffered there. It is important to see how the fortunes of the Royalist army were reported—and received—in various parts of Europe. Contradictory, and supposedly authoritative, reports of the progress of the army reached the Continent. News of a Royalist victory was supposedly greeted with great happiness by de Haro, "because it [the Commonwealth] had not attached so much value to the recognition and friendship of this crown as was expected."[3]

The confusion about Charles was especially great in France. On 19 August, news of a great parliamentary victory was reported in Paris. The Queen of France, "no ways a friend to the Parliament of England," had the news withheld from Henrietta Maria, for fear of upsetting her.[4] Anne was said to be disturbed because she blamed herself for having allowed Charles to go to Scotland and place himself in danger. In the midst of the bad news for the Royalists, she showed great kindness to Henrietta Maria. This solicitude was interpreted by some French Protestants as the opening stage of an alliance that Anne was trying to arrange between herself, Henrietta Maria, and the papacy, the purpose of which was to restore Charles and overthrow the Reformed religion in France. There was a widespread feeling in France that only the internal disorders of France stopped Anne from doing more to aid the Royalists.

In a fortnight, the news from England was more optimistic for the Royalists. Charles was reported to have entered England at the head of a victorious army. There was a joyous reception of this news in the Louvre, and the court was full of reports that the French

are more disposed to believe, from their enmity to the Commonwealth. They are appointing an ambassador to go to the King, believing him in so hopeful a posture that he will soon be the master of several seaports. .

. . Poor as the French court is, they will strive hard
to send the King munitions and other supplies unless
he be suddenly suppressed.[5]

The reports that reached London about the reception of
Charles's "victories" must have seemed familiar. The same
fears that had dogged Parliament in the first Civil War were
repeating themselves. Distrust of France was enunciated in
the statements made by the parliamentary army that
marched into Scotland in 1651. Its commanders stated that
they were fighting Charles, "who endeavoured commotions
at home . . . commissioned Rupert and the French . . . to
the end he might destroy the people of God and the peace
of the three nations: and now being, by his Mother and the
Popish interests abroad, counselled thereto."[6]

The question of future French support for Charles was
rendered academic by the crushing defeat inflicted on the
Royalist and Scottish armies at Worcester on 3 September
1651. The King was left to make his own way, in a most
dramatic and romantic fashion, back to France. Any plans
the Royalists had made, or imagined, for foreign support
were shattered along with the Charles's army. Even the
scheme for an alliance with the Duke of Lorraine—was ended.
Lord Taafe made this clear in a letter to the Duke of
Ormonde.

> The King's disaster [Worcester] has made my negotia-
> tions useless as to the assistance promised the Duke of
> York, nor do I find but it sets a period to the Duke
> of Lorraine as touching his pretensions for Ireland,
> believing it not in his power to redeem them, considering
> how undisturbed and absolute the Parliament have
> rendered themselves in England and Scotland.[7]

Cromwell's victory at Worcester ended Charles's invasion,
but if the Commonwealth had not followed up its advantage,
the battle could have meant little more than the death of
a great many Scots and the flight of the King. After crushing
any remaining pockets of resistance, the Commonwealth had
to make sure that no future Royalist attack would receive

any foreign assistance. This meant, for the most part, stopping France from giving any more support to the Royalists in the future than it had in 1651.

Until the Battle of Worcester, neither English nor foreign observers had cast much doubt upon France's inclination to aid Charles, only upon its ability to do so. English diplomacy had either to change France's feelings or to make France incapable of implementing pro-Royalist sentiments. The most direct solution mentioned was that "Cromwell is resolved the next spring if not sooner, for certain to visit France with a very good army in assistance of Spain."[8] This was discussed among the Royalists, but does not seem to have been considered by Cromwell. Even after Worcester, Secretary Nicholas was sure that "They here [the French] would do something to curb the insolency of the Usurpers in England, were not France by the Prince of Condé's misbehavior [so speak gently of it because he pretends to be affectionate to our Master] so very much embroiled with internal Division."[9]

In the closing months of 1651, the diplomatic position of the Commonwealth was extremely strong. Its military posture was more formidable than ever, and thus it was more eagerly courted by other states. It was free to turn its attention to any threat that might be posed by France. It could count on another formidable weapon: the civil war in France, with its consequences for the war against Spain. It was as if the roles of France and England had been reversed, and the Commonwealth could meddle in the internal politics of France.

The rout of the Scots enabled the Commonwealth to pursue a diplomatic policy that was free of past encumbrances, and to assert its new power with an international scope. New rumors appeared about the Commonwealth's plans to participate in the Bourbon-Habsburg war. The diplomats who tried to predict the Commonwealth's actions saw many, and sometimes contradictory, factors that might influence its decision. Material gain, ideological and religious dispositions of other states, and the treatment accorded the Commonwealth before September, 1651, were the considerations that were discussed most often.

Overlooked in the conjectures about England was the fact that freedom of action included the freedom to refrain from action. It was assumed that England would not remain a spectator in international politics but would use its navy and army in some major project. However, the Commonwealth gave no indication how it intended to act. It benefited by remaining flexible and allowing other states to tailor their diplomacy to possible actions by England. There is no evidence that the Commonwealth consciously tried to build a policy around temporary inactivity, but the distinctive features of its diplomacy—secrecy and amateurism—confounded foreign courts and further bolstered its position.

Foreign acceptance of the Commonwealth's power reinforced the bravado it had already exhibited, and convinced the more skeptical Englishmen of its stature. Foreign opinions about the strength of the Commonwealth were based only partially on its actions. These opinions, in turn, became part of a cycle by which the Commonwealth's confidence in itself was strengthened. This confidence led to the greater unity of purpose that was necessary before the potential power of the Commonwealth could be realized.[10]

The Rump took one important diplomatic initiative before the victory at Worcester. In March, 1651, an English delegation, led by Lord Chief Justice St. John and Walter Strickland, arrived in The Hague to negotiate with the Dutch. The ultimate purpose of the mission, as expressed by St. John, was a confederation of the Protestant maritime powers. Instead, the negotiations became bogged down with the more mundane, and pressing, issues of the commercial relationship between the two states and refinements of the regulations concerning contraband and seizures. In more than three months of negotiations, two points became clear to St. John: the plan for union had no chance of success; and the Dutch intended to retain as much of their commercial advantages as was possible.

By the time the mission left The Hague on 20 June, its members had been frustrated in their negotiations, subjected to a series of delaying tactics by their hosts, and insulted by Royalist refugees. There is little doubt that the experience hardened St. John's feelings toward the Dutch, and his account of the mission added to the anti-Dutch feelings in Parliament.

The Rump's solution to its relationship with the United Provinces was the passage of the Navigation Act of 9 October 1651. It was formally enacted after the victory at Worcester, but had been recommended by the Council of State in August. The structure of the legislation may have represented, in part, St. John's wounded feelings, but there was little that was novel in the act. Its purpose was to insure a role for English shipping in the importation of commodities into the country.[11]

The passage of the act was resented bitterly in the United Provinces. It appeared to the Dutch that Parliament was attempting to destroy Dutch trade. The hostile feelings between the two countries were increased by the decisions of English admiralty courts, which had used the undeclared war between England and France to justify the seizure of Dutch ships bearing French goods. It appeared that the Commonwealth was pressing an aggressive trade policy against the vital interests of the Dutch.

The militant commercial activities of the Rump did not surprise many observers. There had been predictions, some as far back as the first Civil War, that a republic in England would use its potential naval strength in a more forceful manner than had the King.

While Parliament was considering the passage of the Navigation Act, Cromwell was engaged in the campaign against the Royalist army. He apparently made no attempt to use his influence in the question of the Navigation Act, and there is little indication of his feelings toward the Dutch at that time. However, the commercial policy of Parliament had a serious impact on his later actions, and has led to some interesting analyses of the relationship between him and the Rump.[12]

Trevor-Roper has described the Rump's policy as a "Whig policy of mercantile aggression . . . contradictory to the declared views and prejudices of those ordinary Independent gentry whom Cromwell represented."[13] Despite this situation, Cromwell made no attempts to put pressure on Parliament to change its policies or to stop the impending conflict with the Dutch. After Worcester, Cromwell was once again the most important figure in the government. His prestige was unrivaled, and he once again topped the polls for the Council of State. Trevor-Roper has pointed to the Dutch war as showing Cromwell's inability to deal with Parliament.[14] There appears to be more than just lack of parliamentary skill present in his dilemma at the end of 1651. If Dutch opinions are to be credited, Cromwell was not trying to revert to the Elizabethan policy of alliance with the Netherlands; rather, he was a bitter enemy. If conclusions can be based on his later actions, it should also be noted that he did not rush to make peace with the United Provinces after he seized power in England, and that the terms he offered were not lenient.

Other considerations had an influence on Cromwell's attitudes toward the Rump's anti-Dutch policies. He had to face the reality of domestic politics. Despite his personal standing, he did not control Parliament. The council was not in a position to give him the power he needed. Other issues required his immediate attention. There were renewed pressures in the army for the settlement of old grievances—among them the abolition of titles and legal reform. Behind the growing split between the Rump and many army leaders, there lay a question of fundamental importance—what was the power of the Parliament, and how could it be made more responsive to the desires of forces outside it? Cromwell tried to bridge the gulf between the Rump and the army, but his efforts produced little besides a sense of personal frustration.

If Cromwell had wanted to see a change in the anti-Dutch policies of the Rump, the timing for an attack on those policies was not right. Even after war broke out with the Dutch, Cromwell was in no position to oppose it, at the risk of adding new divisions within England. There were aspects of the Rump's policies that recommended themselves to Cromwell. If the Navigation Act could be enforced, it might lead to new prosperity in England. On the other hand, if the Dutch chose to go to war, there were also advantages to be gained. The war would be against a people who had been identified over the past half century with the impoverishment of England, the loss of her trade, and the brutal treatment of freeborn Englishmen who dared the monopoly of the Dutch. War with the Dutch was an opportunity to gain financially and to bring Englishmen together in a sense of national emergency. The possibility of war also meant the chance of new victories and glories—ingredients that had been both omnipresent and crucial in Cromwell's rise. It is interesting to speculate how closely he identified the God-directed success of his own endeavors with the necessity for him to continue an unbroken sequence of triumphs.

Foreign diplomats made another error when they tried to regard England as part of the diplomatic structure that had been raised by the Bourbon-Habsburg war. They ignored the possibility that English interests might operate outside, or in opposition to, the existing struggle. Since the diplomats assumed that England intended to have an activist policy, and that that policy had to operate within the present diplomatic structure, they could find only one answer to the mystery of the Commonwealth's inactivity—the offers made to England had not been high enough or phrased in the proper manner. The important diplomatic guessing game concerned what England wanted as payment and how payment might be arranged.

Shortly after the Battle of Worcester, the Commonwealth received an interesting proposal from Condé. His representative, de Rivière, asked Cromwell for 100,000, 6,000 foot, and 2,000 horse to help the Prince against Mazarin. This appeal showed that Condé recognized England as a potentially, but Cromwell's reply was more significant. He said that he regarded the request as a trifling matter, and that he would personally come with a force of 40,000 foot and 12,000 horse, and would pay for it, "provided the Prince would give his hand to reduce France to the state in which England is today." Cromwell was phrasing his answers in the belligerent manner that had become so characteristic of the Commonwealth. The Venetian representative who reported the episode felt that Cromwell was only mocking Condé for "his imprudence in asking for help from someone who desires only the ruin of monarchies and the Catholic faith." At the same time, the Venetian realized that Condé would continue to seek assistance from England, because "without foreign help, he is obviously going to destruction."[15]

Cromwell's reply to de Rivière opened up a whole new set of considerations about English policy. Unfortunately, most of these were based on whether Cromwell was serious in his offer or whether he was mocking Condé. Some of Condé's supporters, and some outside observers, did think that Cromwell wanted to meddle in the affairs of France. In late October, 1651, Cardinal de Retz (who was sometimes an optimist to the point of self-delusion) stated that he had been visited by Henry Vane, who brought a note of credence from Cromwell. Vane supposedly said that Cromwell was impressed by de Retz's statements about public liberty and wanted to become friendly with him.[16]

In February, 1652, Gentillot said he had learned from "someone with knowledge of the English Council of State" that Cromwell was ready to attack France unless France quickly came to terms with England. Gentillot's informant was positive that most of the council would "joyfully consent" to an alliance with Spain, but there was still a chance to block that action. If the alliance was concluded, England would send forces to Italy and use its fleet against France.[17]

Despite the bad news he had received, Gentillot still thought there was a chance of securing an alliance with England. He had no detailed suggestions, but considered that Dunkirk might be a useful counter in talks with England.[18] Gentillot was not aware that the two issues about which he was concerned—Dunkirk, and English intervention in France—were already being discussed at the highest levels in his kingdom as well as in England.

As early as May, 1651, Dunkirk had become an issue between England and France. At that time, Colonel Popham, the commander of a Commonwealth squadron, complained to the Governor of Dunkirk that pirates from that town were raiding English shipping. Popham said that he had no desire to fight, but that he wanted agents of Charles Stuart, who were using Dunkirk as a base, turned over to him. He also demanded that the Governor disregard letters of marque issued by Charles, because the latter was not a ruler and had no power to commission captains. Popham's demands were not met and he did not press the issue.[19]

By the beginning of 1652, the French hold over Dunkirk was insecure. The city was besieged by a strong Spanish force, and the renewal of the Fronde made it likely that the city could not obtain sufficient reinforcements. One solution for France's dilemma was to turn the city over to England, rather than have it fall into the hands of the Habsburgs. However, Mazarin's first step was to offer it to the Dutch.[20] The Dutch refused the "gift," saying they did not want to antagonize Spain by taking a prize that belonged to the besieging army. There was a more practical consideration facing the Dutch. Had they accepted Dunkirk, they would have been forced to defend it; it was clear that Spain wanted it and that the Commonwealth desired access to it. Furthermore, Mazarin's offer came on the heels of the passage of the English Navigation Acts. The relationship between the two events was probably coincidental, since the timing of Mazarin's offer was dictated by France's military needs. In any case, November, 1651, was not the proper time for the Dutch to make any move that might cost them support from Spain or antagonize the Commonwealth.

After Dunkirk was offered to the Dutch, the Commonwealth renewed its interests in the city. Its Governor was approached by a representative from Cromwell, supposedly bringing an offer that Cromwell would pledge "two million pounds," would furnish fifty vessels and 15,000 foot to join with the armies of the King, and would declare against Spain and all the enemies of France in return for Dunkirk. This offer surprised Governor d'Estrades, who asked for time to consult the court. He accompanied his account of the proposal with a letter stating that he was afraid a rejection of Cromwell's offer would push England into an alliance with Spain. To demonstrate the gravity of the situation, d'Estrades said that he could not hold Gravelines and Dunkirk without assistance from England.[21]

By the end of February, Mazarin had received comments from Gentillot and d'Estrades about Dunkirk. The Commonwealth's desire to obtain the town should not have

surprised Mazarin, but the offer of an alliance must have
come as a shock. However, the Cardinal's reply to d'Estrades
dealt only with the military readiness of the city. Mazarin
said that if it could hold out until mid-May, it would be
saved by massive reinforcements. D'Estrades was instructed
to turn all his attention to the defense of the city and to
forget all other issues.[22]

On the surface, Mazarin was ignoring the chance to establish the type of alliance that he had tried to set up with
England. The obvious assumption about his actions was that
he did not think the proposals made to d'Estrades were
authentic. However, a further consideration entered into the
Cardinal's decision. In March, 1652, d'Estrades received a
message from Paris reminding him that the city must be
held "in order to get a good union and alliance with England."[23] Mazarin had decided to use Dunkirk as part of a
scheme to get an alliance with England, but he was not
prepared to do it on Cromwell's terms. The Cardinal saw
that he could not negotiate with the Commonwealth from
a position of weakness, and he decided that France could
not give up Dunkirk during a time of peril. He was not willing
to give his enemies at home the chance to say he had turned
France into a client state fighting for the interests of the
"regicides" in England.

Mazarin was also taking into account the worsening relationship between England and the Dutch. If a conflict broke
out between them, France would be able to command a
higher price for its friendship. The Cardinal's actions seemed
to be justified when England and the Dutch went to war
in May, 1652. Before the war had started, Nicholas had
discussed its possible effects on Dunkirk.[24]

> If the English make war on this side [the Dutch] I
> am confident they will soon attempt the taking of
> Dunkirk (by the help of the Spanish) as anything, that
> being a place that will be of vast advantage to them
> and that will render them absolute Masters of the
> Narrow Seas and make a good Step toward the mastering
> of these provinces, which doubtless is the principal aim,

tho' these dull Butterboxes will not discern it, nor provide sufficiently against it till it be too late.[25]

Mazarin's calculated gamble, with Dunkirk as the stakes, depended upon the French armies' abilities to save the city. Desultory negotiations continued between France and England until the end of May, but it became clear that Mazarin had decided to maintain the city without contracting any new alliances.

While Mazarin was delaying talks with England, the English council had decided to force the issue. Orders were given to Admiral Blake to use his fleet to intercept French ships bringing reinforcements to Dunkirk. Despite the many rumors about English help for Spain, it came as a great shock, as well as a crushing military loss, to France when Blake virtually destroyed its fleet off Dunkirk. Two days later, its garrison surrendered.

France salvaged nothing from Dunkirk, having lost the city and the diplomatic counter it provided. All that remained for Mazarin was to analyze the new position of France and try to calculate what the Commonwealth's next move would be. Blake had taken only a few ships and no territory from France, but had won a major psychological and diplomatic victory for the Commonwealth.

A Venetian diplomat wrote to his government that the results at Dunkirk showed how much good England could do its friends and how much harm it could inflict on its enemies.[26] He explained that England's aid for Spain had been based on opposition to the continued presence of Charles Stuart in France. The Venetian also stated that the Commonwealth's fear that the Dutch would get Dunkirk had hastened the decision to aid Spain.[27] The latter view was supported by Hyde's informant in The Hague, who stated, "The taking of Dunkirk hath much alarmed these countries who apprehend that it may turn, whilst Spain is in conjunction with the rebels in England, to another Sound, to make all ships trading the narrow Seas pay tribute."[28]

In one blow at Dunkirk, England had reasserted its value as an ally, had ended a potential Dutch threat, and had

thrown France's military plans into turmoil. France's immediate reply was a series of sharp letters delivered by Admiral
Vendome and M. Gentillot. The Commonwealth responded
with silence, and then put on a display of righteous indignation. Parliament maintained that the attack by Blake was
justified by prior French attacks against English merchantmen. Relations between the two states appeared to have
reached the breaking point. But while France was issuing
orders to seize English goods and making belligerent statements, there was a feeling among diplomats that a reconciliation was close.[29] It was noted that in mid-October, England
had received a representative from Portugal, which was
interpreted to mean that Spain did not have much influence
in the Commonwealth.[30] A month later, a Venetian diplomat
commented that England was anxious to make sure that
relations with France did not worsen, even though England
did not fear France, because internal disorders had weakened
France so much.[31] Hyde echoed the Venetian's comments,
and seemed ready to believe a report that Charles would
be asked to leave France because his presence disturbed the
Commonwealth and held back conciliatory steps between
France and the Commonwealth.[32]

After the Commonwealth rejected the protests, France's
anger about Dunkirk cooled quickly. At the same time, the
activities of the Fronde at Bordeaux gave the Commonwealth
another opportunity to strike at the Cardinal's regime.[33]
Mazarin decided that a policy of conciliation toward England
was the wisest course. He did not, as Henrietta Maria and
Hyde phrased it, "recognize the infamous regime in England."[34] However, the arrival of a new French representative
in London showed that the Cardinal wanted to regain the
initiative in dealings with England, and not to leave the field
open to Spain any longer.

Until 1652, no one in England, other than Strickland, had
defined any objectives for a policy toward France. In February, 1652, the Council of State received a report entitled
"A Brief Information of the present condition of those of
the Religion in France, and the way to provide for their
redressment in the present Juncture,"[35] which attempted to
analyze the policies of the Commonwealth in terms of the

condition of the French Protestants. This document extended the religious passions of the English Civil Wars into
international politics. The report brought up a sore point
for many Englishmen—the siege of La Rochelle. Ever since
the siege, the report stated, the Protestants had been denied
their rights at law, had lost their positions in trade and office,
and had seen their churches and schools closed. The government in France had callously ignored the edicts granted to
the Protestants, and attempted to destroy the faithful.
Despite their persecution, the Protestants had remained
loyal to the crown during the recent civil wars. The Queen
had counted on their assistance despite the fact that she
had done nothing for them.

The royal government, realizing that it could not put its
wishes into effect until after the civil war had ended, had
allowed the Protestants to fortify areas like Montauban and
La Rochelle. However, there was no goodwill behind those
actions, and many Protestants thought they were worse off
than before. The Protestants had also been encouraged by
the princes to establish fortifications and take up arms, in
hopes of enlisting support in the battle against Mazarin.
According to the report, the Protestants had not committed
themselves, since they had no confidence in either side. The
example of the Edict of Restitution was too clear in their
minds for the Protestants to take any bold step on their
own. They required a "protector" who could mobilize a
Protestant party throughout Europe for their assistance, one
who could chastise the Emperor for his persecutions and
oppose France and other Catholic states if they should join
in the league proposed by the pope. This protector should
awaken other Protestants to the need for an alliance, and
should cause as much difficulty as possible between Catholic
states. The report revived issues that had been part of the
emotional attacks made by Parliament against James I and
Charles I. The Commonwealth could ignore them in 1652
only by divorcing itself from its psychological heritage.

The "Brief Information" did not leave its readers to
conclude for themselves what England ought to do. It stated,
"The Parliament of the Commonwealth of England, whom
God hath made instrumental for destroying such monsters,

as by an unparalleled cowardice have been the cause of the
ruin of the Protestant faith, and in particular of the French
reformed, seem to be chosen from above in this occasion
and opportunity to repare that breach by the glory of their
reestablishment."[36] Its authors concluded with a four point
plan for Parliament to aid the cause of Protestantism. Parliament should inform French Protestants, through M. Augier, that it knew of, and sympathized with, their position.[37]
Parliament, "since it fought a war to establish the true
religion in England," should fight for the faith in France
and should establish an "in-time union" with the Huguenots.
Parliament should demand that the Huguenots be given the
treatment promised them by edicts, but beyond that, they
should have freedom of worship and full civil liberties
throughout France. Finally, Parliament should exploit the
divisions among the papists in France by consulting with
men like the Count de Davignon, governor of La Rochelle
and the ile de Rhe. The Count was described as a great enemy
of Mazarin, as well as being friendly to the Huguenots.[38]

The "Brief Information" was much more than a statement
of the condition of the Protestants in France. It was an appeal
to their coreligionists to do something to change that condition. The report's oversimplification of the domestic situation
in France was a serious flaw because is authors were describing the situation they wanted to see in France, not the
realities of it. A positive response to the suggestions made
in the "Brief Information" would have defined a new role
which would have committed Parliament to take warlike
actions against France, although it might be possible to limit
them to steps like the attack off Dunkirk. The proposals
in the "Brief Information" had superficial advantages for
England. They could be implemented with a minimum of
trouble and expenditure, they were suited to the forces
possessed by the Commonwealth, and they were directed
against an already weakened foe. The greatest attraction
was that success would wipe away the dark stain of La
Rochelle from England's recent past. The actions contem-
plated in the "Brief Information" would be fought for the
noblest of causes, a purpose for which many Englishmen
still felt the new state had been created.

The "Brief Information" ignored any response by France, which could not be expected to submit tamely to demands or invasion by England. Furthermore, the struggle that would result would mean new expenses for the Commonwealth and might force it to commit itself in the European war.[39] The feelings embodied in the "Brief Information" did help to explain the self-righteous approach the Commonwealth took toward France's protests about Dunkirk. Furthermore, Cromwell's supposed boasts to foreign diplomats and de Rivière about invading France took on more significance if they were interpreted by someone who recognized the presence in England of the sentiments that were expressed in the "Brief Information."[40]

In October, 1652, the Fronde was finally crushed, and Louis XIV entered Paris in triumph. The Frondeurs held only the city of Bordeaux. Their leaders were bound to the cause of Spain; no longer could they claim to be fighting for their monarch. The basic nature of the movement had changed; it was another front in the international struggle between the two great houses of Europe. When the Fronde collapsed, Mazarin was in his second exile. During that time, he saw the necessity to make some drastic move to improve France's position in the war, but the clouds of Münster and the Fronde hung over his plans. The most obvious course open to the Cardinal was to obtain a powerful ally, and the Commonwealth became a likely object for his attention.[41] Mazarin was not alone in seeking assistance from the Commonwealth, an uncommitted state with a strong army and navy. Spain had been careful not to antagonize the English, and de Haro's "government had reason to expect a propitious outcome from its English policy, which was determined by pragmatism, not ideology."[42] England was courted actively by the Bourbons and the Spanish Habsburgs and the diplomacy of the Commonwealth operated within the framework of the advances made to it by the two great powers of Europe.

The Commonwealth might not be liked or admired, but its power was respected. It was becoming clear that it could play a role in international politics. The important question was what that role would be, and on what terms would the choice be made.

4

The Labors of Bordeaux

The loss of Dunkirk hastened Mazarin's realization that he had to establish better communications with England. On 2 December 1652, instructions were drafted for Antoine de Bordeaux, who was being sent to England as a representative of the Cardinal. They stressed the injuries that France had suffered at the hands of the Commonwealth. Bordeaux was supposed to remind the Commonwealth of its failure to act in a friendly manner toward France, and to demand that the "vessels of that new regime are restrained."[1] The remainder of his instructions showed the strained feelings France had for the Commonwealth as well as the respect for its military power. Bordeaux was told to present himself to Parliament, "and after saying that he is not an ambassador," to state that mutual advantages would be gained by closer intelligence between France and England. He was to say that France wanted to treat the Commonwealth with "the same exactness as it did the King of England" and to treat with it "as nation to nation" in the same manner as Louis would from "king to king."

Bordeaux's instructions showed the contradictions in France's policies. He was supposed to influence England's decisions and check the influence of Cardenas, but he was not given the title of ambassador. He was supposed to make sure that the Commonwealth recognized its "guilt" at Dunkirk and compensated France for it, but not to alienate the Commonwealth.[2]

Even before Bordeaux left France, his mission was being discussed in diplomatic circles. Sagredo stated that the release of the Dunkirk prizes was only a pretense for Bordeaux's arrival in England; the real reason was to end the ill will between the two states and stop an Anglo-Spanish alliance.[3] Charles Stuart was extremely bitter, because he had thought that his blood ties would stop France from deserting his cause. When the Stuarts were told that France had "decided to recognize the infamous traitors, notwithstanding all the reasons we have been able to give against it," Charles went to plead personally with Louis.[4] When he failed to stop Bordeaux's departure for England, Charles made plans to leave France. His mother was to stay in Paris and no plans were made for the Duke of York.[5] Before Bordeaux had arrived in England, the Commonwealth had benefited from his mission. The Stuarts' position in France was undermined, the family was separated, and Charles was looking for new allies. However, the situation was not construed as a complete victory for the Commonwealth, since some observers thought that Charles had been assured by Mazarin that France's plans for the Stuarts would change as soon as there were new developments.[6]

Charles's decision to leave France ended a series of steps he had taken to enlist support to overthrow the Commonwealth. In May, 1652, he had tried to act as mediator between Louis and Condé. He had proposed to Louis that Mazarin be sent to conciliate the princes and hasten a general peace with Spain. This idea was enthusiastically endorsed by Royalists like Nicholas, who believed "it may not only prevent any Design that those in England may have upon France, but a good step to a happy and sensible peace between the two Crowns of France and Spain, which all men heartily pray for."[7] Louis's only reaction had been to reaffirm his desire to maintain Mazarin's position in France.[8] The Cardinal's reactions to Charles's attempts to bring peace to France were not apparent, but he could scarcely have forgotten that Charles had also tried to promote the marriage of the Duke of York with Lorraine's daughter a short time earlier. It might be thought that Charles was not only trying to improve his own status at Mazarin's expense but was also acting as an agent for the enemies of the Crown rather than as a peacemaker. In either case, the Cardinal could not have been enthusiastic about Charles's actions.

Secretary Nicholas was sure that Mazarin had turned against the cause of the Stuarts. In October, 1652, he wrote Hyde, "That juggling Cardinal will not suffer the King of France to do any good for the King and I may tell you, I very much apprehend that the design of the Cardinal is (and I pray God some in the Louvre do not concur in it) to keep the King still a pensioner of France."[9] If Nicholas was correct, part of Mazarin's feelings might be ascribed to Charles's peace proposals, but it must also be remembered that Nicholas was writing shortly after the Commonwealth's show of power at Dunkirk. Hyde continued to hope for support from France, but he feared that the military power of England was influencing the Cardinal against the Stuarts. Hyde's main hope was that a series of victories by the Dutch would restore France to the Royalist cause.[10]

Bordeaux arrived in England on 22 December 1652, and immediately started to make arrangements for a parliamentary audience.[11] His first address to Parliament was phrased in general terms, and reflected the contradictions in his instructions. He attempted to show why England and France should be friends. At the same time, he reminded the Commonwealth of its attacks on France, and declared that France could not be expected to suffer these indignities any longer.

Bordeaux tried to emphasize the ties between England and France, and stressed that the union that should exist between states did not depend on their forms of government. England, for example, could become a republic, "but the geographical situation is not changed." The manner in which Bordeaux also criticized Blake's actions at Dunkirk emphasized that it had aided no one besides Spain. In his analysis of international politics, Bordeaux stated:

> You ought to regard him [Spain] as a common enemy, considering the influences of your Parliament, he divides you from your ancient allies [sic] and tries to engage

you in a war with all your neighbors . . . to also reduce you to the necessity of depending upon his assistance. The designs . . . that nation had engaged in against England, their political maxims and counsels of conscience so contrary to your welfare and religion, ought to make you suspect the great zeal with which they have affected to seek your alliance.[12]

Bordeaux was attempting to construct a target against which Parliament would feel compelled to act, by considerations of politics and religion. If the Commonwealth did move against Spain, England would be acting as an ally of France, even if no alliance was concluded. Bordeaux did not confine himself to giving reasons for attacking Spain. He discussed the strength of France: "France has nothing to fear except her own strength. Your divisions, in which she has not interfered, though she was in a position to foment them, and many reasons impelled her to do so, have made you acquainted with the frankness and sincerity with which his majesty is accustomed to treat his allies."[13] He concluded by stating that he knew Parliament would recognize the power of France and would want good relations with it. The latter part of his address was obviously a reminder to Parliament of its past, and possible future, insecurity. He almost made it appear that Louis had been an ally of the Commonwealth while it was struggling for survival.

Bordeaux's efforts were not limited to formal appearances before Parliament and the council. He thought he detected "great zeal for the French cause [among] some of the Colonels."[14] Bordeaux's hopes were raised also by a report from the Portuguese ambassador that the latter had been told by a parliamentary committee that England wanted peace with France and had no intentions of forming any alliance with Spain.[15]

Assurances from sources outside Parliament were the only favorable responses Bordeaux received to his address. On 9 January 1653, Parliament made its official reply, which stated that trade losses on both sides were great, and reasserted that England wanted peace and friendship. It defended, in vague generalities, the seizure of French ships as retribution for the loss of English merchantmen, and gave little satisfaction to Bordeaux.

Bordeaux's early reports to Paris underlined his difficulties in getting any specific replies from Parliament. He tried to convince Brienne that dealings with the Commonwealth would be determined largely by factors over which France had little or no control—the Dutch War, domestic affairs in the Commonwealth, and offers made by Spain. He also noted, with some satisfaction, that Cardenas's audiences with Parliament had produced no results.[16] Bordeaux was reasonably sure that one factor was working in his favor—the Commonwealth had no desire for another war at that time, especially with France. He was aware that his mission was disliked and feared by many Englishmen: some believed that its only purpose was to arrange an accommodation between the Commonwealth and the Dutch; others felt that he represented the interests of the Stuarts and was trying to trap the Commonwealth into a set of alliances and obligations that would set the stage for a Royalist restoration. Bordeaux was bothered by his inability to understand the English position, but was more disturbed by his dependence on official replies to his proposals for some indication of the Commonwealth's sentiments. He was positive that the opinions of the "gens du pays" were crucial to whatever decision would be reached, but he had found no way to discover what that group was thinking.[17]

The difficulty that Bordeaux had in understanding the policies of the Commonwealth was a result of the confused political situation in England, not of his own lack of insight. The big problem facing any diplomat dealing with the Commonwealth was to discover where foreign policy was being made. By the beginning of 1653, there appeared to be no answer to the problem. Cromwell was certainly the most important man in the country. He was becoming the head of state, in fact if not in name, but he was still a servant of the Rump. Foreign diplomats had to exercise great care in dealing with the situation. If they continued to direct their attentions toward the Rump, their efforts might be wasted; but if they attempted to deal with Cromwell, they would probably alienate the "government" of England.

By the time Bordeaux had established himself in London, the political divisions within the Commonwealth had become severe and open. The critical problem was the disaffection shown by the army for the Parliament it supposedly served. The officers and men were increasingly troubled by the Rump's lack of concern for their pay and conditions of service in the army and other reforms it advocated. It appeared that once the army had protected the Rump from its enemies, that the civilian-dominated Parliament was going to ignore its debt to the soldiers. In August, 1652, some army officers had petitioned Parliament for redress of major grievances. The reception of the petition was coldly formal, and nothing was done. Throughout 1652, it became clear that the army was becoming more discontent and that the Rump was unwilling to reform itself to placate its opposition.[18]

Cromwell appeared to share the discontent with the actions of the Rump, but he said little publicly. Throughout the spring of 1653, his attempts to reconcile the Rump and the army became increasingly difficult. The situation had changed dramatically since August, 1652. The army's distrust of the Rump could be satisfied only if fundamental changes were made in Parliament and new elections were held. The opposition to the Rump, even within the army, did not represent a single interest—a circumstance that made English politics virtually incomprehensible to foreign diplomats. This situation, in turn, led many diplomats to create a picture of England with which they could cope, even if it was not an accurate representation of events.

During the early months of 1653, Bordeaux had received only a few unimportant communications from Parliament, had made no specific proposals, and had received no assurance that Parliament wanted to negotiate with France. However, he had worked hard familiarizing himself with the political situation, and had identified the army's growing dissatisfaction, which was dividing it from Parliament.[19] Out of the confusion surrounding the dislike of the Rump, one feature was becoming clear—Cromwell's role was a crucial consideration. Two factions emerged, separated by their opinion about Cromwell's place in a future government.

However, neither of these factions represented a desire to continue the drift of the present situation. Robert S. Paul's description—that the "best distinction perhaps, is to be found in the terms 'Cromwellian' and 'anti-Cromwellian' "—not only summarizes the political situation in England but demonstrates the problem facing diplomats such as Bordeaux.[20] The government of the Rump had one advantage for foreign diplomats—it was already dealing with other states, and thus it had a de facto foreign policy. Neither the "Cromwellians" nor the "anti-Cromwellians" had possessed the responsibility or the power to determine foreign policy. As a consequence, their leaders had said little about the subject. Foreign diplomats were in the unenviable position of knowing that fundamental changes might take place at any time in the English government, but of having little idea which faction they should support or what either faction might do if it gained control over the government.

Bordeaux viewed his task as insuring that France's position in England did not deteriorate. He hoped that he could put France at diplomatic parity with Spain. If he could accomplish this while England's role in world affairs was unsettled, then France could be ready to make a satisfactory proposal when the Commonwealth was in a position to accept it. Bordeaux's first priority was therefore to establish a climate of goodwill and trust with the Commonwealth, rather than to secure any commitments. In order to succeed, he needed great patience, and some good fortune. His personality provided the former; internal divisions in England and the tactics of Cardinal Mazarin, the latter.

By the middle of February, 1653, Bordeaux felt his mission showed some progress. He hoped that Louis's victories over his opponents in France made the Commonwealth realize that France could fulfill its foreign obligations. Bordeaux also thought that the desires of English merchants, "whose profit support the Commonwealth," for more trade with France would combine with the "hatred many have toward Spain" to bring the Commonwealth closer to France.[21] Bordeaux's policy of careful waiting, combined with the new stability of his King's government, appeared to be succeeding when another critical issue arose that demanded his immediate attention.

The remnants of the Fronde had been deteriorating rapidly, and by March, 1653, the rebels' remaining hope was the city of Bordeaux.[22] The rebels who controlled the city made trade offers to the English which might prove attractive to the merchant community. There was also a similarity between the logistical positions of Dunkirk and Bordeaux which could scarcely have escaped Mazarin's notice.

Barrière, the Prince of Condé's representative in London, also recognized that the situation at Bordeaux offered an opportunity to advance his own negotiations. He agreed with Bordeaux that England would take a "moderate course" until its internal disputes were resolved and the Dutch war ended. Barrière also thought that the Commonwealth wanted him to present a specific proposal for assistance to Condé, upon which it would act when the time was right, and that if Condé could raise some money, the Commonwealth would serve him rather than France.[23]

In contrast to Barrière's opinion, the Venetian representative maintained that the Commonwealth was well disposed toward discussing a treaty with France, and that the states "are on the threshold of a definite treaty."[24] The bright picture painted by the Venetian did not correspond with Bordeaux's own description. After discussing a possible treaty with representatives from the Commonwealth, he became resigned to the fact that "there is no longer hope of engaging them in a break with Spain: the sole desire [of the Commonwealth] is to begin a peace with the whole world and not the friendship which would oblige them to accommodate themselves with France." He suggested the possibility that some of the parliamentary leaders might "want to enter some foreign war in order to have some pretext to conserve the army: in the meantime it is certain that the principals want a universal peace [i.e., peace between England and all other states] so as to establish their government more solidly, apart from the fact that the Spanish have many more partisans in this state."[25]

Bordeaux's attitude varied greatly from week to week. In

February, he was so disillusioned that he felt his efforts had "done nothing but diminish the good disposition which England perhaps had for an accommodation with France."[26] A few weeks later, he agreed with a rumor that a tentative agreement had been reached between England and France. Bordeaux thought that the breakthrough in his mission had come when the "general disposition of Parliament seemed favorable [to the reestablishment of trade relations]."[27] The remaining point of contention was the Commonwealth's demands for indemnities for ships taken by subjects of France. Bordeaux thought the question could be handled at a later date, and was prepared to push ahead with a firm agreement that would protect France's honor as well as her interests. However, his government felt he was moving too quickly without obtaining terms that were favorable enough.[28]

Bordeaux had seriously oversimplified the questions that still had to be settled. France's role in the Anglo-Dutch war and the struggle at the city of Bordeaux changed the complexion of his talks with the Commonwealth. M. Bordeaux had been approached earlier by some English officers, who had asked him to assist in bringing about a peace with the Dutch. Bordeaux had told them that his country favored such a peace, but he had taken no further steps.[29] He was aware that his enemies had tried to portray him as a Dutch spy who wanted the Commonwealth to sign a treaty that would deprive it of any possible gains from the Dutch.[30] He avoided raising questions concerning the Dutch war, but at the end of February, a change took place in his tactics. He decided to show the Commonwealth that France was a trustworthy ally, who had the best interests of England at heart.[31] Playing a positive role in negotiations between the Dutch and the Commonwealth might demonstrate his sincerity. Bordeaux held private talks with representatives from both sides about peace proposals and a three-party alliance, and concluded that the responses were favorable enough to offer his services as a mediator.[32] The Commonwealth's response to Bordeaux's proposed role in the negotiations was negative, leading him to complain that members of Parliament are not able to believe in our charity: and when I have wanted to speak to them sometimes about the displeasure that the King of France has to see his friends at war, and that he offers his mediation if they were disposed to accept it, it has been told me that all the world wants to take part, but that when they resolve to come to an accommodation they would not trouble anyone, and that now it is being deliberated whether they should send ambassadors.[33]

Bordeaux had chosen an inauspicious time to try to act as a peacemaker. A series of victories by the Commonwealth made it wary of any Dutch willingness to negotiate. This distrust extended to anyone who seemed interested in aiding such negotiations. Subsequent attempts by Spain to act as a mediator took most of the sting out of Bordeaux's miscalculations.[34] The Dutch were also involved in another situation that adversely affected Bordeaux's position. When he began to interest himself in the Dutch war, there was an effort by some of the leading Royalists to obtain help from the Dutch.[35] The timing of the Royalists' actions almost certainly had nothing to do with Bordeaux or France, but the coincidence served to remind the Commonwealth of the ties between the Stuarts and the French court.

The possibility of English assistance to the city of Bordeaux occupied much of M. Bordeaux's time. Proposals were circulated in the English council to send aid to the beleaguered city and to open a profitable trade with it. When M. Bordeaux asked about these proposals, he was told only that they had not been rejected. He thought it was likely that England might use part of its large fleet to relieve the city, a possibility that prompted him to tell Brienne that the time was right for France to drop demands for reparations for the ships seized by Blake.[36] M. Bordeaux did not immediately change France's negotiating position, but appeared to change the manner in which he acted, leading one member of the council in England to remark that "the King [of France] treats with the Council as tributary kings formerly did to the Roman Republic."[37]

Bordeaux's policies seemed to have the effect he desired. Barrière reported that although some antagonism toward France still existed in England, there probably would be no assistance for the city of Bordeaux. He finally appealed to the council, saying that the city could not survive without English help, and if it fell, Condé would be destroyed. He was operating on the assumption that the total collapse of Condé's forces would disturb the leaders of the Commonwealth. But when the commissioners demanded that Condé offer them cautionary towns in France that were under his control at that time, Barrière had to answer that Condé could make no offer of places along the rivers or on the coast until the Commonwealth helped him obtain such places. He left the meeting convinced that the Commonwealth was not opposed to aiding Condé, but not without his offer of something for security.[38]

The approach that Condé and Barrière tried to use toward the Commonwealth was familiar to anyone who was aware of England's Continental involvements during the reign of Elizabeth. There were, however, great differences between the positions of the Dutch and of Henry of Navarre in the sixteenth century and of Condé in the seventeenth. The former had something of value to offer England in return for its assistance, whereas Condé had nothing to offer besides his nuisance value against Louis. Condé did not have even the psychological link to England that a common religion provided. Even Condé's ally Spain did not think it was worth its efforts to spend much time arguing the case with the Commonwealth for the defense of the city of Bordeaux.

Barrière's failure was not merely a sign of Condé's weakness; it showed also that Bordeaux had done his own job well. Barrière admitted this when he told Condé that "the more Bordeaux works in London, the better proposition [Barrière] is going to have to make [to the Commonwealth]."[39] However, as long as the rebels continued to hold the city of Bordeaux, England could exert pressure on France. In April, the Commonwealth demanded the immediate return of English vessels that had been seized by Prince Rupert and brought into the port at Nantes.[40] Bordeaux wrote immediately to Brienne informing him that the issue of Rupert's "prizes" appeared to be the only thing standing in the way of a treaty between the Commonwealth and France. He requested, as demanded by the Commonwealth, that he be given written authority to complete the treaty.[41] Bordeaux's optimism and sense of urgency were matched by Barrière's pessimism and resignation to the belief that the English commissioners had concluded arrangements with Bordeaux and that a treaty was likely.[42]

Bordeaux received the powers to conclude the treaty, but in the fourteen days it took to reach London, the situation in England had rendered it virtually useless.[43] On 20 April 1653, Oliver Cromwell, with the support of the army, had dismissed Parliament and the Council of State. The divisions that Bordeaux had earlier noted in England had caused the destruction of the Commonwealth. The actions of 20 April not only had shattered the government in England but also had thrown into confusion the diplomats who dealt with England. They had no way of knowing how the new government intended to act toward foreign states, or when it would act. The only practical course open to the diplomats was to wait and hope they did not commit any blunders. Any arrangements with the deposed government, or plans for the future, had to be set aside for an indefinite period. Diplomats showed great respect for Cromwell's strength,[44] and none of them showed any inclination to press the new government into any quick decision.

5

Cromwell Takes Control

Cromwell's dismissal of Parliament added a new dimension to English diplomacy. Cromwell had been at the center of politics in England for years, but he had given little indication of his feelings toward the outside world. Even those foreign observers who had regarded him as the real power in the Commonwealth had no plans for dealing with him. All the diplomats had to readjust their thinking to cope with an unknown commodity.

Bordeaux seemed to have suffered the greatest reversal when Cromwell took control. He wrote Mazarin that "nothing was capable of delaying the peace treaty which was proposed to me" except the fall of the Commonwealth.[1] Bordeaux's first action was to make sure that his government gave him the power to treat with Cromwell and to conclude an agreement.[2] Bordeaux tried to convince Mazarin that Cromwell had greater power and authority than the king of England formerly had, and that Louis should send a note of civility to Cromwell. Bordeaux counseled a policy of caution and restraint toward Cromwell until the new government showed it could control those "people of spirit [formerly in Parliament] opposed to his grandeur."[3]

The many rumors concerning Cromwell's plans centered on two issues: aid for the city of Bordeaux,[4] and a new approach toward the Dutch war. Despite the frequency of these rumors, little happened in England to justify them. The new Council of State appeared to ignore foreign affairs.

The Venetian representative, Palucci, explained this, stating that "diplomatic agents here are very reserved in dealing with it, possibly under the impression that it lacks authority for disposing of important affairs, being liable to change and modification and not offering the appearance of a well regulated and stable government."[5] In the absence of action by Cromwell, foreign diplomats began to depend more than ever on rumor and conjecture as the basis for constructing their policies toward England.

Orders were sent from Paris urging Bordeaux to press the government in England "to conclude the renewal of the alliance."[6] In turn, he had advised Mazarin that the time was not right to raise any important issues with Cromwell.[7] When Bordeaux did attempt to get some official reaction in England about a possible alliance, he received no answer. This treatment did not overly disturb him. He realized that all the other diplomats were treated in the same fashion, and "that all negotiations are postponed until his [Cromwell's] establishment."[8]

By June, 1653, Bordeaux had drastically changed his approach toward the negotiations. Formerly he had tried to portray the advantages of an alliance with France; most of his arguments had stressed the trade positions of the two states, their geographic proximity, and the idea that they were natural allies.[9] The disruption of the negotiations convinced him that the issues about which he had agreed with the Commonwealth were not uppermost in Cromwell's mind. Concerning the new status of the negotiations, Bordeaux wrote Brienne:

> If [Cromwell] is not persuaded to an accommodation with us, one might attribute it to a firm belief that he has that if his majesty had the power, he would wish to aid the King of England. [Bordeaux's position appeared] much more difficult: it is not that the regime wants an alliance, but it fears our power and will be very glad if we would always be occupied in [our] kingdom. That is why the more prosperous it [England] becomes, the more chance there is that they will stir up the party of M. le Prince and the Bordelois.[10]

Bordeaux was convinced that he had to get Cromwell to believe in France's "true affection" for the new government in England. Before serious negotiations could begin, France and England had to settle the pressing problems of the insurrection at Bordeaux and the Dutch war. There was an important difference between the two situations. England could possibly use its resources to aid the enemies of France, but France did not seem to be in a condition to assist the Dutch. The potential danger that France posed was its support of the Stuarts. Cromwell's government was fortunate in its early months that the diplomatic ineptitude of the Royalists made it almost impossible for France to use them as a diplomatic lever against England.

Secretary Nicholas often complained to Hyde about the men who had begun to advise the King. Some of them, like Marmaduke Langdale, were supporting the papist cause, a policy that Nicholas thought was disastrous to the King's position in England.[11] Charles had concentrated his own diplomatic activities on establishing ties with the Dutch. By the time Cromwell seized power, the Royalists had identified themselves with Catholicism and the Dutch, causes that had one thing in common: they were anathema to the majority of politically influential Englishmen. Charles further damaged his position by failing to recognize that an identification with Catholicism had an adverse influence on his standing with the Dutch.[12] Some of Charles's oldest advisers tried to convince him that the only way to restore his kingdom was to combine foreign support with Royalist sentiment in England, and to accomplish this, he must reject Catholicism and become the champion of Protestantism.[13] Charles's response to this advice was to send a representative to Rome to see if the pope wanted to aid the restoration.[14] The follies of Royalist diplomacy helped raise Cromwell's stature in England.[15]

The war with the Dutch appeared to be going well for England, but there was little indication that it would soon end. Shortly after the dismissal of Parliament, a declaration was issued by a large segment of the English fleet expressing its "resolution to be faithful to their country and to fight against the enemies of it, whether Dutch or others."[16] At the same time, there were many rumors in London that the army was opposed to the war and was working for its conclusion. The vital consideration was how Cromwell felt about the war, and he had given little indication of his sentiments. In early May, the Venetian representative reported that peace talks between England and the Dutch were a sham, "and that war is needed for Cromwell's maintenance, especially after his treatment of Parliament."[17] However, a month later, another Venetian diplomat said that Cromwell was trying to end the war because that would bolster his popularity at home.[18] Foreign observers agreed that Cromwell had to resolve the Dutch war in some fashion before he could develop a forceful foreign policy. There was also a consensus that Cromwell's actions would be determined by the impact he thought they would have on the domestic position of his government.[19]

Cromwell's attitude toward the Dutch war has occasioned much commentary from later historians. Generally, they have dealt with three major considerations: Cromwell's dislike of fighting against another Protestant nation; his willingness to see England continue its involvement in an aggressive trade war; and his inability to reverse the policies of the Rump.[20] Cromwell's contemporaries were confused about the ambivalent nature of his actions. He had not taken a position about the Rump's war against the Dutch, but he obviously saw the problems posed by the war. It was another issue that divided factions in England while he was trying to work out compromises. There was a suspicion among some army leaders that the war would benefit the navy at their expense. Money would be spent on the fleet, and the army would have to accept the bitter fact that another organization would reap the glory and be portrayed as the defender of the Commonwealth.

During the winter of 1652-53, the war had not gone well for the English fleet. In addition, some of the army's fears about the Rump were fulfilled. Sailors' pay was increased at the expense of the army. When the situation was rectified after a protest by the officers, the distrust of the Rump was not diminished.[21]

To many observers it appeared that strong pressures—the

feelings of the army and the force of religion—would act on
Cromwell to force him to bring a quick end to the war.
However, he showed little immediate concern about it, let
alone a haste to end it. Cromwell's actions again demonstrated his characteristic willingness to postpone decisions
until they had to be made or when he could be relatively
certain of victory. His overriding consideration in the spring
of 1653 was how to minimize the adverse reaction occasioned
by the expulsion of the Rump. The discontent against the
war was not great enough to turn its conclusion into political
advantage, while any precipitous peace settlement might
make it appear that he had sold out the interest and honor
of England merely to change the policies of the Rump.

The end of the Rump eliminated the old formal government, and made it possible for Cromwell to substitute himself
and his advisers as a policy-making body. This did not mean,
however, that he came to his position equipped with a set
of policies to be implemented. He acted in a manner that
showed he regarded external considerations as secondary to
domestic politics. No serious revisions would be made in
foreign policy unless the changes could be shown to buttress
his position at home. Cromwell's assumption of power gave
him new freedom of action, and also presented him with
a freedom to delay or not to act until he felt conditions
were more favorable.

Bordeaux's situation was weakened by the assumption in
England that France favored the Dutch. In truth, France
had no control over the Dutch, and relations between the
two states were marked by distrust. Actions in the Netherlands further hampered Bordeaux's attempts to portray
France as a friend of England. In June, 1653, Holland
sponsored a resolution stating that the Provinces should not
enter into any treaty with France which might lead to an
alliance against England. This resolution obviously referred
to the abortive league between William of Orange and Mazarin, a chapter from the past which Bordeaux did not want
to become a topic of conversation once more.

Despite the position of Holland, when Dutch representatives were sent to London to discuss a peace treaty,
they were instructed to see Bordeaux as soon as they arrived.

The instructions of the States General stated that it wanted "to obtain a common confederacy between the said crown [France], the government of England and this state ... if there is a treaty between the said commonwealth and this state ... that the crown of France be comprehended in said treaty of alliance."[22] While Bordeaux was trying to stir up English interest in an agreement with France, the Dutch talks still held the center of the diplomatic stage.

Brienne's opinion was that France should not worry about the feelings of the Dutch; in the light of the treaty at Münster, an alliance with the Dutch held few advantages for France. Bordeaux was instructed to make it clear to England that France was willing to make any reasonable concession or adjustment, including restructuring its alliance with the Dutch, to secure amicable relations with England. He was told to inform the English that Louis was trying to convince the Dutch to make peace with England, and that he could act as a mediator between England and the Dutch, unlike Spain, who wanted to foment divisions between the two Protestant states.[23]

Many Englishmen remained unconvinced that France was promoting peace between England and the Dutch. According to the *Mercurius Politicus*, France wanted to help the Dutch, but as long as the rebels held out at Bordeaux, "the French will not do anything that may disoblige or exasperate England."[24] The *Mercurius Politicus* also contended that Mazarin had instructed Charles Stuart to go to the Dutch for help, and that the Cardinal would supply the Royalists by way of the Dutch. Charles, supposedly wary of the proposal, had consented when Mazarin told him that France's negotiations with England would break down soon and that France would give more support to the Dutch.

The charges in the *Mercurius Politicus* echoed a letter of intelligence that Thurloe received from Paris saying that France was trying to "make sure that the United Provinces do not come to peace with England."[25] This provided a plausible explanation for recent actions. It combined the various factors that Bordeaux had stated were halting his negotiations—the Dutch war, English assistance for the city of Bordeaux, the supposed French affinity for the Stuarts,

and the distrust of Mazarin—and used them to accuse France
of negotiating in bad faith.

Despite a lack of progress, Bordeaux showed a renewed
enthusiasm for his negotiations. It may have been occasioned
by a rather enigmatic communication from Cromwell to
Mazarin in mid-June, 1653, in which Cromwell concluded
by assuring "that I feel myself obliged to serve [your]
Eminence on all occasions; and as I deem honorable and
possess the power, I hope M. Bordeaux will facilitate the
means to this."[26] The next set of instructions Bordeaux
received from Mazarin contained a new approach. Until that
time, Mazarin had stated merely that England would benefit
from an alliance with France, but now he stressed that
England and France had a common enemy who threatened
to devour both of them. Mazarin said that it did not seem
possible that after the recent changes in England, "which
were in the true interests of England, that the wise rulers
who now govern will not recognize the power of Austria."
The Cardinal wanted it made clear to Cromwell that the
election of the King of the Romans and the proposed marriage of the Spanish Infanta were laying the basis for a
powerful coalition led by Austria. England and France must
act together to block the aggressive plans of Austria. In doing
so, Cromwell and Mazarin would bring about "a renewal
of those old alliances which were contracted in other times
. . . and that experience has shown are very useful for the
peace of Christendom."[27]

Fear of the Habsburg power was not the only feature in
Mazarin's new instructions. The Cardinal recognized that
Cromwell could consider that as France's problem or view
it as another admission of France's weakness. He wanted
Bordeaux to stress that "a sincere reunion with France and
the United Provinces would be doubly to their [England's]
advantage." Not only would England no longer have to fear
the Habsburgs, but "one would be able to insert conditions
into the alliance which would be made, which would make
secure all that they today fear on account of the notable
changes in their states."[28] Mazarin wanted to make proposals
dealing with the sentiments that supposedly motivated
Cromwell—hatred of popery, desire to end the Dutch war,

and fear for the safety of his government. Mazarin may have been misinformed about the depth of Cromwell's feelings, but these considerations represented one intelligent outside view of the objectives of Cromwell's foreign policy.

While Bordeaux was trying to expand the scope of his negotiations to cover a broader international context, the old issues of Condé and the Dutch war moved into the forefront again. Palucci reported that there was a strong feeling in London that peace with the Dutch was near. He said that he had also learned "that the government favours Condé rather than the court party" and that England intended to aid the city of Bordeaux.[29] Palucci's observations were inaccurate, but talks being carried on in London with the Dutch and deputies from Bordeaux might have led him to his conclusions. Of greater interest was Palucci's prediction of what would happen after peace was made with the Dutch. England would have to use its large army and navy somewhere. He thought that a peace treaty would be harmful to France and Spain because England would take advantage of the Bourbon-Habsburg war to make itself "the absolute mistress of the West Indies." At the same time, "the English would seek to foment civil strife in France" and thus "pretend" to help Spain. Palucci based his analysis on a combination of England's strength and statements that it intended to 'make a noise in the world." He thought that Cromwell was developing long-range plans to use the combined fleets of England and the United Provinces. Palucci was aware that the Dutch did not favor that arrangement, but he was sure they would consent if England dropped claims for a war indemnity. The Venetian thought that Cromwell had plans for more than a series of attacks on Spain's possessions; the cornerstone of the strategy was his desire to "attempt vast conquests."[30]

Palucci's estimate of Cromwell's plans was different from any made previously by a foreign observer. The considerations that underlay Palucci's view were echoed in a policy memorandum prepared by Edward Sexby a few months later for Cromwell. Sexby, formerly an officer in Cromwell's regiment, had been sent to France to gather information about the power of the royal government, the extent of the rebellion

against it, and the position of the Huguenots.[31] His report
contained a far-reaching plan for policy toward France and
Spain, as well as an outline of the basic objectives for
England's foreign policy. According to Sexby, "That it is
in England's and your Highness' interest to prevent the
making of a general peace is so obvious," other considerations
should be subordinated to implementing that idea.[32] The first
step must be to arrange a peace with the Dutch. After that,
England should interfere in France's domestic problems, thus
insuring that France could not defeat Spain and bring peace
to Europe.

The capitulation of the city of Bordeaux on 3 August
marked a virtual end to the armed resistance of the Fronde.[33]
It showed that Mazarin was in control in France and, at
the same time, deprived England of any chance to strike
at France in a situation that seemed uniquely vulnerable
to England's power. The capture of the city caused no
dramatic advance in M. Bordeaux's negotiations. Even before
the event was known in England, Cromwell had "assured
him [Bordeaux] that the treaty is well advanced and that
the only difficulty will be to get consent to all the promises."[34]
M. Bordeaux did not share Cromwell's optimism, and began
to feel that negotiations were coming to a halt. He became
concerned about his inability to understand the intentions
of the English, something he thought he had been able to
do in the past. When the English council finally answered
Bordeaux's proposals, it virtually ignored their substance and
began to discuss the possibility of French support for Charles
Stuart. Bordeaux was not sure whether the council was really
disturbed by the possibility, or whether this was merely a
delaying tactic. His pessimism reached a new low when the
council accepted the fall of the city of Bordeaux with a
mixture of lack of interest and disdain.[35]

Bordeaux continued to make proposals, but by the middle
of August, he was speaking again in broad generalities. In
his communications to Mazarin, he placed the highest priority on "removing the suspicion that the stay of the King
of England at the court gives to this state."[36] Bordeaux scaled
down his proposals, and pressed for a peace based on the
mutual restitution of maritime prizes and a renewal of the

treaty signed between Charles I and Louis XIII. The council ignored the former point and opposed the latter. Before Cromwell's seizure of power, the Commonwealth had suggested the renewal of Charles I's treaty, but the new council had told Bordeaux that "because this government was completely different, they intended to also make new and fundamental treaties."[37]

Bordeaux had a difficult time trying to convince Mazarin that Cromwell's government differed from its predecessor in more than its leadership. A new element had been injected into the negotiations—vanity. The new leaders seemed sure of their power, but wanted to exhibit it to the rest of the world. One way to do this was to force France to meet conditions set by England before discussing an alliance. Since England had made no concrete proposals, it was engaging in a series of delaying tactics. Bordeaux thought it was useless to press England because its leaders derived pleasure from treating other states as supplicants.

Bordeaux also felt that Cromwell's government had brought stability and prosperity to England, and "the affairs on this side being maintained in a high prosperity, apparently my treaty will not be very fast."[38] England's prosperity was evidenced, according to Bordeaux, by the demands it was making on the Dutch for a coalition.

Bordeaux's feelings about a new stability in England reflected his view of the political events of the past few months. Cromwell had been convinced that the Rump would not make the necessary changes in the government and the church and he set into motion the machinery for the selection of a new Parliament. He looked at the new body—the Barebones Parliament, as it has become known—as the hope for the resolution of the problems that had plagued the Commonwealth.[39] Even though the nominated assembly was crucial to Cromwell's plans, he appeared to exercise little direct pressure on it.[40] The members that returned showed few important differences from those in the Rump. Within a matter of weeks, the Barebones disappointed Cromwell and its supporters in the army. Bordeaux's seeming acceptance of Cromwell's bright hopes for the Barebones was tempered by the ambassador's caution to commit himself. His experi-

ences with English politics had taught him one valuable
lesson—optimism about stability in England was no substitute for fundamental changes in the government which made
it clear just where power rested and how it would be exercised. The actions of the Barebones did little to clarify this
situation to Bordeaux. In this respect, his distance from the
English government and the confusion surrounding it enabled him to see its problems more clearly than did men deeply
involved in them.

Bordeaux was determined to avoid issues that might cause
new friction with England, but the hardening of England's
stance in negotiations with the Dutch put him in a troublesome position. A Dutch representative approached Bordeaux
for advice about England's offer of a coalition. Bordeaux
also learned that the English had told the Dutch that France
was in favor of an Anglo-Dutch alliance, not merely a peace
treaty. His reply to the Dutch was to remind them that
England would be the dominant force in any coalition, and
that the coalition would inevitably be driven to war by
England's pride and arrogance. Bordeaux thought he must
prevent the coalition, because he was convinced that Cromwell would use it to embark on some great design involving
a naval power that would be irresistible.[41]

While Bordeaux and Brienne were trying to make some
gesture to show that France was sincere in its support of
the new government, Hyde and other Royalists expected
increasing support from France.[42] Since the city of Bordeaux
was "happily reduced to power by the French King," Hyde
concluded that Mazarin would not have to be friendly with
Cromwell any longer.[43] This view mirrored the impressions
that M. Bordeaux was receiving in London. By removing
a potential weapon from England, France had forced Cromwell to seek other ways to insure that France would not
help the Stuarts. Bordeaux's negotiations appeared stalled,
and he could not get even a response concerning the treaty
that had been resolved by Parliament. Cromwell's reply to
France's proposals made it appear that "he [Cromwell] has
no warmth for France." Bordeaux's discomfiture was only
mildly alleviated by his feeling that he knew the factors that
disturbed England and were delaying negotiations:—the re-

duction of the city of Bordeaux, the placement of the Duke of York in command of Irish troops, and the affection shown to Charles at the French court.[44]

Bordeaux's pessimism would have increased had he known of the actions taken by the English council. On 6 September 1653, it instructed Captain Willoughby Hannum, of the ship *Katherine*, to escort some English merchantmen to Gottenbourg. En route, he was "as far as Providence enables you, to seize and take, and in case of resistance, to sink, fire and destroy all vessels belonging to the United Provinces, or the Kings of France and Denmark."[45] Three days later, the council issued a letter of marque that gave Edward Marston the "power to seize all ships, vessels, arms, etc., of the French, Dutch and any other nation who shall receive any communication, letter of marque, or other authority, for Charles Stuart, the late King's son, or Prince Rupert: as also all ships and vessels going to or coming from any port or place in hostility to Parliament."[46]

The letter of marque did not state explicitly that France was considered "in hostility to Parliament," but in practical terms, the distinction meant little. The Council of State was authorizing attacks on French goods and property, and classifying that state with England's enemies the Dutch and the Stuarts. Bordeaux's fears—that France would be judged by her past performance and her supposed friends, rather than by his statements—had been realized.

The council's actions demonstrated a policy of direct action against France. The Commonwealth had never rejected the idea that France had aided in the illegal seizure of English ships, but the phrases in the letters to Hannum and Marston were not just a restatement of England's right to retaliate; they were commentaries on the international situation. Bordeaux's negotiations seemed to have had no ameliorating effect on English belligerence. Since there had been no recent provocation by France, the explanation for the council's actions must be found in the changed situation in England. Hyde's analysis of the situation provides a valuable insight. He thought that England had lost a potential weapon when the city of Bordeaux had fallen, and therefore Cromwell's diplomatic position had suffered. The way to restore that position was to reassert England's ability to harm France. Any new pressure that could be placed on France would strengthen England's bargaining position.

Bordeaux's attempts to understand the new government in England and to deal with the Dutch war momentarily overshadowed a more serious problem—the possibility of English help for Spain. Cromwell's dismissal of Parliament had had little effect on Spain's policies. Its ambassador, Alonso de Cardenas, had obtained no commitments from the Commonwealth, which also meant he had not bound his own government to a policy that Cromwell might reject. Cardenas's inability to make any arrangements with the Commonwealth had astounded many diplomats. Spain had taken a head start in dealing with England, but had little to show for it. England's actions at Dunkirk had insured the Spanish victory, but had not been part of an agreement between the states and had not led to any other arrangements.

The most apparent factors that militated against Anglo-Spanish cooperation were the hostility that Englishmen harbored for the home of the Inquisition and the Armada and the Commonwealth's recognition of the house of Braganza.[47] Neither could be ameliorated merely by treaty arrangements or diplomatic compromise. Because of the emotional issues involved, Cardenas had avoided pressing the Commonwealth. He preferred to wait until he could offer England a suitable price for its assisance.

Cardenas also showed little enthusiasm in interesting England in assisting the city of Bordeaux. His actions almost drove Barrière and Condé to distraction. They could not understand why their ally the King of Spain was not helping their last-ditch struggle by applying diplomatic pressure on England. Cardenas was more realistic about the situation.He saw that the struggle at Bordeaux had attracted little sympathy in England, and that Spain had no way to bring pressure to bear on England. The only way to involve England would be at a cost that Spain would find prohibitive.[48] In any case, Cardenas thought it most unwise to venture a proposal that England might reject. He kept in the background waiting to see the direction in which Cromwell was heading.

Despite Cardenas's efforts, relations between England and Spain were not always amicable. In early July, 1653, an English ship, the *Harry Bonadventure*, became the center of a new controversy between the two states. While being pursued by Dutch warships, it had entered a Spanish port, where it had been promised protection by the governor. However, the Dutch had sailed into the port and seized the ship. The owner of the *Harry Bonadventure* petitioned the English Council of State to demand that Spain pay reparations for the damages incurred in its port.[49] If the seizure of the ship showed that areas of possible friction existed between England and Spain, the way in which the dispute was handled showed that neither side wanted to push matters toward an open break. Within a month, Charles Longland, a member of the commission that dealt with Cardenas, reported that Spain had seized a Dutch vessel to secure reparations for the *Harry Bonadventure*. Longland explained the Spanish action as another sign of their desire to be friendly with England.[50]

While the issue of the *Harry Bonadventure* was being resolved, another difficulty arose between the two states. Cardenas claimed that English ships had seized vessels and gold belonging to the King of Spain and his subjects. An appeal for the return of this property was made in a calm and orderly manner. Cardenas wanted the issue raised in the "ordinary law courts," and then tried to expedite matters there.[51] There were various explanations for Cardenas's actions: he was sure that the Spanish claim was just, and would be upheld in the courts; he did not think he could exert pressure on the Council of State: or he did not think the issue was important enough to risk antagonizing anyone in England. A more devious line of reasoning circulated at The Hague, which asserted that there must be some secret negotiations between England and Spain, or the King would have been forceful in his protests about a blatant act of piracy.[52] This explanation was plausible, but in reality there were no secret talks or special arrangements between the two states.

Toward the end of the summer of 1653, many rumors of a tentative agreement between England and Spain spread while Bordeaux was having doubts about his own negotiations.[53] Despite the rumors, policy makers in England were not thinking of treaties with France or Spain as the two alternatives upon which their actions would have to be predicated. Cromwell's government had chosen to ignore both France and Spain and to turn to issues that affected it more directly.

6

The End of the Dutch War

The Dutch war was the most important diplomatic problem Cromwell had inherited from the Commonwealth. Unlike other negotiations, it could not be conveniently shelved. The war was a constant source of financial and human expenses, and because it was not universally popular, it was a source of potential discord in England. It was also clear that Cromwell could not make any important foreign arrangements before he settled the war. It is not within the scope of this work to explore the details of the Dutch war or the complicated relationship between England and the United Provinces. However, some aspects of that relationship must be considered more fully because of their impact on the Anglo-French situation.[1]

The negotiations for an end to the Anglo-Dutch war presented a frustrating problem for the participants and a puzzling situation for outside observers. Bordeaux, Mazarin, and Brienne received contradictory reports about the negotiations. The only thing on which the various French informants agreed was that talks were stalemated. In August, 1653, Cromwell personally intervened. He brought up the idea of a coalition, a suggestion that had been made in 1651 by an English mission to the United Provinces, led by St. John and Walter Strickland. Beverningh, the Dutch representative, ignored the suggestion and reported that Cromwell did not have the authority to bring England into a coalition even if the Dutch approved.[2] Beverningh's observation may have reflected his opinion that the calling of a new Parliament meant Cromwell had divested himself of the power to determine English policy. The realities of the situation were unclear. Cromwell did not indicate what powers he would retain, although he did give the impression that he wanted to bring the Barebones into an active partnership with himself and the army. The Barebones's unwillingness to support Cromwell made a mockery of Beverningh's analysis. In slightly more than three months, Cromwell would seize authority that far exceeded what he had when he held the interview with Beverningh.

While the Dutch were listening to peace proposals from England, they were trying to create an alliance with France. Many reports of this reached London, but caused little apprehension there. The men who directed foreign policy in England were aware of the complications standing in the way of an alliance between France and the United Provinces.[3] The political division within the Netherlands between the Orangists and the leadership of Holland was reflected in the United Provinces's dealings with France. The English leaders thought the Hollanders could—and would—block any alliance with France. Furthermore, Mazarin's actions showed little commitment to the cause of the Dutch. He was trying to convince them that Spain was the real cause for the Anglo-Dutch war, and that the Dutch predicament was the result of their abandonment of France in 1648. But while the Cardinal encouraged the Dutch to break with Spain, he rejected any idea for a firm defensive alliance with them. The letters from Mazarin to Bordeaux indicated that the Cardinal feared that Cromwell would declare war on France if it concluded an alliance with the Dutch.[4]

Bordeaux's comments that his negotiations were stalled by the Dutch war showed France's dilemma. The war had to be ended if France could ever hope for assistance from Cromwell, but Mazarin's proposal to act as a mediator had been refused already by England. France could try to influence one side or the other (and the political realities dictated that it would have to be the Dutch) or to throw its support behind one side in hopes of ending the war. The continuation of the war was also causing great harm to France's reputation in England, in a manner over which France had no control. In September and October, 1653, various Dutch states issued manifestos and resolutions concerning the prosecution of the war. These all called for basically the same steps: continued resistance to England, alliance with the Scots and Irish, and the recognition of Charles II as King of England. They also included suggestions for an immediate offensive and defensive alliance with France.[5] France had not suggested any such alliance, but that country was depicted as a potential enemy of England. Once more France was coupled, in the minds of Englishmen, with two great enemies—Charles Stuart, and the Dutch.

By the end of November, 1653, the influence of Holland had made an Anglo-Dutch peace more likely, and Mazarin decided to offer his services to assist the negotiations. Chanut, the French ambassador at The Hague, pointed out to the Hollanders that any alliance against England would work in favor of the Orangists. Chanut did not categorically reject the idea of an alliance between the Dutch and France, but he tried to dissuade the Dutch from making it the cornerstone of their dealings with England. Chanut was speaking against almost the same arrangements that had been made between Mazarin and William II.[6] The situation of the Cardinal and the house of Orange had changed since then, but the important difference was in England. Mazarin no longer looked at revolutionary England as a potential enemy, and he wanted to further any arrangements that might lead to Anglo-French ties.[7]

While the Anglo-Dutch negotiations dragged on, Bordeaux informed the English commissioners that he intended to end his own mission unless some progress was made in a reasonable period of time. The commissioners' reply was to blame France for past delays, and then to ignore Bordeaux. When he reported this episode to Brienne, Bordeaux coupled it with one note of optimism. The climate for his negotiations appeared to be improving, because England was lessening its demands on the Dutch for a political confederation, thus making a peace more likely.[8] He was pleased when he learned that a draft treaty had supposedly been completed, which included an alliance "against anyone who would mount an undertaking against the present regime, [and could] include their allies, the Danes and the French."[9]

The treaty that was finally concluded between England and the Dutch was certainly not a triumph for France's diplomacy. It did not even include many of the elements that Bordeaux believed were sure to be present. The Dutch representative in England tried to convince Bordeaux that he had attempted to include France, but Cromwell had rejected the idea.

When England and the Dutch seemed to be making progress toward a treaty, Mazarin had been anxious to be included in it. Thwarted in that aim, the Cardinal had dropped his protests and had not tried to hamper the conclusion of the treaty. Mazarin undoubtedly realized that further protest could only harm his cause, but many Englishmen, already hostile to him, saw the situation as another sign of the Cardinal's duplicity. One of Thurloe's informants in Paris put all these factors together and came up with a prediction for future actions by France:

> If Mazarin finds that an agreement [between England and the Dutch] shall be made, he will, or at least shall strongly give out that an ambassador extraordinary shall goe from hence into England, soe to keep fayne and amuse both England and Spaine, whilst he shall by some other means trye likewise the Spanish pulse for a general peace, and so will be sure to lay hault of one or another. In the meantime he will continue M. Bordeaux there for intelligence and such.[10]

This facile explanation of Mazarin's policies was echoed in the suspiciousness with which Bordeaux was treated in London. The intelligence report gained more credibility when shortly after Thurloe received it the Cardinal sent an ambassador extraordinary to England.

When France bowed to the inevitable and abandoned its struggle to be included in the Anglo-Dutch treaty, it did so with little grace or tact. Chanut delivered a speech to the States General in which he said France had suggested its inclusion in the treaty only to make it easier for England and the Dutch to reach an agreement. He told the Dutch that they should make peace even if France was not included, and that he objected to a resolution before the States General "to do all they can to advance the agreement of France with England." Chanut stated that France was a great power and did not need anyone to act as her agent in international dealings. He concluded by saying that the Dutch could have insisted on the inclusion of her allies in the treaty, but it did not suit the dignity of a state as great as France to complain after the treaty was written.[11]

Chanut's speech had the sound of a petulant child whose wishes had been ignored and who would not admit it. However, Thurloe's informant at The Hague felt there was more behind the speech than wounded feelings. He felt that Chanut had two reasons for delivering it: either he recognized that the Dutch would go ahead with the treaty no matter what France did, or "France does not need the intervention of this state [United Provinces] because France already had arranged a treaty with England."[12]

After Chanut's speech, France attempted to raise its prestige with the Dutch in other ways. It contended that Cromwell had asked for advice from France before agreeing to the treaty, and that the Cardinal had said, "if the French King had been willing to act in prejudice to the United Provinces France could have come to an agreement with England with as much ease as I can draw on my glove."[13] Mazarin insisted that France had kept the Dutch interests in mind and had resisted when Cromwell had asked France to make concessions that might be harmful to the Dutch. However, Mazarin never specified what those concessions were. Bordeaux's dispatches and his activities in London had demonstrated that France had little influence on the treaty between the Dutch and England. Mazarin was obviously trying to recoup some prestige for France out of its role as an impotent spectator to the Anglo-Dutch negotiations. English officials clearly saw either that Mazarin did not believe the story he told the Dutch or that he was deceived by his own diplomats. In either case, the hollowness of the Cardinal's boast presented the English with another sign of their own importance.

On 5 April 1654 (Old Style), the articles of peace were signed between "His Highness Oliver Lord Protector of the

Commonwealth of England . . . and the Lord the States
General of the United Provinces of the Netherlands."[14] The
first provisions of the treaty dealt with the matter of assistance for rebels and enemies of the other state, and prohibited
any aid that the Stuarts might have hoped to obtain from
the Dutch. Secret articles appended to the treaty provided
for the exclusion of the house of Orange from the province
of Holland, a step meant to protect the interests of the ruling
elite of Holland as well as the revolutionary government in
England.[15]

This treaty marked the conclusion of Cromwell's most
pressing diplomatic problem. It was a triumph for the position he had taken in England concerning the war. It ended
a war to which he was opposed on moral as well as political
grounds.[16] A few concessions had been made to the Dutch,
although a militant element in England had deluded itself
into thinking a harsh peace could be enforced on the Dutch.
The manner in which the treaty was concluded was an
assertion of England's diplomatic independence, a point that
was obvious to Bordeaux, Mazarin, and other policy makers
in France. France had been balked in all its attempts to
determine the course of the negotiations, and had finally
settled for the role of a carping spectator. As far as Bordeaux
was concerned, there was only one satisfactory result of the
treaty—the war was over, and Cromwell might be convinced
to devote serious attention to proposals from France. The
end of the war meant much more than that to the Cromwellian government. It still possessed a formidable navy, and
many of its people and leaders who thought they had scored
a victory looked at the world with an eye toward further
successes. These factors had been noted by many diplomats
in London who had reason to be suspicious of English
ambition.

After the treaty, a new cloak of uncertainty surrounded
Cromwell, and diplomats were once again at a loss to explain
the purposes of his diplomacy.[17] If Bordeaux could begin new
negotiations, they would not be a continuation of his earlier
talks. He had lost whatever gains he had made during the
Commonwealth, and did not have a clear, new frame of
reference in which to operate. The end of the war gave

England the freedom of action to play off several states against one another in competition for its friendship. Further, it left little doubt that Cromwell's policy was freed from many of the restrictions and considerations that had existed during the Commonwealth.

The peace treaty not only gave Cromwell a new freedom of action but also demonstrated the political freedom he possessed at home. The end of the Barebones experiment and the creation of the Protectorate in December, 1653, gave a completely new look to English politics and foreign relations. There was no longer doubt that Cromwell controlled both the armed might of England and the policy-making bodies that determined how that power would be used. His first priority was to consolidate his control and to eliminate some of the causes of political division. The Dutch war represented one such problem. He was in a position to end the war that he had been willing to accept as long as he was walking a political tightrope between factions in England. After December, 1653, he was free to repudiate the policies of Parliament and give the impression of tidying up the loose ends and mistakes of a discredited regime. There were other advantages to be gained from such actions. His new position was a significant break with the policies of the past; a dramatic change in foreign policy might be used to reinforce the determination of his followers to support him.

The failure of the Barebones left Cromwell disillusioned with the experiments of the past year. His high hopes for a righteous government were gone, and he was convinced that he had tried to give up power before such an act was justified. The councillors he chose represented a new conservatism and desire to deal with the political realities of the present rather than to make plans for the future. The fervent republicans and Fifth Monarchists disappeared from the policy-making body. Soldiers like Lambert and Monk, lawyers like Whitelocke, and bureaucrat-administrators like Thurloe set the tone for the Protector's council. Many of his advisers had held positions of responsibility under the Commonwealth, and they recognized the unsettled situation of the constitution. The creation of the Protectorate was their answer to the problem of stability. They were bound to Cromwell as the hope for a stable England and for their own positions.[18]

Despite the political experience of the council, its members were amateurs in the area of foreign policy. Their lack of a ready-made view of the world made it easier for them to solve the most immediate problem—the Dutch war. The war did not appear to be heading for a decisive conclusion, and it was costing a great deal of money. With those considerations in mind, it was even more important to end the war once the decision was made to call a new Parliament. The election was to take place in the summer of 1654, and the treaty was signed in April. By the time Parliament would assemble in September, the Protector could present it with a fait accompli—peace with the Dutch. The peace would be presented as a victory, not only for England but also for the idealism of the Protector's faith. In one stroke, the peace with the Dutch was supposed to add to Cromwell's glory, mollify his religious critics, cut expenditures, and destroy a potential election issue. The peace also left the Protector with a sizable naval force that he could possibly turn to other uses in an attempt to secure broader support for the new government while its first Parliament was being organized. The establishment of the Protectorate was supposed to mark a clean break with the failures of the past in England and the policies that lingered from the Rump.

Bordeaux's inquiries led him to believe that religious considerations would play an increasingly important role in Cromwell's activities after he made peace with the Dutch. It was a question with which Bordeaux had been forced to cope months before the Anglo-Dutch treaty. Condé's representatives had spread rumors in London that Mazarin was persecuting the Huguenots in hopes of gaining support for the city of Bordeaux. At that time M. Bordeaux had been able to show Cromwell that the story was false. The ambassador did not underestimate the appeal that stories about the plight of European Protestants would have in England, "although many of the ministers [of the English government] know that the friendship of France is necessary to them [sic]: that the merchants desire the re-establishment of commerce with a great passion."[19]

Barrière was even more convinced than Bordeaux that religious considerations were vital in dealing with Cromwell. Barrière recommended to Condé that the Prince actively court the Huguenots. The closer England and the Netherlands came to a treaty, the more insistent Barrière became on the value of the "Protestant cause" to any potential ally of Cromwell's. He told Condé that the council in England was surprised that the Huguenots had done nothing to improve their position in France, and if the Huguenots acted against their government, they could count on support from England. Likewise, England would support Condé if he allied himself with the Huguenots.[20] In another interview with a member of the council, Barrière was told that Cromwell received reports that convinced him the Huguenots would stage an uprising if they received outside support. Cromwell was said to be "very passionate about the subject, saying that England had caused the ruin of the party [the Huguenots] and it was up to England to re-establish it."[21]

Bordeaux was not as confident as Barrière was of his own ability to discover Cromwell's motives and plans. However, the French ambassador was "reasonably certain" that Cromwell was planning a foreign war, and that passions in England "will probably drive them to want to help their brother [the Huguenots] who are tyrannized in France." Shortly after the Dutch peace, Bordeaux said, in England it was "also believed that it is impossible to establish a stable peace with France, because of the injustices of the [French] ministers, and as long as it will be ruled by his Eminence or a man of his profession, who are the 'pillars of the papacy.' "[22] Bordeaux regarded this as a distorted appraisal of France's position, but since it was widely believed in England, he knew he had to counter it.

Most diplomatic observers agreed that Cromwell was committed to his view of the "true religion." Their concern was how Cromwell intended to translate his commitment into actions. Barrière was encouraged by a communication from France stating that Cromwell had said that England looked upon itself as the protector of French Protestants against the royal government.[23] Barrière placed so much faith in the belief that Cromwell wanted to aid foreign Protestants that

he asked Condé to consider ending his alliance with Spain
and forming one with the Huguenots.

Barrière's optimism had little foundation, but there were
indications that Cromwell might consider some form of
intervention in France. Any such action was dependent on
two factors: the establishment of closer religious and political
ties between England and the Huguenots, and the weakening
of Mazarin's control in France. At the beginning of April,
one of Thurloe's agents described France as never containing
"so many discontented persons . . . as at present." He
continued, "Our friends in Switzerland, and our friends the
protestants in Languedoc, and Provence, and Geneva, are
inclinable enough to join with any thing or power, or interest,
which probably they can but think will give a larger advantage to their religion." He concluded with a recommendation
for the government in England that if they only realized
the "true situation" in France, they would see how much
they could profit from it. According to this informant, Cromwell had the opportunity not only to secure liberty for
Protestants but also to give the law of the English Commonwealth to the whole world.[24]

The idea that Cromwell was working for a Protestant
coalition was accepted by some leading Royalists as well
as by Barrière. Nicholas hoped the coalition would give the
Royalists new advantages. Writing to Hyde, Nicholas said
he was "glad that the French are so much alarmed at the
Proposition of the Coalition . . . if there shall be, after this,
any Conjecture made between the English Rebels and these
states [the United Provinces], it may justly give all monarchs
jealousies and apprehensions what may therefore come to
pass."[25] On the other hand, Barrière hoped that a Protestant
alliance would not materialize, because he feared it would
dedicate itself "for the service of the Lord, for whom they
[the English] feel a great passion."[26] The possibility that
Cromwell might choose to "fight the Lord's battles" also
disturbed Bordeaux, because the objectives of such a campaign were indefinite and virtually boundless.

The possibility of a Protestant coalition was not a major
concern to Bordeaux. He was sure that the Dutch would
reject the idea and that the coalition would not be established

without them.[27] Cromwell's support for Spain was a more immediate problem. Bordeaux had made it clear in his dispatches to Brienne and Mazarin that it was not enough for France to warn or advise England against cooperating with Spain. England would have to be offered positive reasons for aiding France and be shown that France was a reliable ally.

The correspondence that went back and forth from Bordeaux to officials in Paris showed the confusion surrounding Cromwell's policies. Bordeaux admitted that his own negotiations were uncertain, but he saw little danger of an open break between England and France. He was convinced that a break would occur only if Cromwell thought he could gain concrete advantages from it. Bordeaux did not think Spain was in a position to offer much to Cromwell, and therefore England would have no reason to oppose France.[28] This view of the situation was much closer to ideas held by Barrière than it was to those of Mazarin.[29] The Cardinal said he was convinced that Cromwell intended to launch a large naval expedition against France, in conjunction with Spain and Condé. Mazarin's knowledge of Cardenas's and Barrière's activities showed that France's intelligence system in Spain was operating efficiently, but he misinterpreted the power of Spain. The Cardinal was much surer than Cardenas or Barrière that Spain's proposals would be accepted by Cromwell. Bordeaux provided Mazarin with shrewd insights into Cromwell's interpretation of events, but these were not integrated into the Cardinal's overall perception of the international scene. The Cardinal's views were remarkable in two ways: he was convinced that he had a better understanding of the situation in England than did Bordeaux; but he did not send any instructions to Bordeaux to take new steps to block the Anglo-Spanish alliance.[30]

While Mazarin was expressing his apprehension about an alliance between Cromwell and Spain, Bordeaux thought that the English position toward France was softening. A series of decisions by English courts which enabled captured French ships to be returned to their owners further convinced Bordeaux that Mazarin should not base his policy toward England on intelligence received from Spain.[31] One of Ma-

zarin's agents in London took this point further and stated
that the Council of State in London had instructed the courts
not to act against French ships if the Cardinal decided to
intervene in their behalf. This informant also told Mazarin
that Cromwell would welcome a letter from the Cardinal,
discussing good relations between their states, and "thereby,
little and by little you will come to a general agreement
at last, a thing so much to be desired by all honest men
... and a thing of that consequence in France and [in which]
your particular interest is so highly concerned, being so
deeply involved in the welfare of that nation."[32]

While the Cardinal was trying to obtain a clear perspective
concerning Cromwell, Bordeaux was trying to work out a
set of proposals to prove the value of France as an ally.
Despite his efforts, he was still plagued by the distrust and
dislike of France that had been present in England at his
arrival. France was still viewed in many quarters as the home
of the Stuarts and the "natural enemy" of England.[33] When
the suspicion developed in England that Mazarin was trying
to negotiate with Spain for a general peace, Bordeaux's
position was weakened further. Charges of Mazarin's duplicity were impossible for Bordeaux to refute adequately. If he
denied that negotiations were taking place, the English
assumed he was trying to deceive them. As the rumors about
a general peace gained wider acceptance in England, Bordeaux noticed a decided coldness in the attitude of the
commissioners. By the last weeks of 1653, Bordeaux expressed
greater anger and frustration than he had at any time in
the past, finally stating, "I do not have confidence in any
good wishes of the English, nor in the words of M. le
General."[34]

By the beginning of 1654, Bordeaux had little to show for
his stay in England. He set forth a new series of proposals
for Cromwell's consideration, the main point being that
England should use its fleet to attack and capture Spanish
territory in the West Indies. Bordeaux thought the idea
would have obvious attractions for England. "Nevertheless
I see no disposition towards it, and if M. le Protector had
no change of sentiment, we ought not to count on it."[35] This
rather negative opinion was Bordeaux's first mention of any

attempt to use the West Indies as a lure for Cromwell's friendship. Less than a month later, his negotiations were at an impasse. He blamed part of his difficulties on England's attention to the Dutch war. At the same time, Bordeaux asked Brienne for new instructions, and suggested it might be essential for the king to have a "man of quality and higher rank as ambassador to England."[36]

Before Bordeaux mentioned the possibility of sending an ambassador of higher quality, Mazarin had already commissioned the Baron de Baas to go to England. He was instructed to convey personal regards from the Cardinal to Cromwell, as well as an assurance that Mazarin had no intentions to support the Stuart claim to the throne of England.[37] De Baas did not remain long in London, but his appearance, and the message he carried, showed that Bordeaux's comments concerning the English distrust of France had not gone unheeded in Paris. Since de Baas's mission was an emergency measure, it was reasonable to assume that Mazarin wanted him to deal with the most pressing issues. De Baas received a polite reception from Cromwell, but his arrival raised more problems than it solved. Members of the council were displeased because de Baas represented himself as an envoy from Mazarin and not from the King.[38] The question of diplomatic procedure was raised in a more serious fashion when Bordeaux was curtly informed that Cromwell would not talk with him any longer until he became a properly accredited ambassador. Bordeaux had been accredited to the government of the Commonwealth and Parliament, and no adjustment had been made in his commission after the events of April, 1653. Cromwell's insistence that Bordeaux obtain new credentials came as a bitter shock to the Frenchman. He remembered the difficulties the Commonwealth had caused about his title. He assumed Cromwell was using the same tactics to delay negotiations, a sign that Cromwell was moving away from any agreement with France.

The Cardinal was the only French official who seemed satisfied with the results of de Baas's mission, believing that Cromwell had been convinced to take no actions against France. De Baas felt that Cromwell wanted to exploit the Habsburg-Bourbon war for the consolidation of his own

power in England.[39] Bordeaux saw that de Baas had done
nothing to create any foundation, material or psychological,
upon which to further the negotiations. Within a month,
Mazarin decided to send de Baas back to England in an
attempt to end procedural problems and distrusts of the past.
He was instructed to flatter Cromwell and to authorize
Bordeaux to grant Cromwell "the position to which he wants
to raise himself," but not to give Cromwell any titles that
were superior to those formerly held by the Stuarts.

New instructions were also sent to Bordeaux. If Cromwell
was not satisfied with the title of "Protector of England,
Scotland, and Ireland," then Bordeaux should "make some
arrangements which will counter what titles Spain gives
him," but no concession should be made which would give
Cromwell any satisifaction for England's claim of control
over the Channel.[40] The most important part of these instructions authorized Bordeaux to offer the expulsion of
Charles Stuart if Cromwell wanted that step as a preliminary
to closer relations. The instructions that de Baas brought
to Bordeaux were a long-delayed reply to the pleas Bordeaux
had been making to Brienne and Mazarin for more than
a year. Bordeaux knew that the concessions authorized by
Mazarin would provide only an opening wedge in the negotiations. Their effect might be negated by a recent feeling in
England that there was renewed French support for the
Stuarts.[41] John Thurloe, who was the first English official
to know of the new status accorded to Cromwell, paid little
attention to it, seeing the move as France's attempt to
salvage something from its disappointment at being excluded
from the Anglo-Dutch treaty.[42]

Mazarin obviously hoped, by sending a new commission
to Bordeaux, to show respect, without any cost to France,
to Cromwell, "whose preparations were so greatly feared."[43]
Bordeaux was less sanguine about the relationship that had
been established between England and France. He was dis-
mayed by what he saw as the French court's unwillingness
or inability to see that Cromwell possessed sovereign power
in England. Bordeaux warned his superiors not to be deluded
into thinking that Cromwell might be overthrown. Bordeaux
did not foresee any problems on the question of diplomtic

language; he was sure Cromwell would be pleased to be addressed by the term "brother." This would cause some resentment in France. Since France was the last major power to accord formal recognition to Cromwell, it would have to go further than other states to atone for its past policy. Bordeaux sensed that some English ministers—and even Cromwell—were "entirely disposed to the accommodation, and thought an agreement with France was in the interests of England.[44]

By the beginning of March, 1654, it looked as though the major difficulties hindering Anglo-French cooperation were disappearing. The ambassador happily reported "that even those noises in Parliament of the 'Religionnaires' of France have dissipated themselves."[45] The French ties of the Stuarts were still a serious problem, but Mazarin decided to rid himself of that burden by asking Charles to leave France. The Cardinal told some diplomats in France that he had been forced to accept Charles because of blood ties with Louis, "but as dynasties and governments change by the will of God, he [Mazarin] has no intention of resisting decrees of Providence."[46]

While the tide was running his way, Bordeaux impatiently requested authorization from Mazarin to discuss specific provisions for an alliance with England. He stated that an agreement was within his grasp but that he did not have the power to conclude it. Any delays would damage his position, because the commissioners would regard it as sign of Mazarin's continuing bad faith.[47] Bordeaux might have been overstating his case, in order to hurry the return of de Baas with new instructions from Paris, but other observers supported his views about English reluctance to place much trust in Mazarin's words unless they were backed by actions.

7

New Policies Considered

At the conclusion of the Dutch war, Cromwell's bargaining position was excellent. England had emerged from the war with no international commitments. Then too, it had a powerful army and navy—two assets that led the European powers to strengthen their efforts to obtain an alliance with Cromwell. It was commonly assumed by foreign diplomats that Cromwell intended to pursue a more active foreign policy, but there was little agreement concerning the details of the actions. Cromwell and his advisers were in no haste to commit themselves to a specific policy. They wanted the opportunity to ascertain the motives of their potential allies. This presented a major problem with Mazarin, because of the inscrutable front he presented and his reputation for duplicity.[1] The Cardinal railed against delays by England, but those delays were sure to continue until he took an unequivocal stand in favor of Cromwell's government.[2]

The enigmatic nature of the Protector played a critical role in shaping the policies of other states. The manner in which foreign diplomats portrayed Cromwell helped to determine his actions as well as those of their own governments. Many of the descriptions were inaccurate, but led to concessions that, in turn, changed Cromwell's demands. Out of the mass of confused and contradictory opinions concerning Cromwell, Bordeaux and de Baas focused their attention on two issues—the manner in which Cromwell intended to use his fleet, and the possibility of an alliance between England and Spain.

Bordeaux had passing thoughts that Cromwell might be using the fleet as part of a diplomatic bluff, but the ambassador was not willing to hazard anything on this estimate.[3] When Cromwell allocated the funds to refit the fleet at Portsmouth, most diplomats were convinced he intended to use it. A new series of rumors circulated throughout Europe. At The Hague, it was thought that Cromwell was using the fleet as a lure for an alliance with Spain, the first objective of which was supposedly the reconquest of Portugal.[4] There were rumors that the fleet might be used to assist Spain in the Mediterranean, to aid Condé in an invasion of France, or to put down potential rebellions in Scotland and Ireland. Bordeaux regarded the fleet as Cromwell's means of implementing England's hostile feelings toward all its neighbors. If this was true, there was a good possibility that its first action might be to retaliate against France for the past seizures of English merchant vessels.[5] Even de Baas, who was usually optimistic, was afraid that Cromwell might have offered his fleet to Spain, and reported to Mazarin: "The Protector . . . will have some connection with our enemies."[6] De Baas did not think Cromwell had closed his mind to negotiations with France or that there were any concrete issues dividing the two states. The real problem was to convince the Protector of the sincerity of Mazarin and to wipe out the suspicions that lingered about France.

It took the specter of an Anglo-Spanish alliance to get Mazarin to propose real concessions to Cromwell. Cardenas had offered an alliance to Cromwell, to which the Protector had responded with a concilatory message to Madrid.[7] Cardenas's proposals, the details of which Mazarin learned, involved an offensive and defensive alliance against France, a large cash payment to England, and England's cooperation in an invasion of France. All the conditions seemed reasonable, and rekindled the fears that had been present in France since the consolidation of the Commonwealth.[8] Mazarin was finally convinced that the time for obscure proposals, generalizations, and polite gestures had passed. De Baas was authorized to meet the Spaniards on their own terms and to attempt to top any financial offer they had made. Besides trying to outbid Spain, de Baas was to attempt to convince

Cromwell that France would pay what it offered but that
Spain had a notoriously bad record for paying its debts and
keeping its promises. Mazarin also wanted to remind Cromwell that by breaking with France, he might cut himself off
from Sweden and face new opposition in Scotland and
Ireland. In a more positive vein, Mazarin also wanted to
show Cromwell that cooperation with France would "be more
advantageous a course for their commerce and for an infinity
of other reasons." The Cardinal's instructions to de Baas
concluded by stating that "just the idea of protecting the
crowns that are under his protection should be reason enough
to make him stop to consider his actions towards France
... and it will not be necessary to repeat often to the
Protector how much France can help him to defend and
affirm his dignity and his power."[9]

It was to the preparation of the fleet that Bordeaux looked
for signs of Cromwell's plans. The ambassador was convinced
that no specific plans had been made for the fleet but that
the general temper of the Protector did not bode well for
France.[10] The only positive note in Bordeaux's dispatches
was that an Anglo-Spanish alliance had not yet been concluded, because Spain could not raise enough silver.[11] When
Mazarin was finally convinced that Cromwell was on the
verge of an alliance with Spain, he authorized de Baas and
Bordeaux to offer Cromwell a large amount of money and
a force of cavalry if the Protector wanted to invade Dunkirk
or Gravelines. Mazarin felt that Bordeaux should have no
trouble convincing Cromwell that a break with Spain would
be greeted with "the applause of all the English," [since]
he [Cromwell] would be able to insure himself of an important place like Dunkirk and could also look forward to seizing
much valuable territory in the Spanish Indies."[12]

The suggestion that Cromwell seize some Spanish territory
in the Indies had obvious attractions for the Cardinal. The
lure of wealth and potential power might convince Cromwell
to break with Spain. The Indies also presented an objective
for which the fleet at Portsmouth could be used. If Cromwell
was already considering an attack on the Indies, Mazarin
might be able to create closer ties with the Protector at no
cost to France. If Cromwell had not chosen a target for the

fleet, Mazarin's suggestion might serve as a stimulus to English action. If the fleet was being readied to attack France or its possessions, there was some chance that the Cardinal's ideas might give Cromwell some cause to reconsider.

Ideally, Mazarin wanted to foment a break between England and Spain, and then have England join France as an ally against a common enemy. But the Cardinal's comments about the Indies exposed the impotence of France's policy toward Cromwell. There was no way for the Cardinal to exert real influence to assure that his suggestions were carried out, and it was not clear that France would gain anything if they were implemented. The Protector retained an almost total freedom of action, and any policy he chose to follow would be based on his own set of priorities and would be implemented by his own resources.

Mazarin's idea that England attack the West Indies did not have even the advantage of originality. There was a buccaneering tradition that went back to the Elizabethan age, and there had been a strong feeling in the Parliaments of James I that Spain's possessions were fair game for English and Protestant expansion.[13] A more recent—and persuasive— argument for England's intervention in the Indies had been presented by Thomas Gage, a former resident of that area. Gage appealed to Cromwell to mount a large-scale attack, after assuring the Protector that the plans were not an attempt to draw the fleet away from the British Isles.[14] The power of England's fleet was a sign of God's providence, and the fleet should be used "for faith in the saints, in behalf of God's glory." Gage said he had seen "the flourishing condition and strength of the House of Austria (Rome's chief strength and pillar) and hath observed the Austrian pillar's strength to bee in the American mines; which being taken away from Austria, Rome's triple crown would soone fall away and decay." An attack on the Indies was justified because God was fed up with the sinful and proud Spanish, and "their sinnes would betray and fight against them, if ever any nation shall oppose them." Gage did not rest his case on divine assistance, but further asserted that "within the maine land . . . in the greatest cities, there was no one gun or field piece, or wall, or castle, or any bulwarke." Once the invaders landed, they would be met by Indian tribes who would assist them, and the "Spanish, being a fat, lazy, sinfull people, feeding like beasts upon their lusts, and upon the fat of the land, and never trained up to warres, would not be much opposition." After England had overthrown the Spanish power in the Indies "Godly missionaries" could be sent to convert the Indians and "worke for the greater glory of God . . . and to the ruining and the utter fall of the Romish Babylon."[15]

Gage's presentation included many of the elements that had been identified with the opposition to James I and Charles I, the political milieu in which Cromwell had been shaped. Gage echoed the missions of Drake and Raleigh, the complaints against Gondomar, Parliament's frustration about the Protestant debacle in the early years of war in Germany, the Cromwellian campaigns in Ireland, and the Commonwealth's attempts to bring the light of the Gospel into the far corners of its own territory.[16] "The greater glory of God" ran through so much of Cromwell's descriptions of his own role in the Civil Wars that he could scarcely have ignored Gage's comments. However, "the greater glory of God" was an elusive quantity to define. Even if Cromwell's notion of God's purpose was not identical with Gage's view, the latter also appealed to the economic gain and political opportunism that had been present throughout the formation of the Commonwealth.[17] Gage's presentation was one more example of the "Trust in God and keep your powder dry" attitude that Christopher Hill has pointed out as one of the characteristics of the Puritanism that manifested itself in the Civil Wars, and whose most representative figure was Oliver Cromwell.[18]

Gage was the most recent in a long series of pamphleteers who propagated the "Black Legend" in England. His writings dwelt on the clerical immorality and mistreatment of the Indians in the Spanish colonies. Among Englishmen who wrote attacks on Spain, Gage was uniquely qualified to support his charges. He was a renegade Dominican who, according to his own account, became so disillusioned with conditions in the Indies that he returned to England and became a Puritan. Certainly, his presentations had all the hallmarks of a convert, one who could see nothing but the depravity of his former associates and one who had dedicated his life to the destruction of their power. Gage's total rejection of the Catholic Church and the practices of the Spaniards in the Indies led him to overstate his case. Because he fervently wished an end to Spain's domination of the Indies, he believed it could be easily accomplished—all that was necessary was an earthly agent to set in motion the wrath of divine providence. Gage dwelt not only on the sinfulness of the Spanish but also on their weakness. His writings and his appearance before the council certainly had an influence on Cromwell's view of an expedition to the Indies. Gage made it appear not only necessary but easy to destroy the power of Spain in the Indies.[19]

Gage's traditionalist description of Spain as the support of Rome and the enemy of England raised questions that were more complex than he described. For many months, there had been circulating widely accepted stories that an Anglo-Spanish treaty was near completion. In this context, an attack on the Indies seemed only reasonable to most observers, if carried out in the spirit of "no peace beyond the line." That was not, however, what Gage was describing. The attack he proposed was part of a war against the Habsburgs and Catholicism. It was unlikely that members of the council could have thought Gage was describing another hit-and-run raid. It was also reasonable to assume that Spain recognized the importance of the Indies and would not accept losses without retaliating. They had different ends in mind, but both Gage and Mazarin were using the lure of the Indies to involve Cromwell in an active role in the worldwide struggle against the Habsburgs.

One indication of the paucity of France's offerings to Cromwell was the difficulty Bordeaux and de Baas found in getting a chance to appear before the Protector and the council. Bordeaux and de Baas relied heavily on Gilbert Pickering, a member of the Protector's commission on foreign affairs, to aid them and present France's case in a good light.[20] This confidence had not been rewarded by any positive action, and by April, 1654, Mazarin was beginning to distrust Pickering.[21] A more serious threat to France's situation was

the position of Secretary Thurloe. Not only was Thurloe
one of Cromwell's closest confidants, but most of the foreign
intelligence reports passed through his hands. It was Thurloe
who digested and relayed the information to Cromwell upon
which the Protector based his decisions concerning foreign
affairs. Both Mazarin and de Baas were convinced that
Thurloe was partial to the interests of Spain, and that he
was trying to influence Cromwell in its favor.[22] If this was
true, France was operating at a serious disadvantage in the
contest for Cromwell's assistance.

Mazarin was disturbed when he heard that Cromwell and
Cardenas had agreed on the price to be paid for English
troops, and that specific areas in France where the Huguenot
population was high had been chosen for an invasion.[23] At
the same time the Cardinal received these discouraging
reports, de Baas asserted that his own negotiations were more
advanced than at any time since his arrival.[24] Much of this
feeling was based on conversations with Pickering and a
friend of Thurloe's in which de Baas was assured that
Cromwell had made no arrangements with Spain. De Baas
placed even greater significance on Cromwell's recent questions concerning Mazarin's situation within France, assuming that Cromwell's curiosity was a sure sign of his interest
in Mazarin as an ally.[25] The conclusions reached by de Baas
and Mazarin again demonstrated the Protector's capacity
for masking his thoughts and plans from the inquiries of
foreign diplomats.

While the Cardinal and his advisers were trying to sort
out the contradictory reports they received about Cromwell,
Bordeaux urgently informed them that Cromwell was ready
to make some important decisions. The council was holding
meetings with many diplomats; rumors in London described
a renewed interest in the situation of the Huguenots; and
the Protector sent envoys to many German Protestant states
to inquire about alliances. Bordeaux thought the main purpose behind such alliances was to bolster Cromwell's reputation with militant Puritans in England.

Bordeaux was correct in his assumption that the Protectorate was taking a careful look at its foreign policy. On
20 April 1654, the council had a lengthy debate concerning

proposals to invade the Indies. The debate was made up of a set of propositions, followed by a detailed discussion of the pros and cons of each of them.[26] The discussion started on the premise that since the Dutch peace the Protectorate had one hundred and sixty ships and a large army, which had to be used or disbanded. The question was how these forces should be employed—to attack France with Spanish help, to attack Spain with French help, or to get money from both countries. These alternatives were not up for debate; they were the guidelines under which the discussion took place.

The arguments concerning an attack on France were dominated by the negative position. The first contention was that a war against France would be difficult and unprofitable. There was a suspicion that Spain was only trying to get England and France to fight one another; then Spain would not help England, preferring to see the two states exhaust themselves. The final argument was couched in religious terms:

The weakening of France and the greatening of the Spaniard being the greatest prejudice to the Protestant cause all over Europe, the Spaniard being the greatest enemy to the Protestant in the world, and a nation of great councill, and harder to be dispossessed of any accesse of greatness: the French not soe bitter against the Protestants, a people not to be kept from intestine divisions and easier disturbed and distracted at any tyme.

The considerations that militated against an attack on France were a combination of factors that men with such diverse viewpoints as Strickland, Barrière, and Bordeaux had noted. The weakness of the government in France and the possibility of another Fronde, issues that Barrière had stressed in his talks with Cromwell, actually worked against his cause. The threat of internal collapse did not make France a more promising target for England, but made Spain a more dangerous potential enemy. The council's deliberations underscored a much more important point, on which all the

foreign observers were misled or deluded themselves—that
an attack on France or Spain would force England into an
alliance. The council took it for granted that whatever
decision was made, England could count on support from
either France or Spain without making further commitments.

The council discussed six points favorable to an attack
on Spain: a raid on the Indies would be profitable; aid was
available from France because that country was weak and
could not afford to offend England; Spanish territories were
so large that they "may well admitt a sound losse"; Spain
was the greatest enemy of Protestantism; Spain was the
traditional enemy of England; and conditions in the Indies
made a successful invasion likely. When it was obvious that
the sense of the meeting favored an attack on Spain, the
council turned its attention to various targets and invasion
plans. Two former English residents of Hispaniola, Captains
Hatsell and Lymere, appeared as expert witnesses. They
proposed the capture of Hispaniola and Havana, in order
to dominate the Indies and gain a stranglehold over the
movements of the Spanish fleet. Their arguments were a
combination of Elizabethan ideas and an assessment of the
situation of the Protectorate. They held out assurances that
the treasure fleet could be captured, and that "affairs in
Scotland could better be settled by transporting 8000 to
10,000 men per year." A final point in favor of the attack
was that it was favorable to many of the elements in Parliament. They discounted any chance of failure, asserting that
Spain was so weakened by its war with France that it could
not oppose any attack by England.[27]

Despite the persuasive presentation made by the two
captains, some members of the council raised serious questions about the broader diplomatic implications of an attack
on territory that was so valuable to Spain. There would
probably be a sizable loss to England's trade if good relations
with Spain were disrupted. This was countered by the assertion:

Notwithstanding our warr with Spain in America, it is
possible, if not reasonable to expect that wee may have

peace and trade in Europe, for his necessitye of our trade will replace it, but especially his interest in Flanders, which he hath no way either to relieve with forces of monyes but through out Channell, which if hee have warr in Europe he will certainly be debarred of.

A second assertion was made—that a conflict with Spain might make trade in the Straits more difficult. This was met by the argument that friendship between France and England would open the Mediterranean to more trade and improve the overall position of England's commerce.

The final objection was that the Dutch would gain much trade from Spain, make themselves richer, and then try to gain revenge for the results of the war with England. These considerations were countered by the argument that the Treaty of Münster showed that the Dutch were not a reliable ally in any case. Some members of the council, especially those who thought the exclusion of the house of Orange from power in the Netherlands was vital to the interests of the Protectorate, stressed that France was influential in the Dutch states that supported Orange. The discussion concerning the Dutch abruptly changed focus and revolved around the views and actions France might take.[28]

The council concluded its proceedings by discussing further advantages that would accrue from an Anglo-French peace: the hindering of peace "betweene the two great crownes, assistance for the Protestant cause throughout the world, and discountenance of our rebells in Scotland and fugitives" elsewhere in Europe. The discussion had strayed far from its originally limited topic, and it became evident that propositions about the Indies could not be made without putting them in the context of the Habsburg-Bourbon war. Much of the discussion echoed what Bordeaux had been saying ever since he arrived in London. It would be, however, a great mistake to credit France with having any direct influence over the council's deliberations or decisions. At no time did the council feel it had to make a choice between France and Spain. Comments about a peace with France were based on the smug assumption that France wanted closer ties with England so badly that it would support the

Protectorate if it was allowed the opportunity. The council was looking after its own interests, and assumed its decisions would be met with approval, or at least forbearance, by the major European powers. Three months later, the council held another meeting; this time, they discussed in greater detail the plans to attack the Indies and the possible internal repercussions.

The meeting of 20 April marked a turning point in the formulation of England's foreign policy. The discussion owed some of its form to the bombast of the Commonwealth, but that was being replaced by a calculated self-assurance. The Protectorate had received formal recognition from the leading states; an ambassador extraordinary had been dispatched from France; and England had received offers of alliances and large payments from both France and Spain. England had seen that Condé was considering abandoning his ally and protector the King of Spain to ally with a regicide. The Protector had negotiated with the Dutch a treaty that was favorable to his interests, and had persuaded the Dutch to accept it over strenuous objections from some of the Provinces. The strength of England's fleet had been felt in the Mediterranean, and the assistance of the Protector was sought by Protestants throughout Europe. It was undeniable that the Protectorate had taken giant strides toward establishing itself as a power in the world. Even more remarkable was the fact that the offers of alliances and money that flowed into England were unsolicitied. The future appeared even brighter since Cromwell had made no concessions or commitments. The Protectorate not only possessed power; it also had freedom of action.

Cromwell's decision to attack the West Indies has received more attention by historians than any other action of his in the field of foreign policy. There has been a wide divergence of opinion concerning the motives behind the Western Design, the manner in which it was handled, and the effect it had on future policies. It has been described as: a monumental piece of folly; a forward-looking attempt to establish England's power in the Americas; a blind throwback to the Elizabethan privateers; a sign of Cromwell's implacable hatred of Spanish Catholicism; a desperate attempt to distract Englishmen from their discontent with the Protectorate; and a demonstration of Cromwell's capacity for hypocrisy. There has been general agreement, however, that the Western Design marked the start of an important new phase in Cromwell's foreign policy.

The Western Design was one of the most dramatic episodes in the history of the Protectorate. Unlike Cromwell's other actions, much of the drama was provided by the manner in which it blundered along its course. Despite its outcome, the Western Design was not an impulsive step taken on some whim of the Protector. It was sanctioned by the council after a series of methodical debates had carefully weighed the possible gains and losses involved in an attack against Hispaniola and a possible war with Spain.

The plans for the Western Design were completed at a meeting of the council on 20 July 1654.[29] While the council was making preparations to attack Hispaniola, negotiations between England and Spain had continued. Barrière, Condé's representative in England, stated that the only issue dividing the two states was the question of how much aid Cromwell would receive if he attacked France. He was sure that Cromwell was coming to terms with Spain, and feared that Spain would neglect Condé's interests.[30]

While the Protector's council was discussing its policy toward Spain, Bordeaux and de Baas were shunted into the background. Both complained that they were not receiving a fair hearing, but they would have been less disturbed had they known the direction in which Cromwell's policy was moving. Knowing little about the council's deliberations, Bordeaux must have been reminded of his abortive negotiations before the signing of the Anglo-Dutch peace treaty.

8

The de Baas Fiasco

Throughout the spring of 1654, Bordeaux's reactions to Cromwell's policies were a mixture of bewilderment, frustration, and caution. He complained that the commissioners showed no friendship toward him despite his constant efforts to make proposals that seemed in the best interests of the Protectorate. Bordeaux had the impression that the English were treating him as a supplicant whose main function was to serve as a foil to more serious negotiations being carried on with Barrière and Cardenas. Bordeaux was especially annoyed by the commissioners' habit of speaking to him in friendly terms and then issuing inflamatory statements against France. He cautioned Mazarin to disregard the substance of those statements, "believing that he [Cromwell] should not be presumed to have an attachment to the enemies of his Majesty."[1] Bordeaux thought that any break with England would be the result of miscalculation or misunderstanding on Cromwell's part. In this respect, the ambassador feared that stories of the mistreatment of the Huguenots might cause a breach between England and France, either from a sincere desire in England to support the Huguenots or by giving Cromwell an excuse to ally with Spain. He might support Spain "under the pretext of assisting those of the religion that are claimed to be persecuted."[2] The most difficult part of Bordeaux's position was that there was little he could do to convince the English of the well-being of the Huguenots, short of Mazarin granting Cromwell a protectorate over them—and that idea was politically impossible.

The focus of most diplomatic attention turned to Admiral Blake, who was preparing for sea. Four possibilities were the most widely discussed: to attack Portugal in conjunction with Spain; to establish an English foothold in the Mediterranean; to attack France, in support of the Huguenots; to attack some of Spain's possessions in the Indies.[3] In the reports of many foreign diplomats, some of these plans were combined. There was agreement on only one point—Cromwell intended to use the fleet to implement some aggressive design.

The diplomats were making important assumptions based on their reading of Cromwell's intentions. These assumptions, more than Cromwell's actions, conditioned the way diplomats acted toward him. There is no evidence that he had made definite plans for the fleet, but the council meeting of 20 April showed he had certainly given some thought to uses for the navy. Cromwell appeared to outsiders to have no long-range plans, and therefore whatever tactical victories the fleet might gain could determine his overall policy. Cromwell's actions during the spring of 1654 bewildered most of the diplomats who dealt with him and forced them to constantly reevaluate their own circumstances.

By the end of April, Barrière was confident that Cromwell intended to sign a treaty with Spain, but then the Protector turned his attentions to France. Condé's representative conjectured that Cromwell did not want to declare war on any state at that time, but that he might be willing to allow Spain to hire units of the New Model Army and the navy. Less than two weeks after stating that the Protector wanted to avoid any war, Barrière reported "that he [Cromwell] has resolved to employ [a fleet of thirty ships and a land force of nineteen thousand] men against the French." Barrière concluded that "the religious of the district of Languedoc and Provence are the inducement there, if he has that design."[4]

Bordeaux came to the view that Cromwell was trying to obtain aid from France without having to commit any of his resources or to make any hostile moves against France's enemies.[5] However, the French ambassador's actions toward Cromwell were very different from Barrière's; the former did not have the luxury of impotence. Condé's representative could theorize about Cromwell's policies and treat them in a detached manner, since there was little he could do to influence them.

Even when Bordeaux appeared to have some insight into the Protector's plans, the divisions within the Protectorate complicated matters. Bordeaux recognized the nature of the divisions, but that left him more discouraged at his own prospects. He feared that Cromwell might be willing to attack France to placate some of the council's desire to use the army. Bordeaux had come to the conclusion that Cromwell, much as he was rumored to dislike France, was really the major brake on hostilities between England and France.[6]

Bordeaux and de Baas stepped up their appeals to Cromwell as rumors of Lambert's hostility toward France became more widespread. De Baas flattered the Protector, reminded him of Mazarin's concern for the preservation of the Protectorate, and tried to convince Cromwell "that if we break, nothing could be more disastrous to the Protector than for it to occur at a time when the Scottish party is strengthened."[7] Bordeaux took a more direct approach. After reminding Cromwell that negotiations had dragged on for months, during which time England's trade had been harmed, Bordeaux said he would leave England if no agreement were reached soon. The threat had little effect on Cromwell, leading Bordeaux to complain to Mazarin, "All my reasons did not produce any good response."[8] The only satisfaction Bordeaux and de Baas could find in their work was that the much-rumored alliance between Cromwell and Spain had not been concluded.[9] Nevertheless, the overwhelming diplomatic opinion was that Cromwell favored Spain and opposed France.[10] France was forced to court Cromwell actively and combat Spain for his friendship. This fact was obvious to the English commissioners, and explained the nonchalance with which they treated Bordeaux's threats to leave. He, in turn, warned Mazarin that it was a mistake to push the Protector into making a hasty decision.[11]

There continued to be tremendous confusion surrounding Cromwell's feelings toward France. Barrière, who had been so optimistic about an Anglo-Spanish agreement, felt compelled to reassure Madrid that there was no truth to the rumor of an Anglo-French treaty.[12] His position reflected the views of most diplomats—that their opponent had the inside track with the Protector, and might be close to an alliance with him. The confusion and apprehension among the diplomats in England aided the diplomatic position of the Protectorate. However, there was no evidence, aside from Bordeaux's comments, that the English were consciously fostering these feelings.

The divisions within the council were much more important since the establishment of the Protectorate. It is deceptively easy to view the Protectorate as an autocracy, with absolute power resting in Cromwell's hands. The Instrument of Government, under which he assumed power included limitations on his actions and provided an important role for the council. Beyond these paper considerations, the council played a critical role in the government because of the men who sat on it.[13] John Lambert, "the architect of the Protectorate" and the guiding force behind the Instrument of Government, joined Cromwell and four other generals on the Council of State.[14] The diligence with which Lambert attended its meetings and the vigor with which he spoke demonstrated that he certainly regarded it as more than a formal body. Lambert had few compunctions about arguing with the Protector during sessions of the council, but it appears that Lambert made no attempt to take their differences outside the chamber in which they were originally aired.

The best-known of the differences between Lambert and Cromwell concerned the plans for the Western Design. This disagreement had no lasting effect on their ability to work together; there were more important reasons for them to cooperate. The creation of the Protectorate had alienated the Fifth Monarchists and the republicans from Cromwell forever and, in so doing, had helped forge a stronger bond between Lambert and Cromwell. Lambert's desire to aid the Yorkshire wool traders, with whom he had close ties, may well have led him to oppose Cromwell's plan to raid the Spanish Indies.[15] It was certainly not important enough to Lambert to press the issue after the council's decision had been made. The debate over the Western Design made it clear that Lambert and Cromwell could disagree over specific issues without tearing the fabric of the government apart. The debate also demonstrated that when Cromwell took an unambiguous position in opposition to one taken by Lambert, the Protector's views would prevail.

It is true that divisions existed within the council, and their existence was a constant topic of conversation and concern among foreign diplomats. However, these diplomats were looking at the Protectorate Council of State through eyes they had used during the Rump and the Barebones. The diplomats overestimated both the depth and the importance of the divisions within the council, and were reluctant to act until they could understand or predict the actions of that body. Foreign observers had grown so accustomed to domestic squabbles in England and dramatic shifts in policy that it was difficult for them to accept the obvious as true and to give the proper credence to the apparent policies formulated by Cromwell and the council.

The diplomatic style of the Protectorate was influenced by the lack of well-defined long-range objectives as well as by divisions of opinion within the council.

Aside from the Protector, one figure appeared to play a crucial role in the Council's determination of foreign policy— John Thurloe. Even a cursory reading of foreign diplomatic correspondence makes it clear that Thurloe was thought to have great influence with Cromwell. The opinion of his countrymen did little to downgrade this impression of his importance.

Thurloe had been in the service of Oliver St. John until he became secretary to the Council of State in 1652. At the formation of the Protectorate, Thurloe became Cromwell's sole Secretary of State. The relationship between Cromwell and Thurloe has defied full explanation. Almost every work dealing with Cromwell takes the same approach—that Thurloe was the cool, calculating "civil servant" in whom Cromwell could confide and to whom he turned for sober counsel when he was besieged by the schemes of others. Thurloe appears to have been almost without personal ambition, a situation that might be explained by the position he had already achieved. His roles in the council and as postmaster and head of a widespread intelligence network certainly made him more than a diligent clerk. His correspondence touches on every aspect of the Protectorate, but says little about himself. The impression that comes through is that Cromwell discussed his ideas with Thurloe and placed trust in his talent to evaluate their feasibility. Almost all the intelligence upon which the Protector and the council based their decisions was obtained by Thurloe's agents and made its way through his hands. He had wide discretion in the choice of agents and the tasks he set for them. There is no evidence concerning the criteria he used to choose agents, although the accuracy of their information was the crucial factor determining whether they would be maintained. There is also no evidence about the manner in which Thurloe selected the intelligence to be presented to Cromwell and the manner in which it was presented.

Another way in which Thurloe exercised an influence on Cromwell's foreign policy was through his relationship with foreign diplomats. By the end of 1654, most diplomats regarded Thurloe as the Protector's closest confidant. Given the aloof, inscrutable nature of the Protector, many diplomats looked to Thurloe for signs of what policies they should adopt. Thurloe's importance became almost a self-fulfilling prophecy among foreign diplomats. The more they tried to bring their position in line with how they read Thurloe's actions, the more the Secretary influenced the options that were open to his master.

Thurloe served many purposes for Cromwell. He was the diligent, hard-working bureaucrat, to whom Cromwell could apparently turn for dispassionate advice. He was also Cromwell's link with the diplomatic world, the man by means of whom "trial balloons" could be launched. Thurloe was the Protector's buffer against the interference of foreign concerns when more pressing problems had to be handled. The Secretary's rather dry and colorless approach toward his job made him a perfect man to manage Cromwell's diplomatic policy, which emphasized the positive value of delay and postponement, a care for minute detail, and an aversion to make any commitment until the highest possible price had been obtained. One critical question remains—what was Thurloe's role, if any, in creating the foreign policy he administered so efficiently? It is a question to which I have no precise answer other than to note that Thurloe's comments made during the life of the Protector showed an unusually high ability to empathize with the policy. In his recollections after the Restoration, even when Thurloe might have tried to disassociate himself from the policies of Cromwell, it is clear that the Secretary understood and believed in those policies in a way that suggests greater involvement than that of a clerk. There is no reason to believe the policies were created by Thurloe or forced upon an unsuspecting Cromwell. The Protector and his Secretary achieved a unique meeting of minds which enabled them to create a policy that represented Cromwell's aims and Thurloe's understanding that ideals and goals meant little if no way could be found to put them into practice.

The dilatory nature of English policy forced Bordeaux to develop a more aggressive approach to his negotiations and to find something new to offer. He attempted to start a discussion concerning the term of address that Cromwell preferred in official documents. The ambassador regarded this as an important and delicate point, but the commissioners dismissed it, saying that the Protector "had sovereign authority as great as that of kings."[16] Bordeaux was placed on the defensive again, and was reminded of the importance the new government attached to itself.

Bordeaux and de Baas had shown little ability to coordinate their efforts. Their sources of information about Cromwell were different, as were their views on the motives of other policy makers in England. These differences caused wide gulfs between the suggestions they made to Mazarin for treating with England. For the most part, de Baas was more optimistic, but he had not experienced the delays and insults that Bordeaux had received.

By the end of May, a new set of problems faced French diplomacy. On the surface, the situation had improved. Bordeaux had finally been able to discuss real issues with the commissioners. He was not fully satisfied with the results of the meeting, but his letters to Mazarin showed renewed hope and expectations of better news to follow. In the next dispatch, Bordeaux informed Mazarin that

> There is every reason to expect a prompt conclusion in the affairs ... it seems we ought to conclude according to the intentions of your Eminence since we have remained in agreement in all general propositions ... as he [Cromwell] was not able to find any other pretexts to break off, after having held us for some time. ....
> If his proceeding is sincere, as his ministers wish to convince me, this negotiation will be concluded in a few days.[17]

Bordeaux was right. Major changes were taking place in the English attitude toward his mission—changes that bore out his contention that the success of his negotiations depended on the extent to which Cromwell believed Mazarin's professions of friendship. The ironic feature about the collapse of Bordeaux's negotiations, which occurred in June, 1654, was that he had no control over the events that caused it—intelligence from France which accused Mazarin of plotting against Cromwell and activities attributed to de Baas.

In late May, Thurloe received news describing a new French policy toward the Stuarts. It was reported that Mazarin was waiting for his envoy to return from Spain after soundng out the Habsburgs about a general peace. If the peace was concluded, the Cardinal intended to throw his full support behind a move to restore the Stuarts.[18] The reports were not an accurate description of Mazarin's activities, but presented a view that responsible Englishmen could find plausible. The alleged activities of Mazarin conjured up in the minds of Cromwell's advisers the same fears that had been expressed in the past—the deceitfulness of the Cardinal, the dangers of a general peace, and French support for the Stuarts. The intelligence also portrayed Bordeaux and de Baas as willing tools of their master's devious policies. When de Baas was implicated in a plot against Cromwell's life, the intelligence reports took on new importance.

The conspirators, who had planned an attack on the

Protector, had hoped to gain the support of dissidents in the army and to use them to overthrow the government. The plan had misfired, and the government quickly rounded up its leaders. When the origins of the plot were traced to Englishmen who had formerly resided in France, some member of the Protector's council saw the hand of Mazarin behind the plot. This suspicion gained support when one of the plotters, Dr. Naudin, confessed that de Baas had promoted and organized the conspiracy. Naudin stated that de Baas had grown frustrated with the Protector's delaying tactics and, in April, had approached Naudin and asked him to organize a mutiny in the army. According to Naudin, de Baas had despaired of obtaining any assistance from Cromwell, and had grown convinced that the interests of France could be served only if the Protectorate was toppled.[19]

Cromwell's government exercised restraint in dealing with the attempted assassination, but also showed vigilance and determination to protect itself. Soon after the disclosure of the plot, new questions arose. There was some discussion, primarily in France, that it had been organized by Thurloe to give the Protector an excuse to establish tighter controls in England. There is no evidence to support this contention, but there is little doubt that Cromwell used the plot to strengthen his position.

Naudin's confession was the only link between de Baas and the conspiracy. The timing of the confession was disastrous for Bordeaux, occurring just when he was sure that his suggestion for an alliance had been greeted with "friendly discussion on both sides." He also thought that he had finally convinced the commissioners that France could not, in keeping with its dignity, initiate all the proposals. He was so encouraged that he asked the Cardinal for authorization to conclude a defensive alliance with England. Still wary of further delays, Bordeaux wanted the new commission sent quickly, because "If they [the commissioners] approve this way of treating, we should be able to clear up very soon the intentions of this regime, which one must always distrust, until the signing of the treaty.[20]

Bordeaux did not believe in de Baas's participation in the plot. Despite their cool relationship, Bordeaux felt he would have known about any plan to overthrow Cromwell.[21] The ambassador was forced to conclude either that he had been deceived by his own government or that the Protector had decided to place another obstacle in the path of an agreement with France.

De Baas's actions during the investigations of the plot showed little awareness of the situation. While Thurloe and his agents were rounding up the conspirators, de Baas informed Mazarin that the commissioners had led him to expect "not only . . . an agreement, but a close and prompt liaison." De Baas had noticed "that their manner of acting seemed more suspect than at first," but he attributed that to a desire "to lengthen the negotiations." He finally became concerned when Cromwell abruptly canceled two interviews. De Baas was afraid that if Cromwell continued to avoid him, "our affair is rather far from conclusion." Despite momentary setbacks, de Baas still thought Cromwell wanted ties with France, and told Mazarin that Pickering "has often confirmed it [a treaty between England and France] to me, and said that we had, he and I, the honor of this great work. . . . Meanwhile this important audience [with Cromwell] has vanished and instead of a short and plain path of trust where we were . . . [Cromwell] gives articles for examination which could lead us to infinity." When de Baas "examined more particularly the behavior of Oliver Cromwell," he expressed the fear that the Protector's reluctance to ally with France might be because "Oliver Cromwell does not find me a proper subject to receive and sustain this important secret." This analysis came to the conclusion that the Protector, "being uncertain of the party that he should take . . . in order to maintain himself considerable by the good and the bad he could do . . . still regarded France as a dangerous enemy which he always distrusted because of the English Royal House." De Baas thought that he had calmed most of Cromwell's fears, and could not understand why the commissioners and the Protector still seemed disturbed. There was no mention in de Baas's correspondence of any conspiracy, and he seemed bewildered at the new turn of events.[22]

The plot against Cromwell was mentioned during an interview de Baas had with Pickering, but both men were more interested in discussing the fleet at Portsmouth, the wealth of the Indies, and Cromwell's price for joining an alliance. Pickering supposedly told de Baas to ignore the rumor that France had anything to do with the plot, since it was concocted by the Spanish ambassador. However, de Baas's apprehensions were not stilled; the Englishman "seemed embarrassed by the importance of this attempt [on Cromwell's life] or he had something in his heart he did not wish to explain."[23]

Just as de Baas started to bemoan his situation, Bordeaux was sure that his own position had improved. He learned that Cromwell was leaning toward cooperation with France, and it was virtually certain that he would take some action against Spain's possessions in the Indies. Bordeaux's optimism was dampened by stories that France might be implicated in the plot against Cromwell, but he felt that "after emotions caused by the conspiracy die down . . . nothing will retard the treaty."[24] Despite Bordeaux's confidence that the issue would be dropped, de Baas was ordered to appear before the council. He was presented with a copy of Naudin's deposition and asked to explain it. De Baas felt that he "must not allow himself to be treated as a criminal witness," and declined to answer any questions, saying he would "render account of his actions but to the King."[25] After a short adjournment, the council reconvened and ordered him to leave the country.

Bordeaux's assumption that Cromwell intended to use the plot to postpone negotiations proved incorrect. At the same time de Baas was expelled, Cromwell ordered the commissioners, with whom Bordeaux was dealing, "to draw up a treaty of reasonable and equal conditions," and added that he "did not believe that the King or his Eminence had any part in this enterprise." At a meeting held with Cromwell the next day, Bordeaux tried to convince the Protector that de Baas had had nothing to do with the plot, and alluded to the assistance that France could provide Cromwell in maintainng his position. If Cromwell wanted to stifle future threats, he should agree to the treaty, "which could be concluded in a few hours, since already the general propositions were arranged."[26]

Bordeaux's reaction to de Baas's implication in the plot was a model of diplomatic restraint and clear thinking under great tension. He almost turned a troublesome situation to his advantage by reminding Cromwell that France had not interfered in England's domestic politics. The ambassador took the initiative during the interview with Cromwell, but did not attempt to push matters. The most obvious change in Bordeaux's tactics was his ending threats to leave England. Bordeaux was afraid that any threat coming on the heels of the de Baas episode, might "engage the King in a rupture with England."[27]

Bordeaux's account of the expulsion of de Baas was written more than two weeks after the event. He was obviously pleased by the manner an which he had handled the affair, but the overall diplomatic situation was not satisfactory. Cardenas was having regular meetings with Cromwell; Barrière was telling confidants that Condé could expect help from Cromwell; and the public disclosure of Naudin's confession had stirred up anti-French feelings. Bordeaux cautioned his superiors that France should be prepared for another long series of negotiations. The only good news he received was a report from the council that it was satisfied with the condition of the Huguenots. The aftermath of de Baas's expulsion impressed upon Bordeaux the necessity to convince Cromwell of the Cardinal's sincerity. There appeared little else that the ambassador could do at that time. Despite his bleak appraisal of the situation, Bordeaux informed Mazarin, "That until the treaty may be signed with Spain, I shall not despair of our accommodation, not that I doubt of the bad intentions of Oliver Cromwell, but because it is not possible to arrive at more disadvantages than to have us for declared enemies."[28] Bordeaux had no means of applying pressure on the Protector; his assets were a dogged perseverance and a belief that Cromwell did not want to break with France. Had Bordeaux known about the council's actions of 20 April, he would have been pleased with the situation he had helped to preserve by his handling of the de Baas episode.

Wilbur Cortez Abbott accounted for Cromwell's mild reacaion to de Baas's implication in the plot by saying, "It was regarded by both the Protector and the Cardinal as merely an ordinary move in the diplomatic game which considered the stirring up of rebellion and even assassination as more or less commonplace incidents in the game."[29] However, Cromwell and his supporters had not shown any previous desire to operate their diplomacy according to the rules of the "game." Judged against previous actions, any evidence of French participation in the plot against Cromwell would have dealt a mortal blow to Bordeaux's negotiations. The Protector glossed over the whole matter, but still obtained diplomatic advantages from it. Bordeaux was forced once more to make tangible signs of friendship. The commissioners had a reasonable new excuse for delaying negotiations and a ready answer to Bordeaux's threats to leave England.[30]

9

Cromwell's Policy of Nondecision

The conclusion of the de Baas episode gave Bordeaux an opportunity to turn his attention to other issues. The most pressing problem was the rumored agreement between Cromwell and Spain. Bordeaux received some encouragement when M. de Maseroles, a special agent from Condé, decided to leave London, having been convinced his mission was useless because of "the disposition of the Protector and the powerlessness of the Spanish ambassador . . . [and because] Spain is not able to support the treaty promises it made to England." Cardenas was also finding it difficult to obtain audiences with the Protector."[1] By the end of July, even the ever-optimistic Barrière realized that the Protector had done nothing to implement his supposed friendship for Spain. Barrière blamed this on divisions within the Protector's council, but he completely misinterpreted the nature of the divisions. He informed Condé, "That they have not resolved in the council with which of these two crowns [Spain and France] they should come to an accommodation, and surely they will make war on one of the two. The much greater [faction] want to do it to Spain, on the pretext that the Spanish are the greater enemy of their religion, *but the Protector is not of this opinion*" [my italics].[2] Barrière's conclusions about the direction of English policy were correct, even if his perceptions of the Protector were totally false.

It was clear that Spain was having difficulty raising enough silver to pay for any alliance. Barrière was concerned that "Cardenas was too timid and closed fisted" to gain a commit-

ment from Cromwell.[3] This opinion was unfair to Cardenas;
the ambassador had done all he could to raise the money.
He had already made arrangements with the Archduke to
transfer funds from Brussels to London, but the silver never
appeared in Brussels.[4] The penury of Spain had brought
Cardenas's negotiations to a standstill. He continually regis-
tered protests about the dilatory nature of his negotiations,
and accused Cromwell of breaking a promise to declare war
against France. The situation became all the more frustrating
for Cardenas and Barrière since they assumed the de Baas
episode would be a catalyst to their negotiations. Barrière
was "not able to understand the change in the resolution
of the Protector . . . it seemed that the antics of de Baas
had come at a good time to confirm Cromwell in making
a declaration against France . . . and one cannot see the
reasons for his change."[5]

After the furore about de Baas subsided, diplomats in
London again turned their attention to the fleet at Portsmouth. Most rumors agreed that it was going to attack the
Indies,[6] but Palucci tried to view the fleet in the context
of the recent plot against Cromwell. The Venetian thought
that Cromwell was disturbed at Mazarin's involvement in
the plot and that he was going to use the fleet to seize French
shipping, as a lesson to the Cardinal.[7] Bordeaux appeared
less concerned about the fleet than did other diplomats. He
assumed that Cromwell had no specific uses for it at that
time. The freshest look at the importance of the fleet was
presented by the Venetian ambassador in Madrid. He accepted the idea that England was embarking on a more
aggressive policy. He asserted that it did not follow that
Cromwell would ally with either Bourbon or Habsburg, since
England possessed the power, in itself, to become a new factor
in the European state system.[8]

Throughout his attempts to get a treaty with England,
Cardenas had faced the accusation that Spain wanted the
alliance merely to be able to force a peace on France. All
that Cardenas could do was to assure Cromwell that Spain
would not lay down its arms "until the government of Oliver
was made secure and stable and safe from interference by

outside powers."[9] Cardenas seemed to ignore the possibility that Cromwell could not feel secure once Spain decided to lay down its arms. The Protector was in an enviable bargaining position because he had military power that could be auctioned off to the highest bidder. If peace was concluded, what would happen to the leverage Cromwell possessed?

Condé's role in any peace settlement further complicated the situation. It was unlikely that Spain would abandon him, having already supported him with treasure and words. Philip IV might be able to write off the treasure, but his promises could not be ignored. It was a matter not merely of honor but also of practical policy. Spain could not expect its allies to trust it in the future if Condé was abandoned. In this way, Condé's role militated against a peace settlement and to Cromwell's advantage. However, Condé raised a more general issue—the rights of princes and legitimate governments. Within the framework of a traditional dynastic settlement between the Habsburgs and the Bourbons (especially one that had to pay attention to Condé's claims), was there any place for the revolutionary and regicidal government of the Protectorate? It was reasonable to expect Cromwell to distrust any agreement between France and Spain, but it seemed that Cardenas never saw the paradoxical nature of the assurances he gave Thurloe.[10]

Intelligence reports that Thurloe received from Madrid had repeatedly stated that Spain would retaliate for any attack on its territories by the seizure of English goods. The importance of this threat was lessened by a feeling in England that Spain's resources were so low "that they will do no rash act, or soon repent them."[11] Viewed from London, Spain's policy was riddled with contradictions: Spain wanted friendship with the Protectorate, but was not willing to make any important concessions. Spain asserted that it would protect Cromwell's position, but it appeared to have difficulties defending its own interests. By the end of June, even the members of Cromwell's council who wanted friendship with Spain or opposed an attack on its territories knew that they had received no satisfactory offers from Spain and that it presented an enviable target for the military resources of the Protectorate. Cardenas's efforts to create closer ties with England had the result of bringing the areas that divided the two states into sharper focus.

Although Cromwell had favored an aggressive policy against Spain at the 20 April council meeting, he continued the negotiations with Cardenas. There is a slim possibility that Cromwell was trying to obtain conditions from Spain which would change the position he took on 20 April. It was more likely that he used the talks to satisfy himself that the plans to attack Spanish territory were justified and to mask the plans from Cardenas's view. The longer that Cardenas was unable to satisfy Cromwell's demands, the easier it was for the Protector to bring the recalcitrant members of the council to his way of thinking.

The final decision to launch the Western Design was reached at a stormy council meeting held on 20 July 1654. The meeting was dominated by Cromwell and Lambert. The Protector opened the discussion with a declaration that England could never have peace with Spain, because Englishmen had to become idolaters if they wanted to trade in Spanish territories. Lambert did not reply to these charges, but mounted a four-point attack on the decisions reached at the 20 April meeting. He stated that it was improbable that England would capture any valuable territory in the Indies; that there was still much work to be done at home; that the capture of the Indies would do little for Protestants, or to cure factionalism at home; and that the case for the invasion ignored its vast costs. Cromwell's reply appealed to a sense of mission as well as of practical advantges. He dismissed the complaint about the expedition's cost and timing by stating that if it was postponed until victory was assured, it would never be started. Furthermore, it would cost as much to lay up the ships as it would to use them; by invading the Indies, there was a chance for the fleet to pay for itself. The main thrust of Cromwell's reply dealt with the purposes for which the Protectorate had been established—God had brought them "where wee are but to consider the worke that wee may doein the world as well as at home." The attack on the Indies was especially suited to God's design, since "Providence seems to lead us hitherto, havinge 160 ships swimminge."[12]

Lambert made no attempt to counter Cromwell's providentially based arguments, but returned to the costliness of the expedition. If it did not capture a large treasure, the government would have to ask for funds, a step that would lead to hostile feelings in Parliament. Lambert attempted to clinch his argument by stating that the capture of the Indies was of little consequence because Englishmen could not be persuaded to live in an unhealthy climate. Once again, Cromwell stressed the positive side of the expedition—that it probably would capture enough treasure to pay for itself and show a profit.[13]

Unlike the meeting of April 20, the July meeting included no discussion of alternative policies and no mention of a role for France. The deliberations of the Council were implemented on 28 August when Admiral Penn and Colonel Venables received instructions "to attack the Spanish both at land and at sea in these parts [the Americas]; who hath inhumanly murdered diverse of our people there, taken away their possessions and doth commit all acts of hostility against them as oppon [an] enemie."[14]

The July Council session took place against the background of the election to the first Protectorate Parliament. The arguments raised by Lambert might find support among merchants who were involved in trade with Spain as well as some Army officers who feared that internal security had not yet been achieved in England. Cromwell was thinking in more far-reaching terms. He was interested in finding ways to build a broader base of support for his government. The unwillingness or failure of the Protector to exert influence over elections or to effectively manage Parliament has been noted as one of the major difficulties facing his government. Trevor-Roper's valuable article on this subject has, I think, overlooked a major consideration—the ways in which Cromwell might influence Parliament by actions having nothing directly to do with that body.[15] He might not have attempted to exercise influence in Parliament in the traditional fashion, but he did not ignore the problem. This was demonstrated

by the course of action toward the Spanish Indies, as well
as by the reasons presented for it, decided at the council
meeting of 20 July. The Western Design failed as a device
for building support in Parliament as much as it failed in
its immediate military objective. However, the policy was
conceived as more than an Elizabethan raid or an instance
of foreign adventurism isolated from the political needs of
the Protector.

Cardenas was not aware of the decisions of 20 July, but
there was a growing apprehension in Spain about the English
fleet. A galleon was dispatched from Madrid to Santo Domingo to warn the garrison of a possible invasion.[16] Spanish
fears of a break with England were increased by a new rumor
of an agreement between Bordeaux and the Protector. At
the same time, it was widely mentioned that the Marquis
de Lede, Governor of Dunkirk, was going to England as an
ambassador extraordinary from the King of Spain. His mission was to block the final ratification of any Anglo-French
pact and to offer Cromwell a port in Flanders in return for
an alliance with Spain.[17] The rumor about de Lede's mission
was accurate, but by the time he arrived in London in May,
1655, it was much too late to do anything to stop Cromwell's
plans for the Western Design.

By midsummer, 1654, a recognizable pattern had emerged
in Cromwell's dealings with France and Spain. He held out
the possibility of an alliance to both of them—a technique
that raised the asking price for his friendship. Then, after
months of hectic negotiations and a great many rumors, a
quiet fell over the Protector's diplomatic activities. The
displeasure Cromwell had shown toward de Baas acted as
a spur to Bordeaux at the same time it gave Cardenas new
hope. Cromwell continued to receive offers from both ambassadors throughout the summer, but his policy seemed more
mysterious than usual. Neither ambassador realized that on
20 July, the council had already set the machinery in motion
to implement a policy of hostility toward Spain.[18]

While negotiations with Bordeaux and Cardenas were
shelved, Cromwell's advisers turned their attention to the
Stuarts. Charles's failure to capitalize on the situation caused
by the Dutch war had thrust him into the diplomatic

background. The plot against Cromwell's life reawakened a fear of the Stuarts, even though there was no direct link between the plotters and Charles. On the other hand, Charles's inability to assist the plotters had further diminished his standing among foreign diplomats.[19]

The Royalists who surrounded Charles were bitter at Mazarin's treatment of their master. The most strident critics of the Cardinal—among them, Henrietta Maria, Prince Rupert, and Jermyn—were also the leading proponents of an aggressive approach toward the restoration of the King. They planned to gather contributions from other monarchs and raise an army in France. After that, they believed, there would be little difficulty gaining support in England, assassinating the Protector, and staging a successful invasion.[20] Each step in their plan followed automatically from the previous one—all they needed was an opportunity to begin the process. All their past schemes had collapsed, but they blamed their failures on the treachery of the Cardinal. Henrietta Maria and her coplotters ignored their own impotence and heaped scorn upon Mazarin for betraying Louis's kinsman and for standing in the way of the restoration of true monarchy in England.

The other important faction among the Royalists—led by Hyde, Rochester, Inchiquin, and Nicholas—wanted Charles to take a more cautious approach. They remembered the circumstances that had led to Worcester, and saw how tightly the Protector held his grip on England and Scotland. They advised Charles to break off negotiations with Presbyterians and Catholics, and to build a solid foundation of support among the old episcopal party.[21] Hyde's faction did not trust Mazarin, but they displayed no open animosity toward him. They had a grudging admiration for the Cardinal as a statesman doing an important job for his master and had no delusions that Mazarin would distract himself to aid the Stuarts. They expected no support from him unless Cromwell broke with France.

Since the end of the Dutch war, Charles had been restless with his position in France. In July, 1654, he left for Germany, in hopes of rallying support from the Emperor and other princes. The timing of his departure, coming shortly after the expulsion of de Baas, led some diplomats to assume that he had been expelled as a sign of Mazarin's friendship for Cromwell. More suspicious men saw the departure as another of Mazarin's subterfuges.[22] One of Thurloe's informants in Paris summed up these feelings, saying that Mazarin had started Charles's actions as part of a plot "wholly against the Protector and they endeavor to deceive him."[23]

At the resumption of negotiations in July, 1654, Bordeaux was warmly received by the commissioners. Immediately discussions were begun concerning specific provisions for a treaty, and Bordeaux was informed that the Protector had decided to conclude an agreement if Bordeaux could convince Mazarin to make further concessions.[24] There were mixed feelings in Paris about Cromwell's professions of friendship. Brienne displayed a cautious optimism, assuming that Cromwell finally realized that war with France would harm the Protectorate, but the Cardinal was not satisfied.[25] He wanted Bordeaux to do nothing until Cromwell lowered his demands. Even Bordeaux expressed doubts that a treaty on terms acceptable to England would be beneficial to France.[26] At the beginning of August, he asserted that a treaty might be near, but cautioned that until it was signed, England should be regarded as a potentially hostile state.[27] By the beginning of August, Bordeaux finally persuaded the commissioners to discuss questions of indemnities and pledges of nonagression.[28] He was pleased when they promised to let him know their decisions in two days, but his hopes for a prompt settlement were dashed. After hearing nothing for more than a week, Bordeaux assumed that Cromwell was witholding any decision until the resolution of the campaign in Flanders.[29]

The siege of Arras was a major test of strength in the Low Countries. Most observers were convinced of the imminent success of the Spanish siege, but French reinforcements arrived and broke it.[30] Bordeaux hastened to tell Cromwell about the victory. The Protector appeared pleased with the news, but refused to discuss an agreement at that time. Bordeaux was left with the impression that Cromwell was holding out for greater concessions on the assumption that France needed the treaty.[31]

Jean Baptiste Stouppe, minister of the French congregation in London, provided an explanation for Cromwell's reaction to Arras which went far beyond Bordeaux's cautious remarks.[32] Stouppe thought it was likely that the French victory would oblige Cromwell "to make a league to counterbalance the greatness of France . . . and [it was] a likelihood that France, now puffed up with the conceit of this great victory at Arras, will now refuse to yield so much the more what hath been demanded of them."[33] Stouppe and Bordeaux agreed on one point—negotiations between England and France were approaching a climax, because Cromwell was ready to take a major step in foreign affairs. The second assumption was correct, but Cromwell was not ready to alter his relationship with France.

While Bordeaux's talks were virtually suspended, preparations were being made for the September meeting of the first Protectorate Parliament. It was generally agreed that Cromwell's foreign plans were being delayed until Parliament met. Secretary Nicholas drew an analogy between Cromwell's situation and the foreign fiascoes undertaken by Charles I. Cromwell's international position was based on the power of his fleet, since it "keeps all neighboring princes in awe, but it must be an excessive expense to England to maintain so many ships so long; yet he will have to abate no forces by land or sea until he sees how this Parliament are likely to fix." Nicholas was convinced that Cromwell's international position would be weakened as soon as it became clear that Parliament would not grant him the funds to maintain the fleet.[34] Stouppe was more sanguine about Parliament, saying that it would give Cromwell the legal basis "for all the powers he currently possesses and enough money to implement his policies."[35] He assured his friends on the Continent that the Protector had not abandoned the cause of international Protestantism, and that he would act on behalf of fellow Protestants when the time was right. However, no action could be taken unil after the end of the Parliament's session.[36]

Most observers agreed that there was little chance of a break between England and France. The circumstances under which this was considered possible were: a combined

Anglo-Dutch attack on French shipping;[37] the involvement of France in an attack on the Protector; or France's destruction of the Habsburgs, making the Bourbons the masters of Europe. None of these was considered likely; the first two depended on the folly of Mazarin or Bordeaux, and the last seemed physically impossible.

The conjectures concerning an Anglo-French alliance stressed the advantages Cromwell could gain from it. According to Stouppe, Cromwell could join forces with France and gain territory and wealth at the expense of Spain. Stouppe was positive, on the other hand, that Cromwell would not sacrifice his freedom of action to support the Huguenots.[38]

When it appeared that Cromwell was coming closer to an alliance with France, Bordeaux was urged to press his negotiations. He obtained a new series of interviews, but Cromwell remained firm in his demands. He wanted a commitment about the expulsion of the Stuarts and indemnities for English ships that had been seized during the undeclared war at sea. Cromwell closed off another alternative to Bordeaux by rejecting the mediation of a third party, such as Holland.[39] Bordeaux was convinced that the Protector was sure Mazarin would make concessions rather than end the talks. The ambassador knew that he must show Cromwell the error of his assumptions, yield to his demands, or abandon hopes for an agreement.

Foreign diplomats awaited Cromwell's opening address to Parliament as a guide to his policies. In the speech, he stressed the need for stability and recapitulated the internal problems England had faced since the execution of Charles I. The speech underscored Cromwell's determination to retain his power and his intention to implement the design for which God had established the new state. He condemned the persecution of Protestants in all lands, and praised his regime for bringing a halt to the infiltration of England by "emissaries of the Jesuits" and other "ungodly and disruptive elements."[40]

When Cromwell turned his attention to the international situation, he pointed with pride to the changes that had occurred since he had assumed power. At that time, England had been deeply engaged in a war with Portugal, whereby our trade ceased; and the evil consequences by that war were manifest and very considerable . . . we had a war with Holland, consuming our treasure . . . a war that cost this nation full as much as taxes came unto. . . . At the same time we were also in a war with France. The advantages that were taken at the discontents and divisions among ourselves, did also foment that war, and at least hinder us of an honorable peace. . . . This was our condition; spoiled of our trade, and we at this vast expense, thus dissetled at home, and having these engagements abroad.[41]

Cromwell did not say that his government had solved all the problems it faced, but did assert that major advances had been made. England had

peace with Sweathland . . . a kingdom that not many years since was much a friend of France, and lately perhaps inclinable to the Spaniard. And I believe you expect not very much from any of your Catholic neighbors, nor yet that they would be very willing you should have a good understanding with your Protestant friends. . . . You have the Sound open which was obstructed. . . . You have a peace with the Dutch. . . . As a peace with the Protestant states hath so much security in it, so it hath as much of honour and assurances to the Protestant interest abroad.[42]

In other correspondence with Parliament, Cromwell emphasized that many states sought the friendship of England, and that he intended to use these feelings to conclude honorable and profitable arrangements.[43]

Cromwell's first Parliament did not live up to his expectations. Eight days after his opening speech, he sent a message reminding it not to obstruct the policies upon which the council had decided.[44] The rift between Cromwell and Parliament attracted the attention of all the foreign diplomats, but they could only guess about the effect on foreign policy. Barrière saw new hope for Spain if Cardenas could step in

and make a large cash offer. Barrière was also sure that if
the Protector assumed greater personal power, he could make
an agreement with Spain. This totally erroneous interpretation of Cromwell's position was based on the belief that his
posture of militancy toward Catholic states was only a pose
to pacify the Puritan element in Parliament.[45] In a like
manner, Palucci thought that Cromwell had sent Blake to
the Mediterranean in an attempt to silence critics in Parliament and to aid the cause of international Protestantism.

Even a cursory look at Cromwell's address to Parliament
should have given the French ambassador a feeling of confidence. Other signs—Cromwell's warm reception of Bordeaux
and the increasing number of stories about the Western
Design—were favorable to France. In Spanish territories,
there was also a feeling that Cromwell had to make a
dramatic gesture to restore his popularity, and that it might
take the form of an attack on the Indies.[46] The mission of
de Lede was one response to this threat; another was encouraging "loose talk about a possible marriage between Don
John of Austria and the daughter of Cromwell."[47]

Despite the favorable signs, Bordeaux's negotiations
showed no progress, and he and Brienne grew apprehensve
about the Protector's designs. England's diplomacy was
achieving some of the goals set for it. As Thurloe later
explained, the council wanted to retain good relations with
France and attack the Indies, "but not to meddle with
anything in Europe until the Spanish should make some
move."[48] Thurloe pointed out the factor that eluded foreign
diplomats in 1654, and which most later historians have failed
to grasp—there was no reason for Cromwell to conclude an
alliance at that time. The diplomatic equation into which
foreign observers tried to fit Cromwell did not describe his
view of the situation. Cromwell made it clear to Parliament,
as well as to the council, that he was proud of the independent
diplomatic position to which he had brought England. Why
should he ignore that and thrust himself into any alliances
unless the benefits were overwhelming?

Cromwell made some attempt to involve Parliament in
foreign policy. He informed Speaker Lenthall, "I have, by

advice of the Council, undertaken a design by sea, very much for the honour and advantage of the Commonwealth, and have already made the preparations requisite for such an undertaking." Cromwell said that it seemed proper to inform Parliament when important steps were taken and

> desire you [Lenthall] to . . . acquaint the House with the contents of this letter, wherein I have foresworne to be more particular, because there are several persons in Parliament who know this whole business and can inform the House of all the particulars, if the House do judge it to be consistent with the nature of the design.[49]

The Protector made it clear that Parliament was supposed to implement policy, but that he and the council were going to determine its goals and the best way to achieve them.

While Cromwell's attention was focused on the Western Design, Bordeaux received a new set of instructions. These showed the priorities that Mazarin and Brienne had established as well as their view of the problems facing Bordeaux. Brienne contended that only a few issues separated the two states; the most important were the disposition of English exiles living in France and the titles to be used in the treaty. He thought it necessary to warn Bordeaux, "Affairs are at such a point, that it is no longer any good to flatter one's self with vain hopes." Brienne thought that Cromwell did not want to speed the pace of the negotiations. Nevertheless, Bordeaux should not do anything that might endanger the present state of the relationship. Instead of pressing for a treaty, Bordeaux was instructed to concentrate on learning the objective of the fleets commanded by Blake and Penn.[50] Mazarin was concerned that the fleet might be used to attack the Duke of Guise, who was attempting the conquest of Naples.[51] Although Bordeaux tried to dismiss that fear, the memory of Dunkirk remained strong in France.

The fleet played the most prominent role in diplomatic conjectures about Cromwell. On 8 October, Blake set sail for the Mediterranean. His destination surprised few people;

the important question concerned the fleet's objectives once it reached its destination.[52] Palucci explained that the only thing that everyone agreed upon was that it would "exploit any opportunity to help the Protestant cause."[53]

10

Bordeaux's Negotiations Are Blocked

After Blake sailed for the Mediterranean, the attention of foreign diplomats turned to Admiral Penn. The council had already given him instructions that confirmed the widely held idea that he was going to the Indies.[1] In early October, the fleet attracted as much attention from the council as it had previously received from foreign observers. While Parliament was discussing the Instrument of Government, the men of Penn's fleet, meeting aboard the *Swiftsure*, prepared a petition listing the sailors' grievances. The political style of the petition made it more than just another attempt to obtain better pay and living conditions.[2]

Penn's fleet provided the background for most of the diplomatic moves made toward the Protector. The importance of the fleet can be understood by briefly noting some of the opinions of foreign observers. Palucci regarded the fleet as a potent fighting force, but said: "Time shows that the real objective of the squadron is to use it to cull benefits from current negotiations of both France and Spain, and to secure Cromwell in his seat . . . [because of the fleet] Spain has to remain friendly with England."[3] Palucci realized that the fleet was a mixed blessing to Cromwell, since it was expensive to maintain. It seemed to Palucci that a series of raids on French shipping and the coast of France might enable the fleet to operate at a profit.[4] Beverningh, the Dutch representative, also regarded the fleet as Cromwell's most potent bargaining weapon, but he was positive "that the fleets are not at all destined for France."[5]

Letters of intelligence that Thurloe received from Paris reflected the confusion of foreign observers about Penn's mission. One report claimed that an expedition was being organized against the city of Bordeaux, and that rumors about an attack on the Indies had been created "only to amuse us here."[6] Later reports indicated a belief that Penn might attack both Spanish and French possessions. The impact of England's naval preparations was "that men do wait with impatience for the success of both fleets, upon that business do all other things depend."[7]

Bordeaux's dispatches showed his extraordinary confusion and uncertainty about the fleet. When Blake had sailed, Bordeaux had warned officials in Paris to alert coastal towns in France. He also reaffirmed his view that Penn intended to attack the Indies.[8] Two months later, in mid-December, Bordeaux informed Brienne that Penn no longer planned to attack the Indies, but intended to help the province of Holland against a possible Orangist uprising.[9] On the same day, Bordeaux wrote Mazarin that there were many objectives for which Cromwell might use Penn's forces. It would probably be employed against the United Provinces or France, but there was a possibility of an attack against the Barbary pirates or the Indies.[10] Less than a week before Penn sailed, Bordeaux reported that "France need not fear it, judging by its preparations,"[11] but in a letter to his father, Bordeaux admitted that he did not know the objectives of the fleet.[12]

Despite his uncertainty concerning the fleet, Bordeaux continued to lay the foundation for an agreement with England. By the autumn of 1654, his negotiations revolved around what concessions Mazarin and the Protector were willing to make. The concept of mutual concessions was not as simple or clear-cut as it might sound. Bordeaux complained that Cromwell had allowed the Dutch war, a potential Royalist uprising, and the plans for the fleet to push negotiations with France into the background. The ambassador accused the commissioners of bringing extraneous issues into the talks merely to delay them. Bordeaux finally began to feel that Cromwell was acting in bad faith, and when that view gained some acceptance in Paris, it made it difficult to consider making concessions to England.

In the period from the end of summer, 1654, to November, 1655, Bordeaux was subjected to a series of frustrating diplomatic maneuvers by Cromwell—actions that were caused only in part by the complex issues at stake. At the beginning of that period, Bordeaux saw only two issues—the position of the Stuarts in France, and the precedence of signatures on the treaty—standing in the way of an alliance. He asked Mazarin for new instructions, and was advised "not to lose a moment to advance your negotiations"[13] and to agree to anything concerning the Stuarts which was not harmful to the interests of France. The Cardinal's advisers showed concern for the prompt conclusion of an agreement, but demonstrated little understanding of the obstinacy of the Protector and the problems still facing Bordeaux.[14] Much of the supposedly informed opinion supported Brienne's feeling that a treaty was imminent. The Prince of Tarante stated, "Tis publick more than ever that the treaty with France is upon [completion]," and Dutch and Venetian diplomats thought that only minor details stood in the way of the treaty.[15]

Two months later, the treaty was still unsigned, and Bordeaux showed new annoyance with the commissioners. As soon as he resolved one problem, he said, they raised another. Even agreement to exile the Stuarts led only to new demands. Despite his assuring Brienne that the unresolved questions could be settled, Bordeaux was coming to the view that Cromwell might not want an agreement. At that time, Bordeaux decided to inform the Protector that he was leaving England because his continued, and fruitless, presence was an affront to the dignity of the King of France.[16]

Bordeaux showed his anger at the delaying tactics of the Protector in the dispatches he sent to Paris. In turn, the Cardinal adopted a more rigid policy, sending word that it might be necessary to terminate negotiations. However, the ambassador received a different interpretation in a letter from his father. According to the older Bordeaux, Brienne wanted the ambassador to employ a variety of delaying tactics and to convince the Cardinal that negotiations should be continued. Brienne was sure that Mazarin would regret it later if France broke with England, since the kingdom could not afford a war with the Protectorate. Such regret would work against the fortunes of Bordeaux after he returned from England. Brienne suggested that Bordeaux talk to Cromwell as a private person rather than as the ambassador of the King of France. Bordeaux should try to convince Cromwell that the ambassador was being unfairly maligned in France because of the actions of the commissioners in England. Brienne also stressed that Cromwell should be made aware that steps were already under way to get Charles Stuart out of France.[17] Brienne's letters showed that Cromwell had persuaded France to implement one provision of the proposed alliance without committing himself to do anything.

Bordeaux's predicament accentuated divisions among Mazarin's advisers. One faction at court hoped to use Cromwell's intransigence to discredit Brienne and the Bordeaux family.[18] This split at the French court hampered Bordeaux's attempts to formulate new policies, but it was undoubtedly welcomed by Thurloe and the Protector. Throughout Bordeaux's mission, the Protector possessed one advantage that has been generally overlooked. The negotiations were carried out by the French ambassador in London but there was no corresponding official in Paris. Important dispatches and instructions traveled in one direction; Thurloe's intelligence system and control of the post made the most of this situation. An accurate indication of how far Bordeaux could be pushed and of when to make conciliatory gestures provided an invaluable aid to Cromwell's policy of tactical delay.[19]

Three major factors combined to forestall any agreement that Bordeaux expected to reach before the end of 1654. First, he had not offered the Protector any new concessions that might tempt him into an agreement. Second, the military and diplomatic position of France and the situation of the Cardinal suffered a series of reverses. The Italian campaign of the Duke of Guise was a total failure, and Spain's victories had a marked effect on the papacy. The pope was pressured (or felt free) to express his admiration for Spain and his desire for a just peace, as well as formally to receive de Retz and bestow upon him the red hat. Papal animosity toward Mazarin might have a favorable psychological effect on Cromwell, but the Italian situation meant that France could not offer as much to England.[20] Finally, Cromwell's attention was concentrated on the preparation of Penn's fleet and news of Blake. Palucci overstated the case when he said, "All activities center around the dispatch of the fleet," but the council was more concerned with the fleet than with any of Bordeaux's proposals.[21]

The commissioners did not ignore Bordeaux, but made it obvious that they were not encouraging new proposals. These actions have led some later observers to oversimplify the diplomatic options that were open to the Protector. Neither he nor the Council viewed their situations in terms of how and when to ally with France. Cromwell showed little enthusiasm for dealings with Bordeaux, because there was no reason for urgency or haste. In turn, Bordeaux saw that nothing could be gained by trying to pressure Cromwell.

On 18 December 1654, a letter was dispatched to Cromwell, in the name of the King of France. The avowed purpose of the letter was to clarify the position of France. It began on the pessimistic note that the King had "but small hopes left to us of the reestablishment of a good understanding betweene this Kingdome and your Commonwealth." The letter maintained that France had made concessions to further good relations, and that England had responded by harassing French shipping. The King was no longer willing "to put up with the uncertainty or to have the world believe that France is acting from any motive besides a desire for harmony." The letter concluded by stating that Bordeaux had been instructed to explain the French position to Cromwell and then to return to France. However, the King hoped that Cromwell would make some gesture to convince Bordeaux that England still wanted to establish amity between the two states.[22]

Shortly after the arrival of Louis's letter, Bordeaux was promised a prompt reply from the Protector concerning the relationship between the two states. When this was not forthcoming, Bordeaux still tried to convince Mazarin not to break off negotiations, because "it doth seem more advantageous to agree than to break." Bordeaux warned the Cardinal not to make any decisions based on "the impressions which are given of the instability of the government of England and of the power of Parliament." He also implied that any assumption that his mission was a failure was based on false information, and that positive results could be expected soon.[23] New rumors circulated in Paris that negotiations had failed and that Bordeaux was ruined. One of Thurloe's informants in Paris attempted to show that Bordeaux was "there in [London] to entertaine you with goode words."[24] The portrayal of Bordeaux as a dissembler with little desire to conclude a treaty did him scant justice. Negotiations had come to a standstill, but it was the Protector who was causing the delay.

The impression that Bordeaux's mission was heading toward failure was not confined to Paris. Chanut, the French ambassador to the United Provinces, was troubled, but his assumptions were based on a false report that Bordeaux had been detained by the Protector while trying to leave London.[25] Bordeaux showed increasing signs of dejection and displeasure with his treatment in England, but mainly he was bewildered by the Protector's actions. No important issues appeared to be unresolved, "but without a doubt he [Cromwell] is driven by some particular consideration, which is unknown to me, to maintain a division with France."[26]

In reply to Chanut's letter, Bordeaux wrote, "It doth seem now, as if the Lords here are inclined to peace." However, the disappointments of the past two years led Bordeaux to add cautiously, "Since I have been so often deceived in my conjectures, that I will not engage to secure it from small remisses."[27] In the early weeks of February, 1654, Bordeaux stepped up his efforts. He spoke confidently of a "nearer union that shall be made," and assured Brienne that Cromwell did not intend to assist any of France's enemies.[28] Just when Bordeaux thought the treaty was completed, he discovered that the commissioners had changed the secret articles dealing with assistance for rebels and enemies of both states. Negotiations had to be suspended while Bordeaux requested instructions from France.[29] His reaction to the commissioners' actions displayed the indignation of one who felt betrayed. He had convinced his superiors in France and himself that the treaty was completed; then it had been denied him at the last possible moment. Bordeaux commented to his father that he had never been so annoyed with the English as he was at that moment. Chanut, viewing the situation from The Hague, summed up Bordeaux's position rather well: "Good God! What patience you must have." English objections had so little to do with the substance of the treaty that Chanut could not understand why Cromwell continued to scorn advances made by France.[30] The only sense Bordeaux could make out of the situation was that Cromwell thought "that since we have yielded so much as we have done to come to an agreement, we will not lose our advances, but rather submit to their desires, though never so unreasonable."[31] This bitter assessment of Cromwell and the commissioners had a solid foundation. The English certainly realized they were sabotaging the treaty. The manner in which the changes were made, rather than the substance of the changes, was the significant feature of the whole episode. The Protector had not ended the negotiations and had not rejected the treaty. The motive behind the actions of the commissioners was to delay negotiations, not to terminate them.

One of Thurloe's most reliable agents in Paris described the French view that the "peace with England moves slowly or not at all, because the Protector had faire pretence for delays." There were strong feelings in Paris that English stories of Royalist plots and internal disorders were only excuses to delay negotiations with France. It was believed that the real reason for Cromwell's tactics was to allow him to discover the fate of his fleets, and then "towards winter he will incline to France or to Spain according to their [Blake and Penn] successes."[32] The anger toward Cromwell which surfaced in Paris was shared by Bordeaux. Writing to his father, the ambassador said that the situation was bad, and getting worse. The main problem was that the "obstinacy which the ministers of the Council do declare upon the two propositions [precedence in the treaty and assistance for rebels] . . . doth cause me to apprehend a rupture." Bordeaux was "sick and tired" of his mission, and was planning to leave England within a week. He told the commissioners of his plans, but was unsure that his threat had made any impression on them.[33] He tried to be more optimistic when he wrote to Mazarin, stating that the only problem was the wording of the clause about assistance to rebels. Despite his ambassador's assurances that Cromwell would not help Condé, Mazarin wanted it put in writing.[34]

In much of his correspondence, Bordeaux stressed that the real difficulty in dealing with Cromwell was that his interests changed so frequently that it was impossible to pin him down on specific issues. Actually, the interests of the Protector did not change as much as the methods by which he and his advisers sought to implement these interests. Both France and England had to make tactical changes throughout their negotiations. During the diplomatic sparring that took place in 1655, Bordeaux gave tacit recognition to the fact that the Protector was being wooed and therefore would establish most of the ground rules for the talks.

In the early months of 1655, the Protectorate was emerging from one series of domestic problems and about to be faced with another. There were rumors of mutiny in the army and navy, a Leveller coup, and a Royalist invasion. Parliament provided the focal point of much of the discontent, as well as the hopes of factions that opposed Cromwell.

Cromwell tried to use Parliament to support plans he had put into motion. The decision to undertake the Western Design meant he had committed himself to a more active policy that would require financial support from Parliament. That body must be convinced that the new policy held out benefits for England and was not merely an attempt to extract money to support the Protectorate. The first time Cromwell attempted to use his power in the outside world, he was brought up short by the realities of his position in England. For months Cromwell had attempted to find some way to maintain the Instrument of Government as the basis for his rule and to reconcile the army and Parliament. In April and July, the Western Design seemed a good means of assisting in that process. By November, the divisions in Parliament had grown too deep for him to realistically expect anything but opposition to a plan that would entail expenditures and faith in his decisions. Parliament's discussions about the Instrument of Government had provided a rallying point for Cromwell's opponents. Sensitive issues, such as religious policy and control over the army, were aired in Parliament, but Cromwell allowed no chance to make any important changes.

In a message to Parliament, he stressed that there had been an opportunity to perform great tasks, but that Parliament had fallen apart into "a quibbling body of small minded men." He accused them of considering their own interests while ignoring the higher purpose for which they met. He took great pains to remind Parliament of the importance of the head of government and of the powers vested in him. He mentioned the possibility of a Royalist uprising, but did not attempt to use that as a bogey to gain parliamentary support for his plans. There was no need for such tactics; Cromwell's speech had one real purpose—to dismiss the Parliament that had sat for the past five months.[35]

French observers paid renewed attention to domestic problems in England after diplomatic negotiations were stalled. Bordeaux discounted the importance of the parliamentary session and thought that Cromwell did not have to take the Royalists seriously, but did not discourage the opposite opinion in Paris. The notion that Cromwell was too busy to deal with France was a convenient method for the ambassador to explain his failure to obtain an agreement and to justify the continuation of his mission. In March, 1655, a series of Royalist uprisings were quickly suppressed. In Abbott's view, the risings had demonstrated three important points about the Protectorate: "Cromwell had made careful plans to meet any uprising, he knew, in a general way, the plans of his enemies, and that no such design had any chance of success in the face of such a force and such preparations to meet it."[36]

The largest Royalist disturbance, led by Colonel John Penruddock, took place while Bordeaux was pressing the commissioners for a final decision on the treaty.[37] The uprising did not present an important danger to Cromwell's rule, but served as a reminder of the possibility of future plots.

Many foreign observers—and some later historians—have
treated Cromwell's fears about rebellion as merely another
technique to enforce his will or gain diplomatic breathing
space. He used the rumors of plots for those purposes, but
this in no way gave the lie to his fear of plots against him
and his government. Too many men and factions in England
were opposed to too many aspects of his rule for Cromwell
lightly to ignore their existence. Despite the timing, Bordeaux said little about Penruddock in dispatches to Paris.
The manner in which Cromwell handled the disturbances
made it difficult for officials in France to accept the English
statements that negotiations with Bordeaux had to be postponed. Nevertheless, Bordeaux's only options were to continue his threats to leave or to display the patience that
Chanut had described.[38]

While Bordeaux was trying to impress the commissioners
with a display of righteous indignation, actions by some
officials in France gave England reasons for further delay.
Between 29 March and 13 April, a series of reports in English
newsletters described the seizure of English ships in French
ports. The tone of the newsletters were belligerent, describing
the seizures as proof of Mazarin's perfidy,[39] and saying that
Bordeaux's mission was to delay any steps by the Protector
which might harm France, not to create ties between the
states.[40] The charge against Bordeaux was groundless, and
it must have struck him with a bitter irony, in light of
Cromwell's delaying tactics.

Bordeaux lost no time in telling Mazarin about the English
reaction to the seizures and embargo. Bordeaux's relation
with the commissioners had grown very cool, and he was
sure the embargo was the cause of it. He thought that
Cromwell was likely to make "some commotion" about the
seizures, but that negotiations would not be hindered
seriously. On the other hand, since negotiations were already
at an impasse, the embargo was certainly not going to give
any impetus to them. Bordeaux tried to convince Mazarin
that a quick reversal of the embargo might demonstrate
France's good faith. However, Bordeaux's explanations to
the commissioners certainly did not help his cause. After
first saying he knew nothing about the embargo, he stated

that a French fleet was probably leaving port and that all ships had been detained for security reasons. When his attempt to discount the existence of an embargo failed, he adopted new tactics. He denied to Thurloe that France was trying to put any pressure on Cromwell to sign the treaty, and, at the same time, contended that France had good grounds for the seizure of English ships. The lack of good intelligence concerning the embargo forced Bordeaux to play two roles at the same time. He tried to convince the English of his position as the long-suffering servant of a King who had been harassed and insulted, while telling the English that they should be satisfied with getting their goods and ships restored after peace had been made between the states. Bordeaux told Mazarin that he had concluded the interview with Thurloe by turning the English protest into an attack on the policies of the Protectorate and saying that France had no cause to fear England.[41]

Bordeaux gave his father a different account of the effect of the embargo. The English reaction had been unsettling to him, but he had met it with a display of indignation. The commissioners had responded by setting up another conference in a few days, and Bordeaux thought that "this conference may well be followed by my departure. . . . I see myself nearer than ever to go." He was extremely disturbed by the Protector's reactions, and feared that Cromwell might be trying to force a break. The seeming capriciousness of the Protector reinforced Bordeaux's belief that his mission as ambassador was over.[42]

When Mazarin learned of the reaction to the embargo, he ordered it to be lifted immediately. He instructed Bordeaux to inform Cromwell that the King meant no harm, and "certainly did not want to take advantage at a time when there were risings in England." The Cardinal's parting remark was a subtle reminder that there might be opportunities in the future for foreign states to meddle in England, as well as an attempt to head off any accusation that the embargo was part of a Royalist-French plot to overthrow the Protectorate.[43] There was possibly even a touch of irony in the references to a situation that the Protector had used in his delaying tactics.

Bordeaux's discomfiture was not restricted to his dealings with the English. In the wake of the confusion caused by the embargo, he received a series of letters from Mazarin and Brienne criticizing his actions. The letters made it clear that he was expected to produce favorable results soon. Mazarin complained that if Bordeaux had remained firm, as the Cardinal had wanted, the negotiations would have been concluded with a treaty or the recall of the ambassador. In either case, France would have been in a better position than it would have been if the negotiations were allowed to drag on with no end in sight. Mazarin concluded by giving Bordeaux rather contradictory instructions. The ambassador was supposed to inform Cromwell that negotiations would end immediately if a treaty was not signed, but not to leave Cromwell in a bad temper, and to reassure him that France would never "harken, directly or indirectly, to any propositions of commotion in England." Mazarin stated that the Protector would still believe in France's good intentions, even though Bordeaux was leaving, since France had "never engaged or meddled in anything to his prejudice."[44]

Reactions to the embargo had been varied in France and on the Continent. Brienne and Bordeaux's father feared that it might mark the end of their hopes for an agreement with Cromwell.[45] Charles Stuart (tinged with the omnipresent Royalist optimism) saw it as an irreparable break between England and France.[46] Bordeaux faced the uproar over the embargo with a combination of fatalism and reserved optimism—the former because he realized there was little he could do, the latter because the commissioners had suggested no substantial changes in the agreement. His personal position was probably strengthened by the blunders at Rouen and Dieppe. The embargo gave the commissioners a chance to delay, but it also gave Bordeaux justification for the same policy vis-à-vis the Cardinal's demands to bring negotiations to a conclusion.

As soon as it became clear that Cromwell did not intend to break off negotiations because of the embargo, the Cardinal pressed Bordeaux to conclude the treaty. The ambassador was caught again between the English determination to delay and impatience in Paris. He issued threats that he would leave England, but made no plans to implement them. Bordeaux retained a sense of perspective, concerning his own welfare and the interests of his King, throughout the English delays. His actions were best summed up in a letter he received from Paris, stating that it was good "you are staying in England with some hope of concluding your treaty. . . . [That policy] "was much better than being in Paris with an absolute breach."[47]

11

The Western Design

The existence of a strong English fleet had always been an important element in Cromwell's foreign policy, but Penn's fleet assumed a special position. Most diplomats thought that the blow struck by Penn would probably determine the disposition of the Protectorate in the European struggle between the Bourbons and the Habsburgs.

At the 20 July council meeting, where plans for the attack on the Indies were formulated, there was no discussion of an alliance with France. An attack against Spain's possessions was not considered as either an alternative to war or a prelude to an alliance with France. The crucial consideration about the Western Design was what could be gained from it. The obvious advantages were a foothold for English trade and loot from the rich Spanish colonies. While Penn was preparing for his expedition to the Indies, Cromwell was carrying on negotiations with France and Spain. Both Bordeaux and Cardenas believed there was some likelihood of an alliance with the Protector. These simultaneous negotiations have led some historians to label Cromwell a hypocrite or to contend that his foreign policy was operating at cross-purposes. A recent interpretation by George Drake stated:

It is clear from the correspondence of Mazarin and Bordeaux and Cardenas and the government of Philip IV that Cromwell was determined to ally with one or the other of these countries; depending on which alliance would be more advantageous. . . . This is one of the

few instances where the documents allow us to go behind
the scenes to check Cromwell's professions—and they
reveal insincerity.[1]

There have been attempts to explain the Western Design
as another example of the Protector's desire to utilize militant Puritanism to insure his position in England. However,
these explanations have been based on Cromwell's speeches
after the attack on Hispaniola—speeches in which he sought
to justify actions he had already taken.[2]

The decision to attack the Indies was, as Drake stated,
preceded by "almost detached calculation." This did not
preclude the existence of emotional issues in the decision.
The council decided that an attack on the Indies would
probably not lead to war with Spain. Thurloe, among others,
was sure it would not.[3] In any case, the attack seemed worth
the risk. Balanced against the potential wealth to be gained
from the Indies, what dangers did Spain pose to the security
of the Protectorate? Spain was already fully committed to
the war with France. If Spain declared war on England, it
would probably support the party of Charles Stuart, and
its territories would become a mecca for Royalist plotters.
That assumption made Cromwell favor the attack on Spain
even more than before. If a political marriage of convenience
between Charles and Philip IV was made, Cromwell would
be the matchmaker. This was not the primary intent of the
Protector, but it must have been appealing to him. Charles's
alliance with Spain would make it easier to identify him
and, by extension, all opponents of the Protectorate with
the forces of the antichrist. A bond between the Stuarts and
the Habsburgs would give substance to the charges that
Parliament had leveled against James I and Charles I.[4]

There was little benefit for Charles in an alliance with
Spain. It would give him the chance to hatch plots in places
like Brussels, Madrid, and Rome, but Spain did not have
the resources to implement them. The alliance, when it was
finally concluded, led to such bizarre suggestions as a coalition of the Habsburgs, the Stuarts, and the papacy to conduct
a crusade to restore Charles.[5] This idea was enthusiastically
supported by Henrietta Maria, who remained in France

throughout the Interregnum. Interesting speculations might be made about the reception that Englishmen (even those who were disenchanted with the Protector and the major generals) would have afforded an invading army that marched under the papal banner and whose leaders included a prominent Irish Jesuit, Peter Talbot, later to be bishop of Dublin.

Cromwell decided there was more to be gained from an attack on Spain than from a policy of neutrality or friendship. If he allied with Spain, he would have committed England to a long-term policy involving it in the European war. On the other hand, after the attack on the Indies, England still had most of the freedom it gained with the conclusion of the Dutch war. Even as Penn was sailing for the Indies, there was a feeling in England that Spain might ignore the attack on its territories. For many months, there had been speculation that Penn intended to attack the Indies. Cardenas was aware of this and other reports reaching Madrid which pinpointed Santo Domingo as its target. Still, Spain demonstrated no sense of urgency in its effort to gain Cromwell's support. The Marquis de Lede was sent to London as an ambassador extraordinary, and arrived in April, 1655. He was received with great courtesy by the Protector, and commissioners were appointed to deal with him. De lede recounted the friendship Spain had shown the Commonwealth, and then launched into a four-point attack against a possible Anglo-French treaty. He said that France's interests were opposed to those of the Protector, that de Baas had been involved in a plot against Cromwell, that France was readying troops to aid a Stuart invasion of England, and that Cromwell had nothing to gain from an alliance with France. De Lede made an offer of troops to act in cooperation with the Protector to capture Calais. In return, Cromwell would use his fleet to put Condé and his army ashore at Bordeaux or another port in France. There was no mention of how Spain expected to finance these ambitious plans when it had not been able to supply Cardenas with the funds to implement less grandiose designs. After de Lede made his proposals, he received a response that was familiar to Cardenas and Bordeaux—assurances that the Protector and the council would consider the matter.[6] De Lede's mission operated on a false set of considerations. He was offering Spain's counterproposal to Cromwell's alliance with France, but Cromwell was not seriously considering such an alliance at that time. De Lede said nothing about the much-rumored English attack on the Indies, probably because de Haro, like Mazarin, could not detach Cromwell from their own concept of a world divided into only two competing factions.

De Lede's mission led to no arrangement with England—he had no chance of success. The decision to attack Hispaniola had been made, and Penn was on his way to carry it out. The presence of de Lede in England showed that Spain had not abandoned hope for closer ties with Cromwell, and the cordial reception of de Lede caused Bordeaux to reconsider his own belief that a break had occurred between England and Spain.[7] If the negotiations with de Lede were a charade on Cromwell's part, they were not without a purpose. Any actions that gave French observers second thoughts about the Protector's policies were almost sure to enhance his position in the negotiations with Bordeaux.

The value of Cromwell's delaying tactics becomes more visible when viewed against other events of the summer of 1655. While the Protector awaited word of Penn's fleet, his attention was drawn to the Royalist uprising that broke out under the leadership of John Penruddock. The attempt to raise the west country was a total failure, but its results were by no means unimportant. "History remembers Penruddock's uprising chiefly for . . . the division of England into eleven districts under as many major-generals." It has been pointed out that the major generals were a "serious error of policy on Cromwell's part."[8]

The efficiency with which Cromwell crushed the rebellion had a decided impact on other governments. The hopes of Bordeaux and Cardenas to use Cromwell's domestic weakness as a diplomatic weapon were ended. At best, it would have been impolitic even to raise the issue in the aftermath of the Penruddock rebellion. The uprising also gave Cromwell another reason to put off making any foreign policy decisions until he knew the results of Penn's actions and could calculate their long-range effects. The uprising and its domestic consequence made the results of the Western Design more important for Cromwell. The capture of wealthy Spanish islands or a treasure fleet would enhance his prestige and help stifle some of his critics.

One of Thurloe's informants went so far as to suggest that "the Spaniard have been struck dumb by the dispatch of the English fleets and just wait in fear to hear what happened. About the only defense Spain has, is a belief that God will not let them be defeated."[9] This analysis contained the braggadocio and cockiness that marked England's feelings toward foreign states, but that did not alter the real circumstances. There was little Spain could do except sit back and wait to react to whatever blow Cromwell decided to deliver.

The probability of an English attack on the Indies caused some of Charles Stuart's advisers to discuss plans for closer ties with Spain. Before news of the attack on Hispaniola reached Europe, Hyde thought that Philip IV was ready to support Charles out of fear of Cromwell.[10] After the story of Penn's attack became known, the Royalists stepped up their campaign to get aid from Spain. Peter Talbot suggested that Ormonde and Hyde should be sent to Madrid immediately to conclude an alliance,[11] while Hyde attempted to convince Philip IV that if Spain declared for Charles, many English hips would not sail against Spain.[12]

Spain's first response to the attack on Santo Domingo was to lay an embargo on the goods of English merchants in Spain.[13] Cromwell received a series of petitions from these merchants, asking him to do something before they were ruined.[14] News of the embargo started speculation in other European cities about the inevitability of war between England and Spain.[15]

Thurloe also held the opinion that England and Spain were moving toward war. Writing to Henry Cromwell—the Protector's son, who was in Ireland—Thurloe described the situation: "Wee are like to have an open warre with Spayne, it being confirmed by the letters of this weeke from St. Sebastian, that our merchants estates are seized and their persons imprisoned."[16]

Cardenas asked for an audience with Cromwell as soon as news of the embargo reached London; Cromwell's only reply was to send the ambassador his passport.[17] The Spaniard tried to make a final gesture of amity, and asked Thurloe for a farewell audience with the Protector. The request was refused. Within the limitations of his government's ability to please Cromwell, Cardenas had done an excellent job and was highly regarded by Thurloe and other advisers of the Protector.[18] Cromwell's treatment of Cardenas during the ambassador's final days in England was decidedly shabby. Years of patient service were not enough to warrant his receiving a courteous farewell. It was not surprising that when Cardenas arrived in the Spanish Netherlands, he became one of the most vocal foes of the Protectorate and an ardent supporter of plots to overthrow it.

By the middle of October, 1655, Spain had seized English goods, Cardenas had left for the Netherlands, and there had been many rumors about a state of war between England and Spain. However, no final break had taken place. Any initiative for a break would have to come from Spain, since Cromwell was satisfied to follow the policies he had already implemented. If the Protectorate became involved in the European war, it would be because Spain pushed her into it or because France made it worthwhile. Most discussions of the subsequent war between England and Spain have ignored a factor of paramount importance. Spain did nothing to disturb the English goods that had been seized until a break was almost certain between the two states. Thurloe saw this; on 30 October, he was informed that there was still hope for reconciliation since "our Habsburg King doth not make use of the embargoed goods."[19]

The Protector displayed an unusual lack of concern with the Spanish reaction to the capture of Jamaica. The options that were open to Cromwell were clear—come to terms with Spain and withdraw from Jamaica, press further hostile actions, or do nothing. The last course of action had much to recommend it; it entailed no further risks, and was consistent with the approach that Cromwell had used in diplomatic negotiations. Another situation made it advisable for Cromwell to adopt a wait-and-see policy toward Spain; new experiments in domestic government were a much more pressing issue. The rule of the major generals began in the same month that Admiral Penn captured Jamaica. It is reasonable to assume that Cromwell recognized that this striking innovation would carry in its wake a new set of complaints against his policies. In such circumstances, it would have been foolhardy to act hastily in foreign affairs and thus compound the confusion and discontent that marked politics in the summer of 1656. After the results of Penn's expedition were known, there was time for Cromwell to reflect upon them and decide how to turn them toward the accomplishment of more important goals—peace and stability at home.

From its inception, the attack on Hispaniola had been a calculated risk, with the possibility that Spain would retaliate. The manner in which Spain reacted supported the position of the proponents of the Western Design—that Spain could not do great harm to England. The discontent of some merchants was weighed against advantages gained by the Protector from a break with Spain.[20] Even before the Stuarts went into the camp of the Habsburgs, Nieupoort described the favorable reaction in England to the war: "Several officers of the army, who having shown a dislike formerly against the present government, were retired into the country, come now with great zeal back again, and offer their services against Spain."[21]

The Western Design failed in its primary objective—the seizure of Hispaniola—but it succeeded in other ways. Its visible accomplishment was the capture of Jamaica. The island was to prove extremely valuable to England's role in the West Indies in the next century, but its possession elicited scant joy in 1655. Even Cromwell found it difficult to work up much enthusiasm about it at the time. The imprisonment of Penn upon his return to England is some indication of Cromwell's attitude toward his admiral's "success."

One need not agree entirely with John Bruce's statement

> Cromwell and his Council . . . began to perceive, that a state of peace, when the minds of the English nation might calmly review the steps by which its new Rulers had become absolute Master, might lead to efforts to restore the monarchy, and therefore judged it to be necessary to engage England in a foreign war, in which if success attended him, the fame of victory might divert the public attention from the power and from the crimes of the Usurper and time and events be improved to consolidate his government. . . .[22]

to realize that an open break with Spain might be as valuable to the Protector as the silver that he could obtain through a series of raids on the Americas.

Part of Bordeaux's original mission had been to forestall any Anglo-Spanish agreement and, if possible, to turn Cromwell against Spain. The Western Design obviously pleased Bordeaux, but did not mean that his negotiations for a treaty were much nearer to completion. On the contrary, the Western Design and its immediate consequences afforded Cromwell another reason to postpone talks with Bordeaux, a step that led Mazarin to the brink of recalling his ambassador. The Cardinal stopped short of that, and told Bordeaux to issue another ultimatum to Cromwell about the lack of progress. Bordeaux's situation would have been much better if Cromwell had thought a choice had to be made between France and Spain. The Protector did not think that was the case, a point that was illustrated in the instructions left for Captain Goodson, the commander of the fleet in the Indies after the departure of Admiral Penn. In Article 1, Goodson was told to "Take all vessels belonging to the King of Spain, or any of his subjects in America, or any other who shall assist or aid him."[23] Article 5 said, "To seize, arrest, surprise, detain, and in case of resistance to sink, burn and destroy all ships and vessels of the French King, or any of his subjects."[24]

Cromwell's attack on the Indies had actually cut away from Bordeaux some of the diplomatic leverage the ambassador thought he possessed. Bordeaux had suggested such an attack, but when the Protector carried it out, there was no consultation with, or acknowledgment of, France. Cromwell's approach toward the Western Design and his relations with Spain emphasized France's inability to influence his decisions. Far from pushing Cromwell into an alliace with France, the aftermath of the Western Design showed that Cromwell would create closer ties only when France provided him with a satisfactory set of concessions. Bordeaux had to discover what concessions the Protector wanted and to convince the Cardinal that England's assistance was worth Cromwell's asking price. Bordeaux knew that the Western Design had not brought England into the European war.

Spain had stopped short of the extreme actions it could have taken against English merchants. Intelligence received by Thurloe supported the idea that Spain wanted to patch up relations with Cromwell. There were reports of another ambassador being sent to London and of new offers of gold to join the Habsburgs in the war against France.[25] For almost three months after the embargo, there was no official condemnation of Cromwell in Spain for staging the attack on Hispaniola, no declaration of support for Charles, no encouragement of the Royalists to use the Spanish Netherlands as a base for their intrigues, and no letters of marque issued against England.[26]

Despite Spain's displeasure with the attack on Hispaniola and the expulsion of Cardenas, it was not until January, 1656, that an order was sent "to all the severall ports in this country [Spain] for a sale to be made of all the ships and goods that were embargoed of the English and the money thereof to be remitted to the King's use."[27] This was followed by the issuance of "letters of reprisal given out to the capers at Dunkirk and Ostend."[28] The final step in the break between England and Spain occurred in March, 1656, when "war against England hath been declared and published in Spain by sound of drum and trumpet, and great preparations for the sea are making there."[29] These measures taken by the King of Spain to break with Cromwell occurred after the Protector had signed a treaty of nonaggression and mutual assistance with France. With that in mind, it becomes difficult to maintain the position, held by many historians, that the Western Design and its aftermath pushed Cromwell into the waiting arms of Cardinal Mazarin. Cromwell was not pushed into any alliance; the choice remained his until he decided to commit himself.

12

The Crisis of the Vaudois

During the summer of 1655, the Western Design had been the main consideration in Cromwell's foreign policy. The combination of that and the embargoes at Rouen and Dieppe had blocked any plans Bordeaux had to press for an agreement. Once the problem of the embargoes was resolved, Bordeaux appeared close to the conclusion of his negotiations.

At the end of May, Bordeaux was promised a complete draft of the treaty within eight days. At the conclusion of that period, he sent a summary of his work to Paris, but could not include any favorable news about a treaty. Instead of an alliance, Bordeaux had been given a curt message saying that Cromwell had written an important letter to the King of France, and that negotiations could not continue until the Protector had received an answer. Bordeaux had a brief interview, at which he discovered that his negotiations were doomed to further delays. He also learned for the first time about the Protector's interest in the situation of the Protestant Vaudois, and that Cromwell expected the King of France to aid the Protestants, who were supposedly being persecuted by the Duke of Savoy. This new obstacle to the treaty shocked and surprised Bordeaux, who could see no reason for the Protector to antagonize France. On the contrary, Bordeaux remained convinced by the "assurances my commissioners gave me of an accommodation."[1]

Once more, Bordeaux had stood on the brink of completing his negotiations, only to see success snatched from him and the future of the agreement made uncertain. In a highly emotional letter to his father, he tried to explain the situation. He was visibly annoyed at the deception practiced by the commissioners. He was disturbed by the inference that men in Paris knew more about the situation in England than he did. He wanted his father to remind critics that Mazarin had often been informed "that the intention of the protector and this government was always to amuse us; and not to conclude to the very last."[2] Bordeaux considered that "this pretense [about] the persecution of the Vaudois delaying [negotiations] is a little bit coloured," but that it was the only excuse remaining for the commissioners. He saw a motive for the Protector's actions, since

> this government, it may be, doth think to render themselves agreeable to the people of England by such offices; and that the rupture with France would pass for a war for religion's sake; but the people is disabused, and have learned more wit, having had experience enough of this fallacy in their own wars.

Bordeaux did not think that "informed people" in France (an obviously sarcastic reference to his critics in Paris) would accept "after three years' delay, the justice . . . which the Duke of Savoy doth exercise, ought to produce upon good ground a war between England and France." Once he had vented his anger against critics in Paris, Bordeaux could turn to an analysis of English policy. He could "hardly believe, that the lord Protector doth know himself so ill, that the power of the King, and the weakness of Spain, can cause him to hope any advantage from a war with the one and from a strict league with the other." It appeared certain that Cromwell would ally with France, because "the design of their fleet, which is gone for America, is a sufficient enough argument to induce everybody to believe it." There was no news about Penn, but the rumors of an attack on the Indies were so strong that Bordeaux was pinning his hopes on it.[3]

No one could hope to analyze Cromwell's policies without some reference to the role played by religious considerations. The difficulty in isolating the influence of religion from other

factors affecting Cromwell exacerbated the diplomats' problems. They all attempted to use religion to bring Cromwell
into their camp. Barrière tried to identify Condé with the
Huguenots: Bordeaux tried to convince Cromwell that Mazarin treated the Huguenots well; and Cardenas told Cromwell that an alliance with the Habsburgs would further the
cause of international Protestantism.[4]

Even though Bordeaux's skepticism about Cromwell's
concern for the Vaudois was shared by other diplomats, he
had oversimplified the problem.[5] This was not the first time
Cromwell had shown his concern for Continental Protestants. Furthermore, in naming John Pell to direct the inquiry about the Vaudois, Cromwell chose the man who had
been closely identified with attempts to establish stronger
ties with other Protestant states in the past.[6]

In 1653, Pell had gone to Switzerland to act as an observer
and to convince the Protestant cantons that Cromwell wanted closer ties with them. There was a suspicion in Paris that
Pell had been sent to disrupt the bonds that existed between
the cantons and France. There was some discussion that
Cromwell hoped to use whatever success Pell might achieve
to bolster England's bargaining position with France. There
was also a feeling in France that the Protector intended to
use an alliance with the Swiss to provide a staging base for
an invasion of France, to assist the Huguenots. For months,
Pell could merely assert Cromwell's interest in, and affection
for, the Swiss Protestants. At the end of 1654, the division
between the cantons over the reestablishment of ties with
France became another battlefield in the Habsburg-Bourbon
struggle, into which Pell attempted to insert England's interests. Pell felt there was an excellent chance that the Swiss
would turn to Cromwell for aid if they were invaded "by
France or any of their other popish neighbors,"[7] but he soon
realized that the pro-French forces had control of the Council of Cantons.[8] It appeared that the only way Cromwell
could obtain any influence in Switzerland was through the
good offices of France. Discussions with the pro-English leaders of Lausanne further convinced Pell that an Anglo-French
amity was favored by the Swiss Protestants and was in the
interests of the "true faith" and England's strategic posi-

tion.[9] Pell's experiences in Switzerland caused him to support the conclusions that Durie and Stouppe had reached by observing the condition of the Huguenots—Cromwell could help the growth of the Reformed religion on the Continent by cooperating with Cardinal Mazarin and acting as a moderating force on militant Catholicism.[10]

The reports that Pell sent to London in April, 1655, prepared some observers for news about the Vaudois. He said he had learned that the Duke of Savoy intended to massacre the Protestants in the Piedmont, that France knew of the plan, and that French forces were going to aid the Duke. Pell admitted that he had not checked the authenticity of the story, but he thought that it still should be made known in London.[11]

When the reports (even though they differed in details and were sometimes contradictory) of actions by the Duke of Savoy against the Vaudois reached London, they were met with feelings of anger and revulsion.[12] The news of French participation was particularly unsettling to men, like Stouppe and Pell, who planned to further the cause of Protestantism by closer ties with France. Stouppe thought that the use of French troops had compounded the disaster, but that the Duke had committed a more heinous act by employing "the bleudie Irish (supplied to him by France) . . . in the destruction of said churches." The Duke had supposedly told confidants that all the actions "against the Protestants of the Vallies, hath had the consent and approbation of the French ambassador, resident at Turin, and of the French court." Stouppe's informant denounced France's role in the persecution of the Vaudois, but still concluded that the only way for the remaining Protestants to survive was "through the settlement of the peace now being discussed between England and France." If the peace was not realized, the French reaction might be to give further encouragement and assistance to the Duke of Savoy, and "those sheep [now] in safety, they might be in great danger."[13]

Stouppe adopted a more direct approach toward the Piedmont. He appealed to Cromwell to assist the Vaudois. "The whole Christendome have their eyes fixed on his Highness [Cromwell] and all good men hope that he will avenge, or

rather God will avenge, by his hand, such a hellish bar-
barousness." In Stouppe's view, the crisis in the Piedmont
was the type of cause for which the Protectorate had been
established. "God had given him [Cromwell] great power to
employ to his [God's] glory; an that hath put a victorious
sword in his hand to be a revenger to execute wrath upon
those that do evill." Cromwell should lead an alliance of
Protestant states to defend the Vaudois, but should also be
willing to act alone if a coalition did not materialize. If
Cromwell did that, "the whole world . . . [would say that]
the Protector of Great Britain has become the Protector of
all those that are persecuted for righteousness sake."[14]
Stouppe's approach to succoring the Vaudois bore striking
similarities to the explanations Cromwell had given for his
own actions during the Civil Wars and to the justifications
for the programs he presented to Parliament. Both men saw
the Protector as God's chosen instrument to protect the
faith and spread havoc among those who threatened it.[15]

The reaction in England to events in the Piedmont was
marked by great confusion concerning exactly what had happened.[16] When the situation became clear Cromwell acted.
He wrote the Duke of Savoy and the King of France, asking
the latter to act in behalf of the Vaudois. Letters were also
sent to the Kings of Sweden and Denmark and to the States
General asking them to exert pressure. The only direct actions the Protector could take were to proclaim a day of
fasting in England and to raise a collection for the relief
of the Vaudois.[17]

The outbreak of violent anti-Protestantism in the Piedmont occurred at an inconvenient time for Bordeaux. Negotiations had gone so well that Thurloe had told Pell that
a treaty was near. Less than two weeks later, in another
communication to Pell, Thurloe commented that there was
little likelihood of an agreement at that time. The situation
in the Piedmont was the only factor to which the change
could be attributed. Furthermore, when the ambassador extraordinary from Spain arrived in London, he attempted to
use the plight of the Vaudois to his advantage. The irony
involved in that position escaped the Spanish. The Marquis
de Lede, by playing on anti-Catholic feelings in England,

brought to the forefront the issue that was most often used by proponents of an attack against the Habsburgs. In addition, de Lede and Cardenas had just rejected an English demand for freedom from the Inquisition and from other religious restrictions for Protestant merchants trading in Spanish territories. Having done that, de Lede presented a strange picture as he joined Cromwell in lamentations over the condition of a persecuted Protestant minority. Spain's new steps to establish closer ties with the Protector combined with the resentment in England about the Vaudois to give Cromwell another plausible reason to postpone negotiations with France.[18]

Bordeaux's predicament was aggravated by the clumsy manner in which Mazarin tried to deny French involvement with the Duke of Savoy. The Cardinal's already shaky reputation for truthfulness received another blow when it beame clear that his categorical denial of France's involvement in the Piedmont was not based on fact. It was reported in England that Mazarin had written the Duke of Savoy chastising him, not for the treatment of the Vaudois "but for choosing no better time to doe it, saying that it was not altogether unreasonable."[19]

When it became clear that French troops and other forces under the command of French officers had taken part in the "massacre," it made little difference to English critics whether these troops had been acting under orders from Louis, the Cardinal, or the Duke of Savoy. The central fact remained that French and Irish regiments had assisted in the "massacre" of the Vaudois, and there was a strong feeling in London that it was the obligation of the King of France to atone for the situation.[20]

Two considerations about the Piedmont situation affected Cromwell at the same time: resentment against France for its involvement, and the desire to alleviate the misery of the Vaudois and to prevent a similar situation from developing in the future. It was clear that collections and fasts in England would not accomplish any of the practical results Cromwell desired. Pell suggested that Cromwell convince Louis to act for the Vaudois, since it "will be possible to persuade the Court of France, that it is in the King's interest

to re-establish and support them [the Vaudois]."[21] When
Mazarin and Brienne realized the intense feelings in England against France's participation in the Piedmont,[22] they
tried to discount these feelings as another delaying tactic
or as hysteria brought on by false and exaggerated reports.[23]
Despite Mazarin's attempt to minimize the situation, there
was a sincere revulsion in England against the Duke of
Savoy's and French complicity in the destruction of the Vaudois communities. There was also a revival of the genuine
fear that Protestantism was still in danger, as well as a feeling that it was the Protector's duty to defend it against all
opposition. According to Thurloe, Cromwell decided that no
treaty could be concluded with France while the Vaudois
were still suffering, and that France bore part of the stigma
for the actions of the Duke of Savoy.[24] On the other hand,
Cromwell did not use the situation in the Piedmont to harass
Bordeaux. When the disappointment about the collapse of
the negotiations wore off, Bordeaux and some of his corre-
spondents at the French court were surprised that Cromwell
did not try to make greater political capital out of France's
involvement in the Piedmont.

The French court did not hesitate long before acting on
behalf of the Vaudois. The French ambassador to the Duke
of Savoy proposed a declaration of amnesty for the Vaudois.
The declaration did not deny the validity of the Duke's actions, but proposed freedom of religion for the Vaudois in
the future and reaffirmed past edicts dealing with the practice of religion.[25] Throughout the summer of 1655, Cromwell's agents kept close watch on negotiations concerning
the Vaudois. Pell and Morland sent lengthy reports to Thurloe, but they could do little to influence the Duke or assist
the Vaudois.[26] Pell became more convinced that only the
intercession of France could protect Vaudois, since Louis
had close ties with the Duke, who depended on France for
military and financial assistance. Swiss Protestants reminded Pell that it was in Louis's interests to avoid disturbances
in the Piedmont, in order "to keep the way open out of
France through the Piedmont into Italy." The leaders of
the Vaudois were also convinced that Protestant states had

no way of rendering military aid if the Duke tried to subjugate them once more.[27]

By the end of August, open hostilities between the Vaudois and the Duke of Savoy were ended by the Treaty of Pignerol. The treaty papered over many issues. It gave the Vaudois the right to worship in freedom, and pledged the Duke to undertake no repression of them.[28] Many Protestants objected to the treaty's assertion that the Vaudois had acted against their ruler. The circumstances under which the treaty was concluded left no doubt that it was dictated by France, and it was implicitly recognized that the King of France would enforce its provisions. Louis had become the protector of a small group of Protestants whose welfare had caused such great consternation in England.

Mazarin's activities in the Piedmont were dictated by its strategic location as well as by the concern shown by the Protector. When the treaty was concluded, Mazarin did not hesitate to remind Cromwell of France's role in protecting the Vaudois.[29] The treaty was bitterly denounced by many Englishmen, but the Protector voiced no objection to it.[30] Even reports that the Vaudois were dissatisfied did not cause Cromwell to attempt to modify the treaty. He recognized, as Bordeaux noted, that Louis's intervention had saved the Vaudois from further suffering. Cromwell had seen that he was powerless to intervene directly to help the Vaudois.[31]

The "massacre" of the Vaudois had turned them into pawns in a much larger diplomatic game. They, as well as their oppressor, had lost control of the final settlement of the situation. In the early summer, it had looked as though the "massacre" would damage Bordeaux's negotiations seriously. When the issue was finally resolved, Cromwell and Mazarin had seen another area in which their cooperation worked to the advantage of both states as well as of the religious scruples of the Protector. Bordeaux's moribund treaty was not suddenly activated by the Treaty of Pignerol, but it was clear that his position was improved.

Some contemporary observers—and later historians—have complained of Cromwell's hypocrisy or his lack of dedication to his religious principles. It is true that his foreign policy was not dictated by religious considerations, but it is equally true that he did not act against them. His actions during the crisis of the Vaudois showed a pragmatic application of his religious concerns. Cromwell did not achieve the freedom that Vaudois or their militant supporters desired, but he did not try to accomplish that goal. He put diplomatic pressure on Cardinal Mazarin and, in so doing, helped to stop the suffering of his coreligionists and hastened the treaty that assured their survival.

Cromwell's actions reaffirmed to Mazarin that he was dealing with a responsible statesman, not the mystical religious fanatic that Cromwell's opponents had portrayed. The situation of the Vaudois demonstrated the Protector's ability, developed through years of crises, to set a course by means of which the best aspects of potentially conflicting policies could be brought into one plan of action. He showed that he understood the international situation, the extent of England's influence, and the ways in which that influence could best be used. Once again, Cromwell the political leader triumphed, not by destroying, but by tempering, the desires of Cromwell the idealist.

As the summer dragged to a conclusion, Bordeaux was in approximately the same position as he had been a year earlier; there seemed little chance of a break with England, but there was no indication of an alliance. This indecisive situation led to renewed impatience at the French court. There was a strong feeling that since the Protector had no reason to oppose France, his procrastination meant that he did not want an agreement. French policy makers were hindered by their inability to grasp two essential factors about Cromwell's actions: his picture of international politics did not coincide with the view from Paris; and he did not intend to make any alliance until he was convinced there was nothing further to be gained from waiting. French anger toward Cromwell's delaying tactics was tempered by uncertainty about the designs of his fleet. When Brienne informed Bordeaux of the impatience of the King, he also warned that negotiations should not be broken off until there was definite news about Penn. Brienne assumed that the fleet was going to attack Spain's territories, and that the attack would cause a breach between England and Spain. He also thought that the Protector wanted to carry his actions against Spain further than an isolated attack on the Indies, and therefore "He will agree with us, to the end he may the better carry on his designs, the Spanish forces being employed to defend themselves against us."[32] Brienne was over optimistic, and his error compounded the anxieties that plagued Bordeaux after news of the Western Design reached London.

13

The Treaty of Westminster

By August, 1655, most observers felt that events had worked out well for Bordeaux. The crisis in the Piedmont had ended, and France had aided the Vaudois; news of Penn's failure at Hispaniola had reached Europe, and led to suspicions of a break between England and Spain; and France had won a series of victoris in Flanders against the Habsburg armies. Since Cromwell had put down a potential rebellion in England, he could no longer reasonably say that domestic turmoil prevented him from concluding an alliance. Despite all these favorable conditions, negotiations on Bordeaux's treaty showed no progress.[1]

The delay prompted interesting reactions from some of Thurloe's agents in France. They had some reason to believe, for the first time since Cromwell had seized power, that France, rather than England, was holding back the negotiations. The combination of English humiliation in the Indies and France's victories in Flanders led one agent to state that the Cardinal "seemed to expect better terms from your lord protector than formerly they would have accepted."[2] If it was true, as another informant said, that "France desired peace chiefly with England to keep off their assistance to Spain against France,"[3] there was no reason for Bordeaux to press for the completion of a treaty. Bordeaux was not satisfied with the situation. He continued to push for an agreement, and the commissioners continued to delay. One cause for the delay was the recent French successes. The English had worked too hard at a policy of negotiating from strength to reach an important agreement with France when their own fortunes were at a relatively low point.

Cromwell had other reasons to put off the conclusion of a treaty with France. In the late spring of 1655, the Royalists had stepped up their campaign to secure assistance from the papacy and support from Catholic monarchs. Charles's serious consideration of this improbable plan was one indication of the level to which Royalist fortunes had fallen. He tried to convince the pope that Cromwell's position was weak, and that a restoration could be accomplished with papal assistance.[4] Intelligence sources in Rome contradicted Charles's claims, and the pope made no commitments to the Stuarts.[5] However, the Royalists were informed that the pope wanted to assist them if it could be accomplished within the framework of a broader set of alliances. Father Peter Talbot and Colonel Sexby set about to arrange an alliance between Charles and the Habsburgs, hoping to involve the papacy in it. It soon became obvious that Spain could do little for Charles until the end of its war with France. There was one solution to the dilemma facing the Stuarts, Spain, and the papacy—the conclusion of the war in Europe. The possibility of a general peace might not be great, but it represented a definite threat to Cromwell's security.

Reports reached England that the pope had revived his attempts to negotiate a settlement between France and Spain. These reports seemed reasonable enough to cause Condé to fear he might be abandoned by his Habsburg allies.[6] At the same time, Mazarin held a series of conferences with a Spanish Dominican who was supposedly on a mission to discuss peace between all Catholic states.[7] Each of these incidents might be trivial, but they combined to make English diplomats fear that France and Spain were heading for the conference table. As the summer drew to a close, more stories, some of which originated in such reliable sources as the Swedish ambassador, reached London saying that a general peace was being arranged by the papacy.[8] Suspicions about Mazarin's plans increased when Cromwell attempted to send George Downing to France. Mazarin was cold to the idea, and Cromwell had to insist before Downing was received in France.[9] In a long conversation with Downing,

the Cardinal tried to show why England should conclude
an alliance with France. One of Mazarin's promises was that
"he would engage, that no treaty or peace should be made
in Spayne, but with his hyghnesse [Cromwell] consent."[10]
Mazarin appeared to believe that his talk with Downing had
swept away Cromwell's hesitations concerning the treaty
and had convinced him that France would not interfere in
England's domestic politics.[11]

In a letter to Bordeaux, Chanut summarized feelings in
Paris about the negotiations, "There remains nothing now
to hinder the conclusion of your treaty." There was a chance
that England might continue to delay, but it seemed unlikely "that there can yet lie underground some new cause or
delay at a time when the Protector doth disoblige Spain,
and when many reasons should induce him to make
friends."[12] Bordeaux was not so sanguine, fearing that Cromwell would continue to press demands as long as he felt he
could obtain more concessions. By the middle of September,
Bordeaux was finally of the opinion that Cromwell was convinced that France would offer nothing more; therefore an
agreement was almost assured.[13] Despite his optimism, Bordeaux was still impatient with the slowness of the negotiations. Occasionally he wrote of his desire to end the negotiations with either the "conclusion of the treaty, or a rupture,
in a short time."[14] These feelings were temporized by a
reminder from his father "not to pursue the signing of the
peace till such time that the protector hath finished his demands and pretences."[15] Bordeaux tried to put some pressure
on the commissioners, reminding them that the treaty had
long been ready and cautioning that no further concessions
would be made.[16] His impatience was increased by the apprehension that Spain was ready to make new advances to the
Protector to avoid a break with him, and by the fear that
the Cardinal might send a new ambassador to England to
secure the treaty.[17] Bordeaux feared that he would be dis-
graced if a new ambassador finished the negotiations. Furthermore, the new envoy would get the credit for Bordeaux's
efforts, which appeared on the verge of success.[18]

French correspondence throughout October, 1655, showed
great optimism about the treaty, but Thurloe demonstrated

an unusual degree of uncertainty. At the beginning of the month, he informed Henry Cromwell, "Wee have concluded a peace with France, and the articles will be signed this weeke."[19] The treaty was not signed within that time, and two weeks later Thurloe wrote, "The issue of our treatie with France is also doubtfull; all things are agreed, and the treaties engrossed fitt to be signed, and now the ambassador refuseth to sign upon a pretense." Thurloe asserted that Bordeaux balked at signing the treaty because of the term of address used for the King of France. Bordeaux was annoyed at the form of the treaty, and he may have used it as a final gesture to restore the dignity of the King as well as some of his own pride, but he certainly had no intention of blocking its conclusion.[20] The dispute was finally resolved through the mediation of Nieupoort, the Dutch ambassador in London, and on 3 November 1655, the treaty, for which Bordeaux had worked so long, was finally signed.[21]

The articles of the treaty fell into six major classes: promises not to assist rebels against either state or future followers of such rebels; and end to all hostilities between the states and all their subjects; the regularization of commercial and admiralty rules; a refusal to receive any pirates and a promise to return any of their prizes; and a promise to have past commercial disputes adjudicated; and an agreement that the treaty should be ratified and made public within a fortnight.[22] A series of secret articles were appended to the treaty, the most important of which concerned individuals to be exiled from France and England. Cromwell promised to expel some of Condé's leading supporters, like Barrière, while Mazarin agreed to expel Charles and James Stuart, the Duke of Ormonde, Hyde, Nicholas, Langdale, and other Royalists named by Cromwell.[23]

According to an account by Thurloe, the secret articles gave Cromwell a series of important promises and forced the Royalists to reestablish their base of operation. Because of the treaty, Cromwell "could depend upon the Friendship of France in case of any future dispute with the Low Countries." The Protector was promised that the Huguenots would receive good treatment and enjoy the privileges of their edicts, and this "should be the Cement of this Union

and Friendship with Them [France]." Finally, Cromwell was
assured "that there were no treaties in progress between
France and Spain," and none would be undertaken without
his participation.[24]

The treaty brought mixed reactions throughout Europe.
There was little discussion in England about its influence
on future policies. Cromwell and his advisers seemed to pay
slight attention to any effect it might have on their relations
with Spain. Its immediate result was to convince Spain that
future negotiations with Cromwell wouldbe fruitless, and to
hasten the decision to sell the embargoed English goods.[25]
Consequently, the treaty accelerated the Royalists' drive to
obtain support from Spain. Charles was anxious to move
to Brussels, where he hoped to set up a series of plots against
Cromwell.[26] However, even Father Peter Talbot, who saw
Spain's opposition to Cromwell as a God-sent opportunity
to the Stuarts, realized that Spain was not going to provide
assistance just because Charles was the rightful ruler of England. The Habsburg leadership wanted assurances that
Charles could support his claims to the allegiance of his subjects in England, especially the sailors.[27] Some of Charles's
most influential advisers—Hyde in particular—had no confidence that Spain would be helpful in the foreseeable future.
This feeling had two roots: the King of Spain did not want
to think that war with Cromwell "was inevitable"[28]; and it
was believed that "true Englishmen . . . will join heartily
in revenge against that bloody popish people."[29] Most of
Hyde's fears were realized. Spain did declare war on England. Spain's war effort was not pressed with any great vigor,
and the "bloody popish people" gave Cromwell a popular
target for English hostilities.[30]

The consequences of the treaty had a great effect on the
personal lives of the Royalists. The secret articles worked
the greatest hardship on the Duke of York. It was clear,
even to men who knew nothing about the secret articles,
that the Duke would have to leave France. Nevertheless,
he tried to find some way to remain in Louis's army, where
he had become a respected subordinate of Turenne.[31] These
hopes were doomed, and even Henrietta Maria saw that it
was not "expedient that . . . [James] should stay in the

French army any longer."[32] The hurried Royalist response to the treaty caused further disorder in their ranks. Hyde was described as being especially anxious because "he is fearful of being laid aside."[33] Charles's need to reorient his policies added new divisive issues to his already factionalized supporters. Cromwell's agreement with Mazarin came as a major psychological shock to the Royalists and a blow to their pride. The responsibility for the "loss of France" caused heated discussions amongst Charles's followers. The question was raised that if Charles's councillors could not insure at least the neutrality of the homeland of his mother, what could they be trusted to do? The men who figured prominently in the formulation of what passed for Charles's policy had to bear the blame for the Treaty of Westminster. This criticism must have been especially bitter for Hyde to accept, since he had realized the inability of Charles to do much to stop the treaty.

The Treaty of Westminster was a nonaggression pact, but many observers believed it would soon lead to more formal military arrangements. It was widely accepted that Mazarin wanted to change the nature of the treaty—a view that was correct. Shortly after the treaty was signed, the Cardinal wrote Bordeaux, "As for a nearer alliance, all of which I can say unto is, that his majesty doth desire it, and will always be ready to embrace it . . . but we must foresee what propositions they will make unto you."[34]

The author of one plan for closer ties stated that the presence of English troops on the Continent would give Cromwell more power to protect the interests of his own state as well as those of Protestantism.[35] Cromwell resisted the suggestion that he enter into an alliance against Spain and send troops to aid France's war effort. Nevertheless, his actions still had a beneficial effect on France's war effort. The attack on Hispaniola forced Spain to divide its naval forces, giving France greater freedom to transport its troops and the threat of renewed raids caused Spain to postpone the sailing of a treasure fleet from the Indies. The longer that fleet was delayed, the more difficult it became for Spain to hire and maintain the forces it needed to fight France.[36]

The Dutch found little to appreciate in the Treaty of

Westminster. Their most extreme fear was that France and England might combine "to drive the Spanish out of Brabant and Flanders, and England [would] become Master of Dunkirk, whereby they [England] will get a footing on this side of the seas to prosecute any greater designe."[37] The treaty was signed at a particularly difficult time for the Dutch. Their vital interests in the Baltic were in an uncertain state, owing to the aggressive conduct of Sweden. Because of the close relations between England and Sweden, the Dutch were afraid that Cromwell might obtain lower rates in the Baltic. In the view of some Dutch observers, the treaty with France removed an area of possible trouble which might have distracted Cromwell from the Baltic.[38] The probability of war between England and Spain posed another dilemma for the Dutch. It would lead to attempts to seize merchant shipping—a situation that would be inimical to Dutch commerce and could provoke new clashes with England. There was some discussion in the United Provinces about reaching an agreement with England to prohibit the seizure of neutral ships, but chances for it were slight.[39] Reports received by Thurloe contended that the King of Spain was suddenly held in high esteem in the United Provinces because he was opposed to Cromwell, and that the Dutch considered sending an ambassador extraordinary to Spain.[40]

The province of Holland was put in an especially difficult position by Cromwell's break with Spain and his closer ties with France. The opposition to an Orangist revival was centered in Holland, giving its leaders a common cause with Cromwell. However, raids on Dutch shipping might give the Orangists an issue to spearhead a campaign to overthrow the ruling elite in Holland.[41] Stories also reached England that Spain was trying to enlist Dutch aid in the war against the Protectorate or at least to get the Dutch to convoy the silver fleet from the Indies to Spanish ports.[42] Either activity would have had grave consequences for Anglo-Dutch relations, but the issues remained hypothetical. The Dutch did not respond to Spanish proposals, and even postponed the decision to send a new embassy to Spain because such a move might disturb the Protector.[43]

The Treaty of Westminster had a pronounced impact on Cromwell's position among some of the Continental Protestants. In Pell's words,

they [Swiss and German Protestants] will be glad to heare of England's peace with France and Warre with Spain. For it is in these countries a general observation with hardly any exception, the papists are for Spain, the Protestants are for France. And although at this time they have no great reason to love France, yet as long as the House of Austria is so great, they do not wish France less powerful than it is, lest the balance should become more uneven.[44]

The treaty effectively ended the hopes of the pope and de Haro of contracting a peace, or at least an armistice, between France and Spain.[45] Cromwell had considered that the subject of a general peace was important enough to include it in the treaty, and he had obtained more than Mazarin's word as a barrier to peace. The treaty gave Mazarin new advantages in the struggle with the Spanish Habsburgs, and held out the hope of further assistance.

The possibility of peace appeared to weigh heavily in the decisions taken by the Protector. He viewed the Habsburg-Bourbon war as a life-and-death matter for France. The convictions with which Cromwell had fought the war in England, as well as his providential outlook, might have led him to a distorted view of the Cardinal's attitude toward the war with Spain. These considerations, combined with Cromwell's feelings about the enormous power of the Habsburgs, provided a set of assumptions about international politics upon which the foreign policy of England might be based. The Protector's outlook on the world, often described as Elizabethan, appeared closer to that of Richelieu and Father Joseph. Since the war was finally going well for France, and showed signs of getting better in the future, English observers saw little reason for the Cardinal to sit down to make peace. If he did violate the treaty by negotiating with Spain, he would lose Cromwell's aid. This action would, in effect, strengthen Spain, and it was unlikely that Mazarin would weaken himself at the time he chose to negotiate. The Protector might well expect Mazarin to postpone any negotiations with Spain until Cromwell agreed, because that policy, as seen from Whitehall, was in the best interests of France. In this instance, Cromwell and his advisers fell into the same trap—the failure to recognize the viewpoints of other statesmen—that had plagued Brienne and Mazarin during most of their dealing with England.

The treaty gave Cromwell another way to strengthen the true religion and to strike at the papacy by adding to his stature among Continental Protestants.[46] Cromwell's attack on the papacy was two-pronged. He sabotaged the general peace which, if successful, would have added to the cohesion of international Catholicism and the prestige of the papacy. When Blake demonstrated that England's power could reach Italy, Cromwell's bellicose statements about the inseparability of Spain and the papacy could not be ignored. Thurloe was informed that many Italians "began to think theyr beloved papacy is in as great a danger by this war as the King of Spain."[47] Cromwell did not mount any attack against the papacy, but he convinced others that close ties with Rome might not be advisable.

By the beginning of 1656, Cromwell and Thurloe regarded the Treaty of Westminster as a closed issue. No plans were laid to use it as the foundation for a larger system of alliances or to involve England more deeply in a European war against Spain. The treaty had already given Cromwell some benefits. The customary confusion among the Royalists had been compounded, and the King had been cut off from his natural base of support. As a bonus to Cromwell, Henrietta Maria was left, with some of her favorites, to engage in her conspiracies and plots without the restraining hand of Charles or Hyde to stop her from embarrassing her son. The Stuarts had been delivered into the hands of the Habsburgs, enabling Cromwell to identify Charles with the home of the Inquisition and the support of Rome. War with Spain gave Cromwell a chance for profit and an enemy against whom he could rouse the emotions of a people who were wearied with the regulations of the Protectorate. The treaty gave him some assurance that he could conduct the war against

Spain in his own fashion, with little fear of outside interference. If the situation ever warranted, Cromwell could turn to France for aid against the common enemy.

The treaty with France was not the first international agreement into which Cromwell entered, but it was the most important step he had taken thus far. The treaty with the Dutch had the specific purpose of ending the war, and the agreements with Portugal and Sweden had not involved serious alternatives. The Treaty of Westminster demonstrated that Cromwell had finally decided between France and Spain, and his vigorous statements against Spain reinforced the point. The treaty weakened the Stuarts and elevated Cromwell's position in England at virtually no cost to him. The treaty demonstrated not only the priorities established by the Protector but also the ease with which he was able to obtain them. The Protectorate was in a formidable bargaining position because of its own strength and the shifting situation in the Bourbon-Habsburg war, which divided most of Europe into two armed camps.

14

Lockhart's Mission to France

In the Treaty of Westminster Cromwell committed England to a policy of cooperation with France, which had the net effect of hardening the hostile situation between England and Spain. Once he had entered into an agreement with France, he changed his approach to diplomacy. The pressure on Bordeaux was lessened—a circumstance that was accelerated by Cromwell's decision to send a representative to Paris. Cromwell maintained the whip hand in his dealings with France. After Westminster, it was actively exercised, as opposed to the passive policy of delay and retrenchment he had practiced before November, 1655. One obvious symptom of this change was the less important role played by Bordeaux. His activities no longer provided the key to understanding Cromwell's policy; Cromwell, Secretary Thurloe, and Ambassador Sir William Lockhart occupied the center of the diplomatic stage until the death of the Protector in September, 1658.

The Treaty of Westminster satisfied the objectives for which Bordeaux had originally been sent to England. However, by 1655, the Cardinal wanted Cromwell's active cooperation in the war against the Habsburgs. Mazarin wanted a "closer alliance," but he also wanted Cromwell to make the first proposals.[1] However, the Protector was in no hurry to suggest any major changes in the relationship. About a month after the treaty was signed, Bordeaux left England and returned to France for consultations with Mazarin.[2] At the same time, Cromwell sent a message to the King of

168

France about the treaty, in which he praised Bordeaux's conduct: "We think it ought to be attributed for the most part to his faithful and prudent service as ambassador, that the conscientous desires and endeavours of both parties were brought to such a fortunate issue."[3] The Protector made no attempt to keep Bordeaux in London, and sent no suggestions with him for consideration by the Cardinal. This is understandable—why should Cromwell press matters until he had gauged the reactions of other states to the treaty?

When Bordeaux returned to France, he discovered that the Cardinal was not satisfied with the treaty. Mazarin wanted the secret articles amended to allow the Duke of York to remain in the service of France. The Cardinal argued that James's exile would "be prejudicial to both England and France. . . . His [James's] stay shall cause no jealousy, for he shall be employed in such a country where the royalists can have no advantage of it."[4] Mazarin did not want James to join the Spanish, because he was a competent soldier, and Irish troops would desert France to join him.[5] Despite the Cardinal's arguments, Cromwell insisted that the secret provisions be enforced, and James left to join his brother.[6]

Shortly before Bordeaux arrived back in England, Cromwell made a move that radically altered arrangements with France.[7] Until that time, England had maintained informal representatives and observers in France. Representatives had been sent by the Commonwealth and Protectorate to discuss specific issues with Mazarin, but there had been no English ambassador in France. This absence had not hampered the Protector's diplomacy, but after the treaty he decided that his policies could not be implemented without an English ambassador in Paris.

Mazarin counseled against sending an English ambassador to France. He said that he would be glad to have a representative from Cromwell, but that there were too many Irish and Royalists in France to insure his safety. Mazarin assured Cromwell that, even without an ambassador in France, "he [Cromwell] shall have a perfect account of the states of affairs in France given him from time to time."[8]

On 19 April 1656, Sir William Lockhart received orders

from the council to obtain bills of exchange and proceed to France to assume the position of ambassador.[9] Lockhart, who was thirty-five years old when he became ambassador, had lived a hectic and exciting life. He had served in the French armies as a young man, and had fought in the Earl of Lanark's regiment during the first Civil War. He had been knighted by Charles I at Newark in 1646. While he was in the "engagers" army, he had surrendered to Lambert. After obtaining his liberty for the payment of £1,000, Lockhart planned to serve in the army that was formed in 1650 to support Charles II. He resigned when an attempt was made to force him to share his command. However, he returned to volunteer his services personally to Charles II. The King snubbed the offer, and Lockhart returned to his home, where he remained while Charles's army marched off to its destruction at Worcester.

Lockhart had chosen a different course from that taken by his father Sir James who had been commissioner for Lanarkshire in a long series of parliaments and had held other important offices. He had been deprived of his offices in 1649, and had assisted Charles II's invasion in 1650. Sir James was imprisoned in the Tower in 1651, shortly before his son appeared in London. In 1652, Sir William had an interview with Cromwell in London. In May of that year, he was appointed one of the commissioners for justice for Scotland and a member of the privy council. Lockhart also served as an M. P. for Lanark in the parliaments of 1653, 1654-55, and 1656-58. Lockhart played an active role in the administration of Scotland. During his tenure there, he worked closely with George Monck. The ways in which Lockhart and Monck had become supporters of the Commonwealth and Cromwell had certain similarities. Their acquaintanceship probably helped bring Lockhart to Cromwell's attention later. The choice of a second wife in 1654, Robina, a niece of Cromwell's by her mother did nothing to harm Lockhart's prospects.

Cromwell recognized the importance of the appointment he made as ambassador to France, and Lockhart had much to recommend him for the position. His service in the French armies gave him experience of which few of Cromwell's officials or advisers could boast. Lockhart's conversion from the service of the Stuarts had occurred long enough ago to make him reliable, and his performance in Scotland had left little doubt of his loyalty or ability. Cromwell could certainly have chosen other men who had been diplomats or officials abroad. Instead, he chose a soldier with a reputation for administrative talents, independence, and confidence in his own judgments. Lockhart's appointment brought to the fore a man who was not associated with the foreign policies of the Commonwealth and who had an understanding of the military situation on the Continent. This selection indicated that Cromwell intended to emphasize the military aspects of his realtionship with France, and that he did not expect his ambassador to be merely a courier.

Since Lockhart became the focal point for Cromwell's dealings with Mazarin, the initial instructions given him must be considered in some detail. After making the normal gestures of friendship, Lockhart was told to inform the King and the Cardinal that Cromwell wished to come "soon to a nearer union and more intimate allyance than is settled and established by the Late Treaty."[10] He was to tell the Cardinal that there were mutual interests between him and Cromwell, and that "he [Mazarin] shall find upon experience that there is no person in Europe who will be more certain and constant friend to him and the affaires of France than myselfe." Cromwell wanted it made perfectly clear to Mazarin that the Treaty of Westminster had not been signed because of any break between England and Spain, and that assurances of good treatment for the Huguenots were a vital factor in the continued harmony between England and France. Furthermore, Lockhart was to tell the Cardinal, "I [Cromwell] doe finally agree with what was proposed by the said French ambassador at the time of his departure hence theat now is the time for both sides to consider and take counsell concerning Spain, the common enemy of both states . . . how our confederate may be usefull to the other in any designe against him." There were no specific suggestions about the form that joint actions might take, but Lockhart had "the power to discuss and argue proposalls with Mazarin." If Lockhart received a favorable reaction to his talks, he was supposed to communicate immediately with London to obtain new instuctions.[11]

Lockhart's instructions made it clear that Cromwell wanted him to do more than merely transmit intelligence to Thurloe, a function that had been ably performed by Augier and Hugh Morrell.[12] Lockhart's arrival in France also meant that Cromwell would have to abandon or strongly modify the delaying tactics that had served him so well in the past. The Protector could hold back instructions from Lockhart and tell him to postpone replies to the Cardinal, but delay would be more transparent in the new situation. Lockhart's presence in France, as well as his instructions, showed that Cromwell had moved toward closer ties with Mazarin.[13]

Lockhart arrived in Dieppe on 6 May 1656, and received a warm reception from local officials. He gained the impression that the Treaty of Westminster was well accepted in France and that there were expectations that both sides would obtain great advantages from it.[14] On 8 May, Lockhart met Louis XIV and Mazarin for the first time. The ambassador's conversation with the Cardinal reaffirmed the desire of Cromwell to create closer ties with France. Nothing of substance was discussed at this first meeting, but both men agreed that further talks would be held soon. Lockhart was certainly not in a position to discuss specific proposals. He knew little about the talks that were going on between France and Spain, and had not had time to acquire any first-hand knowledge of the situation in France. Lockhart was acutely aware that he was dealing with a man who had the reputation of being an able diplomat and an elusive and devious negotiator.[15]

Once the ambassador was established in Paris, he was sought out by many persons who had suggestions for Cromwell. In his first weeks in Paris, Lockhart received one proposal that recommended itself to him—plans for the surprise seizure of Dunkirk by an English army. However, he refused to discuss the plan with its author, reminding him that Cromwell would not undertake anything in Flanders without consulting Mazarin. Lockhart continued to be wary in his conversations about Cromwell's plans, fearing that the Cardinal would send "spies . . . to find my pulse."[16]

In the middle of May, discussions started with the Cardinal about transforming the treaty into a closer alliance. When Mazarin showed interest in the activities of an English fleet sailing off Cádiz, Lockhart replied that Cromwell might be willing to use it in conjunction with a French attack in Flanders or on the coast of Spain. When Mazarin suggested the possibility of an attack on Mardyck, Lockhart tried to dismiss the idea. The Cardinal persisted, adding that the capture of Mardyck would enable Cromwell to transform the city into a Protestant settlement where "the liberty of conscience to the popish need no more be insisted on."[17] Lockhart transmitted the suggestion to Cromwell, and received new instructions almost immediately. The Protector looked favorably upon the idea of beseeging a port in Flanders, "although his highnesse hath disposed of his designe against Spain in another way, yet he will endeavour to bring such a fleet before that place as may be able to beseege it at sea, and keepe all reliefe from that way." Cromwell did not intend to supply any of his "standing army," but he would send forces to join France's armies "upon such termes as shall be reasonable."[18] The message to Lockhart also showed the Protector's caution about entering into arrangements with Mazarin, pointing out that after the capture of a port, it would "be in the power of the French army [and] therefore good assurances ought to be given us, that the places shall be put into our hands."[19]

By the middle of June, 1656, Cromwell had established the framework in which Lockhart's future negotiations were carried out. The central issue was the seizure of a port in Flanders and its occupation by English troops. The campaign to gain possession of a port on the Continent, as well as the rest of Cromwell's foreign policy, required financial support from Parliament. Cromwell was attempting to use one of the ends of his proposed alliance with France as a means of giving him the means to implement his policies. It was crucial that he have something important to show from his negotiations with France before Parliament met. By June, the decision had been made to call another Parliament, and in July, writs for the election were issued. By that time, Lockhart was already pressing hard to obtain for

Cromwell the concession that might convince the Protector's critics that his actions abroad might lead to great advantages for England.

The immediate problems facing Lockhart were distrust of Mazarin and the exact choice of targets. The manner in which Mazarin acted after making his "offer of a port in Flanders" added to Lockhart's suspicions. The Cardinal began consultations with a friar suspected of being a messenger from de Haro, an action which seemed contrary to the spirit of the Treaty of Westminster. In addition, the Cardinal did not answer Lockhart's communications concerning Flanders, and postponed scheduled discussions about other issues of mutual interest.[20]

Lockhart's discussions with Mazarin began to show some results. The Cardinal agreed to advance the money needed to stage an attack in Flanders, and promised to turn the captured cities over to Cromwell's forces as soon as they were taken. Mazarin asked Lockhart to have the discussion put in writing and transmitted to the Protector for immediate consideration. The talks went smoothly until Lockhart mentioned that Cromwell wanted security for Mazarin's promise. The Cardinal reacted angrily to this, and told Lockhart that the only security he would promise was "the word of his master and the respect he has for Cromwell."[21]

When Lockhart complained that Mazarin was delaying the conclusion of an agreement concerning Flanders, the Cardinal apologized for his behavior. He explained that his attention was focused on the uncertain outcome of the French siege at Valenciennes. Mazarin gave assurances that the projected attack in Flanders would go forward regardless of what happened at Valenciennes, but the injection of a new consideration into the discussions disturbed Lockhart. He raised another serious issue at the same meeting—the rumors about a peace between France and Spain. The Cardinal tried to dismiss these rumors, saying that "many who want to separate France and England have been creating these rumors." He admitted that there were some "biggott friars" who came to France "bringing proposals from the nuncio [and] the pope." Mazarin commended those men for their zeal, "but nothing else," and said he had ignored their ideas.[22] This explanation quieted Lockhart's fears about a peace, but did nothing to convince him of Mazarin's sincerity concerning an attack in Flanders.[23]

Mazarin's apprehensions about Valenciennes were well founded. Shortly after the meeting with Lockhart, news reached Paris about the disaster that had struck the armies of France. Spanish troops, commanded by Don John and Condé, had captured most of the beseiging army and its commander le Ferte. Turenne had been able to salvage most of his army, although unable to assist le Ferte. France's gains of the past year were in jeopardy, and plans for the future were uncertain. The defeat also caused rumors about another situation that was potentially dangerous for the Protectorate. The news was welcomed by elements in France that harbored hatred of the Cardinal and admiration for Condé. Although Mazarin's position in France was really not weakened, Thurloe received alarming reports about the situation. One of his informants presented a logical and disturbing appraisal, "Frenchmen as well as Spaniards rejoice at it, being in hopes, that it may produce a peace between France and Spain."[24]

Once more, distrust of the Cardinal's motives clouded the Protector's relationship with him. Mazarin's reaction to Valenciennes was crucial to continued amity with England. Thurloe and Lockhart predicted that the Cardinal would respond in one of two ways: to use the defeat as an excuse to make peace with Spain, with the effect of isolating England; or to use support from England to attack with renewed vigor. In either case, they agreed with the summation made by William Swyft, one of Thurloe's agents, "This summer will showe the English how farr they may trust the Cardinal, who pretends to doe something ere long to expresse how much he values the amity of England."[25]

Throughout the summer of 1656, correspondence received by Thurloe contained many reports about peace negotiations between France and Spain. Many of the reports came from agents who had supplied him with reliable information in the past. Strong rumors about the peace were circulating in many major Continental cities, and gained significance when a representative from Mazarin appeared in Madrid.[26]

Intelligence reports from Spain presented Thurloe with a disturbing picture, because they placed peace negotiations within the framework of a broader political agreement. The proposed treaty supposedly included the marriage of Louis and the Infanta, as well as provisions for the crown of Spain if Philip died without a male heir. Furthermore, Condé was supposedly ready to return to France if he regained his estates.[27]

Lockhart thought that the French court had shown a lack of leadership and direction in its reactions to Valenciennes. This situation made him feel less secure about closer ties with France. The reaction in France to a proposal to use English troops in the war against Spain—"the heightening of the dissatisfaction of the clergy and the biggott parties who impute the cause of this losse to the King's employing a protestant generall, and his alliance with you, whom they call hereticks"—did nothing to restore Lockhart's confidence in an alliance.[28]

In the last week of July, Lockhart attempted to pin down the Cardinal about a peace between France and Spain and the capture of Mardyck or Dunkirk, The Cardinal tried to explain the mission of de Lionne to Madrid, and

protested, that he [Mazarin] had condescended to the propositions of peace upon no other account, but to stopp the clamor of the pope and the French clergy. He knew the King of Spain's demands would be so high, as all honest Frenchmen would think it fitt and just to continue the war. The issue hath answered his expectations, for the Spanish demands are so unreasonable, as even the clergie offer to contribute largely for the carrying on the warre against them.

One Spanish demand had a particular interest for Lockhart—"Henceforth [France and Spain] should have common friends and enemies . . . [France should] renounce the friendship with his highnesse." Mazarin tried to convince Lockhart that a break with Cromwell "was the hardest condition of all." Lockhart wanted more security than the Cardinal's word.[29]

After discounting de Lionne's mission, Mazarin tried to discuss how France could regain the military position it had had before the defeat at Valenciennes. He wanted to contract for three or four regiments of Cromwell's best troops, which would land at Calais. After that, they could be employed as the spearhead of a siege at "Vallenciennes, Cambrai or Doway." Lockhart encouraged Mazarin's hopes of obtaining troops, but warned him that Cromwell might have to withhold them "to interpose his own interest and authoritie for it, which I durst not wish him to doe, except he would alter his desygne and resolve to attack some place in Flanders." After assuring Mazarin that Cromwell would "deny no assistance" to France, Lockhart asserted that "he [Mazarin] could give no greater testimonie of his friendship at this time than be willing to go on with the old business [plans for an attack in Flanders]. It was the only probable means . . . for recovering his reputation in this campaign."[30]

The Cardinal attempted to avoid discussions concerning Flanders, but Lockhart persisted. Finally, "with a great deal of appearance of being satisfied, he [Mazarin] at length agreed to the siege of Dunkirk and Mardyck." No specific plans were made for the attack, but Lockhart was sure that operations in Flanders would be undertaken soon. His appraisal of arrangements with Mazarin—"The Cardinal hath great need of your contenancing him at this tyme; and if I be not mistaken, it is your interest at the present to do that [which] can be done for his preservation"—showed that Lockhart regarded it as the basis for closer ties wih France.[31] The view that Mazarin needed assistance from England encouraged the ambassador to press for quick implementation of the agreement to attack a port in Flanders.

On 26 July 1656, Lockhart and the Cardinal held a meeting at which steps were taken to create an offensive and defensive alliance with specifically defined objectives. Lockhart's conduct made it clear that Cromwell had decided to take the initiative in determining the conditions of the alliance. The tone of the negotiations had undergone a marked change since the Treaty of Westminster. The diplomatic techniques that had operated before November, 1655, were reversed in many ways. In the past, Bordeaux's conduct had been the key to understanding relations between the two states. Most of the proposals had originated with him, and his reactions showed the manner in which Cromwell had chosen to deal with France. Although Bordeaux continued to transmit proposals from the Cardinal to Cromwell, the critical issues were discussed by Lockhart and Mazarin. In one other way Lockhart's position in France resembled Bordeaux's mission—in the constant delays and frustrations to which the latter had been exposed.

Less than two weeks after Mazarin had agreed to an attack in Flanders, Lockhart raised the subject again, "but found him absolutlie averse to it."[32] The Cardinal complained that an attack on Dunkirk might weaken France so much that its armies would suffer losses in other areas. "To lose another place, and deliver up what he [Mazarin] had gott their [Dunkirk or Mardyck] to his highness [Cromwell] would render him so odious to all France, as he durst not venture upon it at any rate."[33]

Lockhart's attempt to give real substance to his agreement with Mazarin ran into a major snag that appeared to be outside the scope of English competence—the supposed instability of Mazarin's rule in France. This came as no great surprise to Lockhart. Shortly after his arrival in France, he had stated that Mazarin's failure to deal in a more direct fashion with England was not "from his unwillingness, but affairs here are in a ticklish posture; he is necessitated to be everie day with the assemblie of the ecclesiastics in the morning, and with the counsell in the afternoon."[34] Furthermore, "discontents are verie high hear, and vearie generall." Lockhart assumed that the complaints would end if the French armies were successful, but if the armies "met with Problems . . . I apprehend great disorders will follow upon it."[35] When Mazarin attempted to use discontent in France to delay an agreement about Dunkirk, Lockhart tried to turn the issue into an advantage for himself. He suggested that a joint attack on Dunkirk would strengthen the Cardinal's position, since "his enemies would give over the thoughts of further plots against him, when they see him fortyfied by all the force he might draw from England, whenever his interest in the government should be questioned."[36]

Once again, Lockhart's stance resembled Bordeaux's former role; when Bordeaux's negotiations had been delayed by fears about the security of the Protectorate, he had pointed out that France could buttress Cromwell's government in a struggle against the Royalists and other dissidents.

Lockhart tried to persuade Mazarin that a campaign could be mounted during the winter, which would surprise Spain and result in easy conquests in Flanders. The Cardinal rejected the plan as too risky, but agreed that if

> the execution [of an attack against Dunkirk] were delayed till next spring . . . he was readie to sign articles for it; and if my master should not thinke fitt to persyst the agreement concerning it now, that in January next he would begin a treatie both concerning it and concerning a joyne prosecution of the war for that whole campayne.

This did not satisfy the English ambassador. In a letter to Thurloe, Lockhart suggested that he return to England immediately, "for if it be thought fitt to take the Cardinal's offer, the articles may be agreed upon and syned in eight days time; and if that treatie be delayed until January next, my stay here will be a vast and unnecessary expense." Breaking off talks would be in the interest of the Protector, "for you will find the Cardinal to be of that temper, that he will need a little rownd dealing."[37] Lockhart's feeling that he was being delayed unnecessarily resembled Bordeaux's complaints, but the similarities ended there. Bordeaux often theatened the commissioners with his intention to leave. Lockhart made his comments to his own superiors, not to the men with whom he was dealing. Lockhart's plan to leave France was predicated on the assumption that Mazarin knew he needed the alliance with Cromwell.

15

Dunkirk and the Alliance with France

The future of the city of Dunkirk became the central point in Lockhart's negotiations for an alliance. To be sure, other issues were raised by both sides, but these were subordinated to the discussions about Dunkirk. One obvious reason for England's interest in Dunkirk was its strategic importance. It was a base from which the enemies of the Protectorate could act. Even if the Royalists and their supporters could not mount an invasion, they could harass English shipping.[1] During the summer of 1656, Thurloe received many reports of seizures of English merchant ships by raiders from Dunkirk.[2] The Protector's council discussed the possibility of blockading the port, but rejected the idea because it would have forced the diversion of a large part of the fleet from other missions.[3] After Spain declared war, the situation at Dunkirk presented Cromwell with a cruel paradox. He might have to divert his fleet from objectives over which he had caused the break with Spain, in order to protect his merchants against the consequences of that break.

The other solution to the problem presented by Dunkirk was to seize the town. Cromwell had discussed its occupation with the French governor in 1651 and 1652, at which time England might have received the town as part of a treaty with France. In 1656, Cromwell would have to invade and conquer it as an ally of France.[4]

By the middle of October, Lockhart and Mazarin were finally agreed on the major issues.[5] The remaining obstacle to a treaty was the same point that had caused so much difficulty during the past—apprehension in England about the trustworthiness of the Cardinal. Lockhart repeatedly warned about the possibility of a peace between France and Spain, even though the Treaty of Westminster prohibited unilateral agreements by either France or England.[6] Intelligence received from Brussels and Madrid assured Thurloe that peace negotiations had broken down completely. The supposed reasons for the break—Spain's inability to determine what the Cardinal really wanted, and that "noe man can give credit, [to] what Cardinal Mazarin intends"—were not heartening to Thurloe.[7] The theme of Mazarin's unreliability was repeated in correspondence of all the parties that dealt with him. Condé distrusted him; Lockhart felt he was carrying on double negotiations and stalling about the agreement to invade Dunkirk; and de Haro thought he was using peace talks to allow France's armies to recapture Valenciennes.[8]

Mazarin, recognizing the distrust with which Lockhart regarded him, tried to neutralize it by showing how France would benefit if Cromwell was to retain his power in England. The Cardinal "renewed his accustomed professions of zeall for his highnesses [Cromwell's] interests and aversione to Charles Stewart, upon the account of his ingratitude to France, and to himself in particular." In an attempt to illustrate his disinclination toward the Stuarts, Mazarin contended that it would be better for France if England was conquered by Spain than if Charles was restored. In the former case, the English people would rebel against domination by a foreign power, "especially that of the Spanyard." But if Charles was restored, England would probably unite under him, "and he being a weak prince, obliged to the Spanyard for his restoration, and charmed into an implicit belief in their counsells, might be acted by them into a very dangerous enterprise against France."[9] One might question the Cardinal's opinion of Charles, but the statement made clear what he thought was the best way to dispel the Protector's distrust. Mazarin also asked Lockhart to infom

Cromwell "that if his highness did doubt of the reality of his [Mazarin's] kindness upon the account of his affection, he might assure himself of it upon that of his [Mazarin's] interests."[10]

Mazarin's professions of good faith were not enough. It would take action to dispel the distrust shared by Lockhart, Thurloe, and Cromwell. The improvement of France's military situation, in the autumn and winter of 1656, deprived the Cardinal of one excuse for not acting against Dunkirk.[11] Finally, in November, 1656, Lockhart and Mazarin agreed to stage a joint attack against Dunkirk or Gravelines the following spring. If Gravelines was seized first, it was to be held "as a pledge for Dunkirk." If Dunkirk was taken, "it is to be putt into your [Cromwell's] hands absolutely."[12] No specific arrangements were made for the attack, because the Cardinal raised new questions about the size and cost of the forces Cromwell would provide.[13] The military plans were discussed by Lockhart at a meeting attended by Mazarin, Turenne, and Servien. The ambassador argued that the attack should be undertaken as soon as possible, an idea that Turenne rejected completely. He expressed fears that a hastily planned operation would give new hope to Spain, and "might occasione jealouisies and differences betwixt England and France." He placed a final stamp of disapproval on Lockhart's plan by refusing to command any expedition against Dunkirk. He was willing to lead an attack on Gravelines, despite doubts about its success.[14] Lockhart raised no serious objections, and the meeting ended with agreement to attack Gravelines as a preliminary step to the capture of Dunkirk.[15]

On 13 March 1657, a treaty was concluded between the Protectorate and France. The most important public provisions dealt with a combined expedition to Flanders. Dunkirk and Mardyck were to be placed under siege in April by an army of 26,000 working in conjunction with the English fleet.[16] If success did not seem likely at Dunkirk, the army was to be diverted to Gravelines. When Gravelines was captured, Mazarin promised to turn it over to the Protector's forces until they could take possession of Dunkirk. New assurances were given that neither party to the treaty would make any agreement with Spain, and they agreed to renew the treaty "so long as the two states shall be fitt to continue a joyntt war against Spain."[17] The treaty contained glaring differences from the Treaty of Westminster. The new treaty was not just a defensive and nonaggression pact. It committed England to supply troops for a campaign on the Continent and to support France in the war against the Habsburgs. The Cardinal also hoped it would lead to further participation by England in the war. He had already suggested to Lockhart that if the emperor violated the spirit of the Treaty of Münster, "it would be fitt [for Cromwell] to enter into as strict a league against him as could be agreed upon."[18]

Secret articles appended to the treaty less than six weeks later pledged the signatories to assist one another in a war against a third state with which one of them might have cordial relations. Cromwell promised to assist France in gaining "revenge against the Dutch" for actions in the Mediterranean which "highly offended the King." When Sweden conrolled the Baltic, English and French ships were to be given equal freedom.[19] The secret articles also stated that "the offensive alliance' between the two states should be expanded to include any state that wanted to fight Spain.

The plans to capture Dunkirk might appear almost insignificant against the larger designs to which England was committed. However, it was clear that the treaty would not have been concluded without the provisions about Dunkirk. Its capture would be more than a strategic victory for the Protector.[20] It would give him a base in which to station forces on the Continent. The value of that had been noted by Colonel Bampfylde as early as December 1656. He wanted the Protector to have the potential to intervene militarily in future disputes between Catholics and Protestants. Bampfylde ignored the logistical problems involved for troops from England to support fellow Protestants, but he did see that a foothold on the Continent would enable Cromwell to make a symbolic gesture to his coreligionists rather than to act through the offices of a prince of the Church.[21]

Dunkirk served as a performance bond for the Cardinal. The other provisions of the treaty would not go into operation until Cromwell was convinced of good faith concerning

Dunkirk. Dunkirk also gave the Protector a concrete target upon which to focus attention in England, and against which he could use the army. It was a logical objective for a state that prided itself on the strength of its fleet and its new army. The Protector could obtain further psychological advantages from the capture of Dunkirk. The reestablishment of England's power on the Continent might bring back memories of its last stronghold, Calais, which had been abandoned by that figure of popish treachery, Mary Tudor.[22] Cromwell could wipe away that stain at the expense of the home of the Inquisition.

Cromwell concluded the alliance with France in the wake of serious signs of discontent in England.[23] The session of Parliament that had begun in September, 1656, had been a source of trouble for the Protector. His opening address showed that he intended to use his foreign policy to influence the conduct of Parliament. He delivered a moral lecture in which he stressed the war against Spain, the immorality of Spain's role as the leading supporter of the antichrist, and Spain's alliance with Charles Stuart. The Protector warned Parliament of the union between Stuarts, Don John, and the Jesuits, which planned to invade England and impose an ungodly tyranny upon it. He took great pains to show that France, although a Catholic state, had not been party to designs against Protestantism. He also asserted that European Protestants had gained a great deal from the closer ties between England and France.[24] The arrangements that were embodied in the existing treaty with France did not justify the claims Cromwell made in his speech.

Cromwell saw this Parliament as an emergency measure. He hoped to raise money and stop Parliament from affecting any other changes. His opening speech stressed many of the dangers facing England, but he did not mention the most sensitive problem—what to do about the major generals. Parliament started its session on an unsettling note—the exclusion of many members who were unacceptable to the army.[25] The reconstituted Parliament began to raise questions about the cost of the war with Spain and the meager results shown thus far.[26] By the end of 1656, even a staunch supporter of the Protector thought the situation in Parliament looked bad. The problem was not "enemyes abroad, but troublemakers at home. . . . We have not all this tyme raised one penny towards the Spannish warre, nor are like to do after this rate till we heare of him [Charles Stuart] upon our border."[27] The war had not had the effect on national unity which Cromwell's advisers had predicted. Parliament's refusal to provide funds for the war created more friction with the army.[28] Many army leaders expressed fear that Parliament was using the war to justify attacking the government.[29] In February, Parliament voted some funds for the war but Cromwell was not pleased with the size of the appropriation or the manner in which it had been obtained.[30]

During Cromwell's battle to obtain funds from Parliament, Bordeaux feared that the Protector might be forced to make peace with Spain to assure his position in England.[31] This judgment concentrated on the financial problems of the Protector to the exclusion of other considerations. An end to the war would have been a blow to Cromwell's stature in England, regardless of its consequences to his relationship with France. The rhetoric in which Cromwell described the war had elevated it to a crusade. He could scarcely afford (even if he could reconcile it with his own conscience) to admit the moral hypocrisy of his foreign policy. Furthermore, there was strong support in the army for the war, at a time when his ties with the army were already strained by the discussion concerning his acceptance of the crown.

The offensive alliance with France, with the seizure of Dunkirk as one of its central features, gave the Protector a new cause to present to Parliament and the army. Once the treaty was signed, he lost no time in making public his desire to attack Dunkirk and in preparing part of the army to fight the Habsburgs.[32] In an astute analysis, Bordeaux asserted that the treaty was advantageous for Cromwell, because he would "have a pretext to strengthen his troops through new levies and to use outside those who could be opposed to him on the inside. It must be said that this consideration got the treaty published. As soon as the news arrived it was used to answer questions [in] London."[33]

The Protector's fears of a general peace played a vital role

in determining the form of the treaty. He was sure there
was a better chance of blocking peace if he could keep the
Cardinal bound to an alliance. The capture of Dunkirk
should cement the alliance as well as provide a valuable prize
of war. Spain's loss of the city would strenghten France's
military position, a point not overlooked by policy makers
in England. The danger of a peace between France and Spain
had been greatest when French forces had suffered defeats.
The conclusion drawn from this was that the promise of
future victories might deter Mazarin from contracting a
peace with Spain. If peace talks ever reached the serious
stage, the possession of Dunkirk would give the Protector
some security. Cromwell's insistence on the capture of Dunkirk underscored his interest in the European conflict, giving
further credence to an observation made by one of Thurloe's
agents in Utrecht, "since [the treaty of March, 1657] . . .
concerning the general peace, we apprehend rather a general
war."[34]

The treaty was not immediately implemented in a manner
that was satisfactory to either England or France. Part of
the difficulty lay in a series of administrative complications
that had arisen during the preparation of the treaty. Further
confusion was added by the different perspectives from which
Cromwell and the Cardinal saw the alliance. The Protector
viewed it in the more limited context of the political needs
of the Protectorate and the Cardinal looked at it as part
of the struggle against the power of the Habsburgs.

Cromwell had to decide between supporting the major
generals and continuing to woo Parliament. His need for
money, occasioned in part by the expenses of the Western
Design and his active foreign policy, tipped the balance. He
turned against Lambert and the new decimation tax. In
January, 1657, the major generals lost their battle in Parliament. The Protector received some of the funds he needed,
but some of the leadership in the army thought that the
price he had paid was too high. They fearfully predicted that
Parliament would try to exert new authority.

Cromwell still had to come to terms with the discontent
in the army. Most observers agreed with the view, expressed
months earlier, that he must do something to "provide for

the honest party in the army, if he be let along, for since Scotland and Ireland will not consume them, there must be some honourable pretences found to send them to some part of the Indies there to perish."[35] This appraisal saw the Protector's need to find a use for the army, but ignored a reasonable objective—the Continent. An aggressive military alliance with France would take some of the army out of England and give the men something to think about besides the political situation in England and the recent actions of Parliament. There were victories to be won which would be worthy of the past glories of the New Model. Even though Cromwell would not lead the troops personally, they would be fighting at his command and as part of the design he had created. The potential campaign was a way to increase the power of England and, at the same time, to strengthen Cromwell's standing with the army and the broader populace.

Before the negotiations for the treaty were completed, the Cardinal was already making plans to widen its scope. He wanted to encourage peace between Sweden and Denmark and bring them into an alliance with England and France to protect the German princes against the Habsburgs. Brienne contended that Cromwell would join those plans "out of his own interest . . . and to stop the power grab of the House of Austria."[36] This view failed to take into account the most difficult international question facing the Anglo-French alliance—the role to be played by the Dutch. The closer Cromwell came to France, the more difficult it was to maintain ties with de Witt and other Dutch leaders.

In the last months of 1656, many accounts reached London about the belligerently anti-English attitude of the Dutch. They were strengthening their fleet, and were boastfully confident that they had nothing to fear from England. War between England and Spain gave the Dutch a chance to strike at England and realize a profit at the same time. Spain made inquiries about having the Hollanders "conduct the money from the Indies."[37] It was reported to Thurloe that the Dutch bragged "that the Spanish fleet from the Indies should never be plundered any more by the English; and that these provinces will take care to conduct and preserve them from the like dangers."[38] It was difficult for Thurloe

to dismiss this account as idle boasting. The same theme
was repeated in much of the intelligence he received, and
seemed consistent with past statements by the Dutch.

The Protectorate's relations with the Dutch were strained
further by English comments about search and seizure at
sea, an issue that struck at the vitals of Dutch prosperity.
Boreel had cause to be disturbed when he reported that
Cromwell had said he would search every Dutch ship "to
pass through the [narrow] seas," and would confiscate those
ships carrying Spanish goods.[39] Nieupoort stated that England's attitude was based on the French maxim "that the
goods of an enemy confiscate those of a friend." He remained
unconvinced by Cromwell's assertion that such rumors had
been started maliciously by Spain in order to cause divisions
between England and the Dutch.[40] Intelligence reaching
Thurloe said that there were strong fears in Holland that
any cooperation between England and France would extend
to the restriction of Dutch trade with Spain.[41] The Dutch
response to the supposed threat to their commerce was
contained in instructions issued to de Ruyter in December,
1656. He was told to avoid hostilities with English ships
unless they attempted to search or seize Dutch vessels. In
that case, he was "to resist with all power."[42]

The anti-English sentiment in the United Provinces was
heightened by a personal dislike of the Protector. This
hostility had varied roots: the execution of Charles I, the
plight of the Stuart family, and the growth of England's
naval and commercial power during the Interregnum. There
were also strong feelings that Cromwell was a hypocrite who
used his professions of faith to support the selfish interests
of England against its coreligionists in the United Provinces.[43] Christopher Hill has depicted Cromwell's "imperial
and foreign policies as part of a single grand design."[44] He
contends that when Cromwell had to make shifts in his
policies, there was still no change in its commercial orienta-
tion. This interpretation gives Cromwell too much credit for
ability to control the situation and to make long-range plans.
His opposition to the Dutch might be explained in commercial terms, but there were other forces at work. The Dutch
became a hindrance to his closer ties with France, and the

alliance with France had more than economic advantages to recommend it.

Cromwell used France to help secure his government from outside invasion and foreign coalitions. The next step was to search for ways to use foreign policy to improve his political situation at home. The possibility of conquest on the Continent and a useful purpose for the army made a port in Flanders an admirable target for the Protector's attentions. Commercial advantages might be obtained from the conquest of Dunkirk just as they might be from the Western Design. Cromwell certainly did not create a foreign policy that went against his commercial interests any more than it went against his religious scruples. The policy he developed found ways to work toward more important goals without sacrificing immediate and visible ends. Closer ties between Cromwell and France led many Dutch to question further the sincerity of his feelings about international Protestantism.

An open split between France and the Dutch caused harsher feelings between England and the United Provinces.[45] Mazarin unveiled a plan to restrict Dutch trading rights in France in retaliation for Dutch cooperation with Spain.[46] Persistent rumors appeared in Paris that war was imminent, and Boreel's efforts to dispel them merely added to their acceptance.[47] The breach was widened further by de Ruyter's seizure of French ships in the Mediterranean. The "great rejoicing" in The Hague which greeted news of the capture was tempered by apprehension that France might declare war.[48] There were heated demands in the French council for war, but "moderate opinion," supported by the Cardinal, proposed the seizure of Dutch vessels that were in French ports.[49] The States General responded to the mood in France by telling its admirals to make preparations to counteract moves by France and "to protect the property of citizens of the United Provinces."[50]

Policy makers in England recognized the gravity of the situation developing between France and the Dutch. Lockhart was drawn into it when Brienne asked his advice about future policies. Brienne wanted to know if Cromwell would "resent" actions taken by France against the Dutch.[51] This

placed Lockhart in an uncomfortable position, and he avoided making any commitments until he consulted the Protector. At the same time, Lockhart tried to calm the situation
by cautioning Brienne "That a rupture with Holland in this
juncture would not prove very feasible." He attempted to
use this delicate situation to solidify the bonds between
England and France. In explaining his actions, Lockhart
stressed, "I was with all careful to give hopes, that nothing
of that nature [a break between France and the Dutch] will
alienatt his highness inclinations from the interests of France
for whose friendship he hath so particular a zeal."

Lockhart held meetings with the Dutch ambassador in
Paris, and tried to establish himself as a mediator in the
dispute, a role made more difficult by the anxiety and
frustration that were building up in France and the United
Provinces.[52] Strong feelings were expressed in France that
the issue was an insult to the dignity of the King as well
as a threat to the war effort against Spain. According to
Brienne, there was a feeling that the King "is resolved to
go to extremeties rather than not to have satisfaction for
the injury done him . . . and that at present the affairs of
the King are in so good condition, that we shall not fear
the joining of their [Dutch] forces with the Spanish."[53] The
possible conjunction of the Dutch and Spain bothered the
Protector, who wanted no interference in the war at sea
against Spain. Paradoxically, the feeling of confidence in
France which might have led her to war had much of its
foundation in the support she expected to receive from
England.

After the alliance of March, 1657, the threat of a French-
Dutch war increased. Bordeaux received reports that in The
Hague "they speak of nothing but war . . . they will rather
suffer any extremity; that is to say they will join with Spain,
rather than suffer any contempt to be put upon them by
France." The Dutch feared that France intended "to ruin
their commerce." Even reports that the States General "doth
rather incline to moderation than war" expressed the danger
that a feeling of desperation could lead the Dutch into a
war that served only the interests of Spain.[54] Lockhart's work
as a mediator was hampered by pressures operating on him

from different sides—the necessity to carry out the letter and spirit of Cromwell's agreement with France, and the Dutch fear that the Protector was using the situation to destroy them without having to go to war.[55]

By the end of May, there were finally indications that the trouble between France and the Dutch might be contained short of war. Mazarin informed Lockhart that he was willing to end discriminatory regulations against the Dutch, and to return embargoed goods as the start of a compromise. When the Cardinal asked Lockhart to set up new negotiations, Cromwell warmly supported the idea.[56] The Protector also tried to assure the Dutch that England would take steps to end the dispute without loss to either party.[57] Thurloe was not optimistic about the readiness of the Dutch to accept mediation, "however they express great confidence in his highness."[58] Once negotiations were started, the Dutch expressed their pleasure at Lockhart's conduct.[59] His efforts to end the threat of war received valuable assistance from de Thou, the French ambassador at The Hague. The activities of Lockhart and de Thou showed that the issues went deeper than the restoration of the property seized by both states. Commercial rights and the position of neutral states were the real questions.

The Dutch commissioners, meeting with de Thou, tried to explore another approach—a defensive alliance between France and the United Provinces. The purpose of the alliance would be the protection of trade, and it would not be directed against any state with whom either France or the Dutch were at war when it was signed.[60] The proposal was enlarged to include England in the alliance, but discussions did not proceed far.[61] Both parties were discussing different questions from different positions. The primary concern of the Dutch was to avoid being dragged into the Habsburg-Bourbon war. This was hampered by the aggressive role that Cromwell had chosen to play in that struggle.[62] The distrust and commerial rivalries between the Dutch and England, as well as the sea power possessed by both, increased the occasions for friction.[63] The suggestion that ihe Dutch sever commercial relations with Spain was totally unacceptable to them.[64] They also refused to join an alliance with France or England if it meant a break with Spain. The Protector made his position clear when he told Nieupoort that a defensive alliance with the Dutch was meaningless if the States General "did not enter into the interests of England and France" and join them in the war against Spain.[65]

The dispute between France and the Dutch placed Cromwell in a new and uncomfortable position. The necessity to support an ally denied him the freedom of diplomatic action he had protected so zealously. War was avoided between France and the Dutch, but at the cost of reopening divisions between England and the Dutch.[66] The question of whether "free ships make free goods" was not settled, and was left to cause new problems in the future.[67] Cromwell continued to approach the Dutch about closer ties. Much of his rhetoric resembled that used by the Commonwealth when it had proposed a confederation.[68] Unless the Protector was suffering from a political myopia that he did not demonstrate in other circumstances, he must have known that the ties with France had ended the possibility of an alliance with the Dutch. The gains from the arrangements with France outweighed those that might be obtained from closer ties with the Dutch. The Anglo-French treaty of March, 1657, demonstrated Cromwell's recognition of that fact.

The most dramatic consequences of the alliance between England and France were the appearance of English troops on the Continent and the capture of Dunkirk. Things did not proceed as smoothly as the Protector or Mazarin had assumed they would. The Cardinal had expected English troops to land on the Continent within two months after the ratification of the treaty.[69] There were none available, and a commission was not given to the commander of the force, Sir John Reynolds, until 5 May 1657.[70]

When the troops arrived in France at the end of May, Lockhart had to insure that they were housed and provisioned until they went into active service.[71] New problems arose about the manner in which they were to be deployed. Mazarin suggested that they immediately besiege Cambrai, rather than Dunkirk. This brought an immediate complaint from Lockhart. He was told that it was impossible to do anything at Dunkirk "so long as the army in Flanders was in that posture they then were in."[72] Lockhart restated his dissatisfaction with the Cardinal's plan, but did not press the issue, since it coincided with the climax of the dispute between France and the Dutch. Mazarin also tried to treat the problem as a minor issue between close allies which could be settled easily. A feeling of trust, or at least an absence of suspicion, finally marked the relationship between Mazarin and Lockhart.

Plans for an attack on Dunkirk were delayed at the beginning of June, when a French force was routed at Cambrai.[73] This gave Turenne new evidence with which to support his opposition to the attack on Dunkirk. Lockhart continued to press for an immediate campaign, but the Cardinal evaded the issue. There was, however, little rancor in the discussions concerning Dunkirk, even though Cromwell became more insistent in his messages to Lockhart.

In September, after a summer of fruitless expectation, the Protector wrote to Lockhart:

> Wee desire . . . that the designe by Dunkirk rather than Gravelinge. . . . We shall not be wantinge, at the French charge, to send over two of our old regiments, and two thousand foot more, if need be, if Dunkirke be the designe. . . . I desire you to take boldnesse and freedome to yourselfe in your dealinge with the French on these accounts.[74]

Instead of pressing the issue with Mazarin, Lockhart tried to show Cromwell and Thurloe that it was impossible to take Dunkirk at that time and that the Cardinal was acting in good faith. He was satisfied that Mazarin intended to press an attack against Mardyck and would turn it over to the English forces.[75] Lockhart's summation of the situation concluded that the Cardinal felt his own interests were served by cooperating with Cromwell and following the provisions of the treaty.[76]

In September, 1657, Turenne captured Mardyck and started to attack Gravelines. After failing to capture the city, he withdrew into winter quarters. Although Lockhart disagreed with the Protector's suspicions about Turenne's campaign, he was nonetheless bothered by the Cardinal's refusal to discuss plans for an attack in 1658. During the winter of 1657-58, many rumors circulated that the Protector or Mazarin intended to abandon their alliance, but no breach occurred.[77] Dunkirk was again the major irritant. Mazarin and Turenne tried to prove to Lockhart that the town could not be taken, but he ignored their arguments. As the renewal date for the treaty moved closer, Mazarin's opposition weakened. When the Cardinal promised that an attack would be staged against Dunkirk, and that France "shall not declyn that enterprise upon any pretense whatsoever," the path was cleared for the resumption of close ties between the states and the renewal of the treaty in March, 1658.[78]

A siege was established before Dunkirk in May, 1658, and English forces played an important role in the final stages of the battle.[79] The news of the victory at Dunkirk and of the English participation in the Battle of the Dunes was received with great joy in London. It appeared as though the Protector's policy toward France and Spain had been justified by God on the field of battle. Another victory by the New Model revived memories of the glories of the Civil War, and provided a sorely needed boost for the popularity of the government in England.[80]

After the capture of Dunkirk, there was some apprehension in England that Mazarin would not turn the town over to the English army. The fear was unfounded. The possession of the city was not, however, an unmixed blessing for Cromwell. Lockhart, who served as its governor, realized that great care was required to defend the area. He would need financial and military assistance from England to maintain his position. There were also some uneasy moments for the Cardinal after English troops took control of Dunkirk. Complaints arose from the militant Catholic party in France that he had betrayed the interests of the Church by sacrificing a city inhabited by the faithful to the rule of English heretics. These charges were mixed with the assertions of his political opponents that he had relinquished a port whose possession was essential to the maintenance of France's power.[81]

Once Cromwell assumed control of Dunkirk, the Cardinal suggested that the allies start new ventures. He seemed annoyed when he received no affirmative reply to his suggestions. Any hopes by the Cardinal of expanding the activities of the alliance, as well as Cromwell's plans for England, were brought to a decisive end on 3 September 1658 by the death of the Protector. The future of the government in England was uncertain, and Cromwell's foreign policy could not be carried out in the turmoil following his death.

16

Cromwell and France:
The Policy in Retrospect

Edward Gibbon's statement—"Cromwell was one of the men who should never have been born or else should never have died"—is certainly applicable to Cromwell's foreign policy.[1] It is crucial to remember that the inability of Cromwell or his successors to carry out his designs did not change the motives behind them, motives often hidden in the recesses of his mind or in the tone of his rhetoric.

We are provided with one glimpse of his feelings in a speech delivered to Parliament in January, 1658. Much of the speech concerned foreign policy (it must be kept in mind that Cromwell wanted Parliament to provide financial support for the policy he was describing), and he saw fit to discuss the ends for which the policy had been formulated. He began with a warning, "You are not a nation, you will not be a nation, if God strengthened you not to meet with those evils that are upon us." The Protector's analysis of the "evils" and their remedies led to a lengthy discussion of England's role in international politics in which he stated that the purpose of the nation was to preserve Protestantism. England had, in Cromwell's words, undertaken a great design to stem the tide of Catholicism. He painted a dark picture of a world in which Austria was arming "to destroy the Protestant interest"; the King of Sweden, who had "ventured all for Protestantism," was in mortal danger; and the Jesuits and their supporters in England were a greater threat than they had been in the reign of Elizabeth.[2]

The Protector's speech repeated many of the Puritan shibboleths about the dangers of popery. Not content with a denunciation of the crimes of Catholicism, he offered solutions to the crises facing England: "You [Parliament] have accounted yourself happy in being environed with a great ditch from all the world beside. Truly you will not be able to keep your ditch, nor your shipping, unless you turn your shipping into troops of horse and company of foot, and fight and defend yourself in *terra firma*."[3] The great danger facing England was a general peace.[4] If it was achieved, "England will be the general object of all the fury and wrath of all the enemies of God and religion in the world." He asked Parliament to support him in the trust he had placed in the alliance with France, and not to be deceived by false friends.[5]

The Protector's speech was delivered shortly before he was ready to renew the alliance with France. It was natural for him to phrase his address in terms that would insure the greatest possible support. At the same time, there was nothing in the speech inconsistent with the steps he had taken in the previous four years.

Before the alliance with France, there had been much discussion of the purposes for which the armed might of England should be used. These conjectures had at least one thing in common with the foreign diplomats who tried to anticipate the Protector's actions—a belief that he would not adopt a passive policy.

A year after Cromwell had dismissed Parliament, many diplomats were still sure that if he intended to ally with any Catholic power, it would be Spain. Such predictions proved nothing more than the diplomats' inability to understand the Protector's goals. Even Bordeaux was not immune to the mystery that surrounded Cromwell's government. In November, 1654, the ambassador was sure he had secured a treaty, but for another year he had to face new proposals and the Protector's refusal to make any commitments. Even Bordeaux's threats to abandon the negotiations made little impression. Cromwell's policy toward Bordeaux operated on the assumption that Mazarin would not be goaded into losing the chance of a valuable alliance. The constant delays enabled Cromwell to press for further concessions (demonstrating a firm belief that nothing would happen to weaken his position) and to evaluate the results of his attacks on Spanish territory.[6]

When Bordeaux arrived in England, his first priority was to block a rumored Anglo-Spanish alliance. The discussion in the Protector's council, during which the relative merits of the two alliances (with France or with Spain) were argued, was one turning point in Cromwell's foreign policy.[7] George Drake has tried to demonstrate that since Cromwell was conducting negotiations with Spain, his later justifications for war "reveal insincerity."[8] In terms of private morality this might have been insincerity, but Cromwell was acting as a political leader. In addition, his actions were consistent with his past measures. Cromwell remained sincere to his own ideals and his view of how to implement them.

Cromwell exemplified earlier Puritan feelings toward Spain, "the [representative of] all the Puritans hated most."[9] In the 1620s, Spain was equated with the papacy and the forces that threatened the existence of Protestantism. The fury that greeted the Spanish match indicated Puritan feelings toward Spain, a hatred that led to "a belief in an anti-Spanish policy, which . . . was a policy to use France . . . another sign by which true, Protestant Englishmen were known."[10] The striking difference between Cromwell and the dissident members of the 1621 Parliament was that he possessed the power to implement his view of the outside world.

Most analyses of Cromwell's relations with Spain have centered on the consequences of the Western Design. A widely accepted interpretation has been that he was operating within the Elizabeth concept of "no peace beyond the line," and was surprised by Spain's reactions. On the contrary, the council considered the possibility of war with Spain, and decided that the attack on Hispaniola was worth the consequences. Even after the news of Penn's abortive raid reached England, Cromwell still could have continued talks with Cardenas, but he showed no inclination to smooth over relations with Spain. The expulsion of Cardenas and the Treaty of Westminster demonstrated Cromwell's attitude, and led Spain to make the final break.

After the Treaty of Westminster, the Protector had to consider new options: what type of arrangement should he develop with France, and how should he conduct the war with Spain. The attack on Hispaniola was not considered by Cromwell or his council as necessarily the prelude to ties with France. In signing the treaty, Cromwell lost his ability to play France off against Spain to obtain larger concessions from both, but he did not lose his freedom of action. It must be stressed again that the treaty was not the result of a declaration of war by Spain, but was the final step that convinced de Haro that Spain must have war with Cromwell. The war meant added expenses, and might cause some loss in trade, but it did give Cromwell a greater opportunity to demonstrate his hatred of popery. The tradition of Hawkins and Drake might still have been alive, but the picture of Gustavus Adolphus was more relevant to the 1650s. The war also gave Cromwell a chance to use the military might created by the new regime: an opportunity to keep the army and navy occupied and to justify asking the nation to pay for their maintenance.[11]

Thurloe's notes showed that he and Cromwell assumed Spain would welcome the Stuarts if war broke out with England. This assumption was correct, which meant a reversal of the Protector's policy of isolating the Stuarts. This apparent contradiction was part of a new policy to identify Charles with the forces of the antichrist and to revive the Puritan cries of the 1620s against the Spanish match and James's reluctance to support the cause of Protestantism in Germany.[12]

The immediate result of the Treaty of Westminster was to create new ties with France. No mention of an alliance against Spain was made in the treaty, although Cromwell knew Mazarin wanted such an arrangement. Thurloe's memorandum stated that the Protector "did not much apprehend the Usefullness of so strict an Alliance ... and wanted to fix upon a particular design that ... would be mutually advantageous." As long as Mazarin was convinced that

Cromell might aid France, the Cardinal was not likely to go back on his word and support the Stuarts.[13]

After repeating the propaganda victories by nudging the Stuarts into the Habsburg camp—as well as providing the added bonus of leaving Henrietta Maria unrestrained, so that she could spin more plots to embarrass her son—Cromwell had to make sure that Spain could not give any substantial assistance to Charles's cause. Closer ties with France might accomplish that purpose, but Cromwell showed no haste to bind himself in an alliance "which [does] intricate and entangle affairs, but [is] seldom performed on the part of any."[14] In the absence of an anti-Spanish alliance between England and France, the two countries still aided one another by the blows delivered against the common enemy.

The loose nature of the Protector's commitments in the Treaty of Westminster determined Lockhart's role as ambassador to France. The original impetus to send an ambassador, despite Mazarin's attempts to delay it, was to have someone check on the way in which the Cardinal was implementing the treaty. However, Lockhart's instructions showed that he was more than a symbolic figure or an intelligence agent. His primary task was to determine how the Protector could gain more from his arrangements with France. Lockhart had to impress upon Mazarin that Cromwell, although an enemy of Spain, was still acting as an independent power, and that any new agreement would have to include specific advantages for him. The milieu of Lockhart's mission showed that the treaties of 1657 and 1658 were not merely extensions of the Treaty of Westminster.

No discussion of Cromwell's actions can long avoid the role played by his religious convictions. There was nothing in his dealings with France which was contrary to his professions of faith or the manner in which he had practiced that faith. His concern for the Vaudois was the most obvious instance when religious and diplomatic ends coincided. Cromwell halted negotiations with Bordeaux to protest France's role in the Piedmont and to demand that Louis protect the Vaudois. Although Bordeaux expressed skepticism about the sincerity of Cromwell's concern and described him as a dissembler, the ambassador admitted that Cromwell had acted in the interests of his faith. The real test of that faith would have come if he had been forced to make a decision between political gain and religious conviction. He was not pressed into that position—a situation that can be explained either by the unity of the two or by the ability of the men who formulated foreign policy to reconcile them.

In the decade after Cromwell's death, his foreign policy was bitterly attacked. One often-repeated comment was that he had been a dupe in Mazarin's hands. Another charge was that Cromwell had been a political innocent with no plans other than to perpetuate himself. Thus, Mazarin had led him into plans that strengthened France and weakened England.[15]

Strange as it may have seemed, an early defender of Cromwell's foreign policy was Clarendon, who stated:

> But his greatness at home was but a shadow of the glory he had abroad. It was hard to discover which feared him most, France, Spain, or the Low Countries, where his friendship was current at the value he put upon it. And as they did all sacrifice their honour and interest to his pleasure, so there is nothing he could have demanded that either of them would have denied him.

Clarendon used two examples to describe how Cromwell used his power abroad to gain important advantages for England—the protection of the Vaudois, and the assistance rendered to the Protestants in the province of Languedoc when Cromwell had the court of France do his bidding.[16]

Slingsby Bethel delivered the most detailed and scorching attack on the Protector's policies toward France. He accused Cromwell of hypocrisy in the formulation of the policy and incompetence in its operation. In *The World's Mistake in Oliver Cromwell*, Bethel said that Cromwell had come to power when England's strength was at its height; trade was prospering, the treasury was full, the army and navy were at top strength, the Dutch had been brought to their knees, and every major European state ardently sought an alliance with England. As soon as Cromwell gained control of the state, he committed three great follies: he misused a God-given victory over the Dutch, and came to a humbling peace with them; he made an unjust war with Spain, "contrary to our interests"; and, finally, he "made an impolitick league with France, bringing thereby Spain under, and making France too great for Christendom: and by that means broke the balance betwixt the two crowns of Spain and France, which his predecessors, the long Parliament had always wisely preserved." The Protector had used Protestantism as an excuse for war, being too ignorant to realize that the only way to protect the Huguenots was by making sure that Louis XIV needed their support. By removing the danger of Spain, Cromwell had "enabled the King to resume his persecution of the Huguenots."

Bethel went on to criticize Cromwell's Western Design, his policy in the Baltic, and his relations with the Dutch. The most severe criticism was reserved for the treaties between France and England. The treaties had some honorable articles, but conditions were so bad in France that Cromwell should have demanded many more concessions. Bethel regarded the treaties as the greatest act of Mazarin's ministry, because Louis "became the first French king since Charlemagne to have no factions and worries about any foreign power." On the other hand, Cromwell got nothing, but

> doubtless Cromwell's over-weening care to secure his particular interest against his majesty, then abroad, and the long parliament, whom he had turned out; with a prodigious ambition of acquiring a glorious name in the world; carried him on to all his mistakes and absurdities, to the irreparable loss and damage of the famous kingdom.

Bethel tempered his criticism with the view that Cromwell was not able to define long-range policy goals while the daily problems of maintaining the Protectorate continued. *The World's Mistake* . . . was an attempt to criticize the Protector in terms of his foreign policy, but the validity of Bethel's arguments was undermined by his refusal to consider that Cromwell's policies might have been sabotaged by the actions of his successors. The comments must be considered in the context of 1668 and the effect of the Restoration on the increased power of France.

Despite Bethel's distaste for Cromwell, his discussion of the Protector's motives provides a valuable framework for a more dispassionate analysis of foreign policy. Bethel recognized the close connection that Cromwell had made between domestic and foreign policies, even if Bethel's conclusions were flawed by his assumption that the interests of the Protector were opposed to those of England and Protestantism.[17]

The greatest difficulty in any discussion about Cromwell is the absence of statements made while he was still considering his plans. The lengthy summaries that Thurloe wrote after the Restoration concerning Cromwell's dealings with France and Spain fill in some of the gaps in our knowledge about the Protector's motives. Thurloe stated that a desire to drive a wedge between Charles Stuart and France was the original reason for Cromwell's wish for closer ties with France. By the same action, it might also be possible to aid the Protestants in France, a step that would have favorable effects on opinion in England.[18] Thurloe said that the primary aims of the Protector's policies toward France were secured by the Treaty of Westminster. After that, Cromwell decided to suspend negotiations for any further alliance. He supposedly began new talks only after deciding to involve England in the Continental war in order to gain a foothold in Europe. Thurloe was firm in his assertion that possession of Dunkirk was the basis for the treaties of 1657 and 1658, but gave no clear reason why the Protector changed his past policy of noninvolvement. The only hint was a final comment that Cromwell intended to make further arrangements with Mazarin, which were cut short by the Protector's death.[19]

All the important accounts of Cromwell's foreign policy— from Thurloe and Clarendon to the recent work of Michael Foley—have stressed the Protector's desire to prevent the restoration of the Stuarts.[20] This theme was never absent from his dealings with France, but it went through important changes as the negotiations progressed. By 1657, the power of the Protectorate made the possibility of a military con-

quest by the Stuarts rather remote. However, Cromwell
never ignored the potential for plots and conspiracies against
his regime. Plots against his life, and the commotion caused
by them, reminded him of the uniqueness and vulnerability
of his position. The goals for which Cromwell had accepted
and maintained power—the rejection of the Stuarts, the
cause of Protestantism, and stability in England—were subordinated to the survival and strengthening of the government. Cromwell was positive that none of these ideals could
be implemented if he lost his position as head of the state.
This aspect of Cromwell's situation was illustrated by Christopher Hill's analysis of the Protector's relationship with
the army:

> his genuine desire for a parliamentary settlement
> continually raised hopes that he might yet square the
> circle. But, just because Oliver owed his position to the
> army, he could never in the last resort break from it.
> He had created it, yet without it he was plain Mr.
> Cromwell.[21]

Samuel Rawson Gardiner captured part of the spirit in
which the negotiations with France were carried out after
the Treaty of Westminster:

> In Oliver's time there was no apparent danger from
> any prominent power. If France and Spain did not weigh
> equally in the balance, neither of them decidedly kicked
> the beam. No other power—and England least of all—was
> much afraid of either. There was therefore no room for
> a policy directed against an overwhelming predomi-
> nance. There was, however, room for a policy of aggres-
> sion calculated on the weakness of one or the other of
> the leading states, and it remains to be seen how far
> Oliver could succeed in persuading himself or others that
> a war of aggression might be based on the highest
> motives.[22]

It was clear that Cromwell convinced himself that war
against Spain and an alliance with France were "based on

the highest motives," because he equated them with his immediate problem, the retention of power. It was a fortunate coincidence (or, as Cromwell might have viewed it, the hand of God) that war against Spain reinforced the desirable policy of maintaining righteous rule in England. Gardiner's view that there was "no overwhelming predominance" was phrased in Elizabethan or nineteenth-century terms. Viewing the situation in the 1650s, Cromwell could not ignore the possibility of the creation of an "overwhelming predominance" if the Catholic powers concluded a general peace. Furthermore, he expected that the Protectorate, Protestant and regicidal, would be the first target of the united forces of the Bourbons and the Habsburgs. The aim of Cromwell's policy toward France was to insure that the coalition was never formed.[23]

Throughout his dealings with France, Cromwell operated on the assumption that Mazarin strongly wanted England's support in the war. When Cromwell finally promised to use his army on the Continent, he received cash, a renewal of the Cardinal's promise not to hold separate talks with Spain, and Dunkirk.

Thurloe's comments stressed the importance of Dunkirk— that a campaign in Flanders was intended to weaken Spain and force it to use troops that might otherwise be employed to assist the Stuarts. The possession of Dunkirk meant much more to Cromwell than the campaign for it. The control of this valuable port denied an invasion base to Charles, and, according to Thurloe, Cromwell "carried the Keys of the Continent at his Girdle." It may have been another example of the boasting that marked the Interregnum, but Thurloe stated that Dunkirk gave Cromwell the opportunity to invade the Continent "whenever he wanted."[24]

Cromwell's speech to Parliament in January, 1658, demonstrated Thurloe's contention that Dunkirk might be the staging base for further English activities on the Continent. The desire to possess Dunkirk might be seen as another attempt to implement the designs of Elizabeth's more bellicose councillors. But if Cromwell's glance was backward, it might be extended even further, to the loss of the last English Continental stronghold by a popish queen. Regaining a port at the expense of Spain, for whom Mary had lost Calais, must have been an added attraction.[25] In any case, it was inconceivable that Cromwell could have forgotten the farce of Buckingham's expedition to La Rochelle. In Marvin A. Breslow's description of the Puritan reaction, "No other single occurrence of this period produced the intense feeling of national dishonour, which gripped England, after the retreat from Rhe and the capitulation of La Rochelle."[26]

In a letter to Lockhart, the Protector stated the pressing reason for demanding the seizure of Dunkirk, "because this action will probably divert Spain from assisting Charles Stuart in any attempt upon us . . . wee shall doe all reasonable on our part."[27] The memorandum attributed to Thurloe contained a more complex analysis for Cromwell's desire for Dunkirk—arguments that were scorned in the denunciation of Cromwell which followed the Restoration but which gained wide acceptance in the 1670s.[28] "Being on the continent and considered as the Patron and Protector of the Protestant religion" added to Cromwell's prestige and support at home. Control in Flanders was also "desired as a Bridle upon the Dutch," and an alliance with France would enable both states "to throw their combined weights against the rising Dutch power." There was the hope that Cromwell, with support from France, could bring peace to the Baltic, ending a war that benefited only the Dutch. Thurloe also said that as long as Cromwell kept Dunkirk, Mazarin would live up to his obligations, "in particular that of not making Peace, but by his [Cromell's] consent." Thurloe concluded that as long as Cromwell maintained his position at Dunkirk, France would make no alliances without him, "because they left a back Door behind them in Flanders which might be made aide of the overthrow of France while they were engaged elsewhere."[29]

To be sure, these comments about the importance of Dunkirk were made after Louis XIV had purchased the city from Charles II. Thurloe might have been trying to show the wisdom of policies that he had helped to formulate, but his statements were consistent with the actions taken between 1655 and 1658. The sale of Dunkirk led to a renewed discussion in England about the wisdom and farsightedness of Cromwell's policies.[30] His critics maintained that he had harmed the cause of Protestantism and endangered the security of England by aiding the King of France to become too powerful. Thurloe's contention was that the "King of France was so careful to get Dunkirk out of the Hands of the English into His own, before he openly engaged in those great designs he seemed upon."[31] In Thurloe's opinion (an opinion that had much support in the 1670s), it was the failure to implement Cromwell's vision of Europe which weakened the position of England and Protestantism.

Michael Roberts has established the most sensible guidelines for analyzing the formulation of Cromwell's policies, "in terms of what was politically possible and desirable for England in the context of the times and how far Cromwell's actions squared with that." Roberts realized the importance of religious and economic considerations, but he insisted that new attention must be paid to "the main political considerations which must sway this ignorant (but shrewd) government . . . at all events, the key in their policy was not fanaticism, but fear."[32] During the Interregnum, there was a constant sense of insecurity in England. The execution of the King had launched the new state along an uncharted course among other states that felt its policies to be abhorrent and unnatural.[33] Even when the threat of armed invasion was remote, the Protector could not relax. The management of the state, the legitimization of his regime, and dealing with internal factions presented constant crises that seemed to outweigh the importance of foreign policy.[34] In that one area, however, Cromwell was free to negotiate as he pleased, because he had power that others coveted. Despite the position of strength from which he negotiated, he entered into international arrangements to end his apprehensions about the basis for his power.

In its crude way, the cartoon showing the Kings of France and Spain vying to "help the Protector clean his breech" explained his diplomatic tactics. The longer he was able to delay a decision, the more the other powers worried about the disposition of England's armed forces. The rush to promise Cromwell concessions developed its own momentum. The longer France and Spain vied to assist Cromwell, the

less attention they paid to ending their own grievances. To
carry off this policy of productive procrastination, Cromwell
had not only to be desirable as an ally but also to appear
available when the terms were equitable. The armed might
of England took care of the former; Cromwell's ability to
understand the Cardinal and the Spanish leadership, the
latter. In Cromwell's hands, delay was not a policy of drift
but a means of building from strength to greater strength.[35]

Cromwell's dealings with France demonstrated Roberts's
comments about the role of fear in the policies of the
Protectorate. The fear was not of France or Spain but of
a general peace and a French-led attempt to restore the
Stuarts. Each step in Cromwell's policy toward France was
intended to dissuade Mazarin from concluding a peace with
Spain. The Treaty of Westminster accomplished part of this
goal, and the offensive alliance directed against Spain concluded the process. However, before Cromwell was willing
to end his diplomatic freedom of action by entering into a
commitment with France, he secured concessions that appeared to bind France to his cause. Mazarin had already
pledged his word that France would not support the Stuarts,
but Cromwell wanted further assurances. England's entrance
into the war was the final step to bind Mazarin to the
Protectorate. The alliance with France provided protection
against both possible results of the war—if Mazarin was
convinced that he should continue the struggle, the threat
posed by a general peace was obviated; if Spain was defeated,
Cromwell would be present at the peace negotiations as a
major power.

The alliance served the immediate needs of the Protectorate better than neutrality or an alliance with Spain. In
the former case, Cromwell would be relegated to the role
of a passive spectator. The rejection of an alliance with Spain
was even more clear-cut for Cromwell. The psychological
differences between him and Spain were enormous, but even
more decisive was his consideration of the Stuarts. An alliance with Spain would have strengthened Charles's position
in France, and would have had an adverse effect on public
opinion in England. Cromwell stood to gain little from any
attack on France or its possessions, but much from attacking

Spain. On the other hand, assistance from France was valuable, and Spain could offer only the promise of future payment.

The final factor that tipped the balance toward an offensive alliance with France was the change in Cromwell's view of the Cardinal. Despite the Protector's distrust of Mazarin, he felt that the Cardinal had an acute sense of what was in the best interests of France.[36] Cromwell also thought that the Cardinal's position was insecure, and that he had to continue the war with Spain until he gained a victory.[37] This was a flawed view of French politics, but it did not damage the policy based on it. By the time the offensive alliance was signed, Cromwell and Mazarin had developed an admiration for one another's pragmatic approach to their problems and their relationship. After Cromwell's death, the ties with France survived. His diplomacy accomplished its most crucial task—preventing a general peace. The Peace of the Pyrenees was not the treaty that Cromwell had feared. Only the disintegration of the state upon which Cromwell had based his power ended the diplomatic structure he had created.

The success of Cromwell's policies can be viewed even in the comments of critics like Bethel, who maintained that he had fought against the wrong state in a war that was not in the interests of England.[38] These critics did not give Cromwell credit for being convinced that a Catholic coalition directed against *his* England was a distinct possibility. The arrangements with Mazarin solved the problem to which Cromwell gave highest priority.

When Cromwell formulated his policies toward France, he did, as George Drake described, set up a balance sheet and "was coldly calculating." There was nothing hypocritical about the procedure. He was the ruler of England, the possessor of a sacred trust. It was natural and correct to calculate the effects of his actions. The mystical religious aura surrounding Cromwell has for too long stopped commentators from realizing that he had to make political decisions based on how *he* saw political reality. William Lamont, in his recent study, has brilliantly demonstrated how Cromwell's concept of godless rule led him to a new sense of political reality.[39] Cromwell had to protect and further his religion, but not in the narrow ecclesiastical or theological sense. Foreign policy was another arena in which he could fight God's battles, without some of the restrictions he faced at home and with the weapons most readily available to him. The aggressive use of the military and diplomatic power that God had placed in his hands came naturally to Cromwell.

Some historians have been able to see Cromwell as a hardheaded statesman. Christopher Hill's description of him as a "pragmatic revolutionary" deals with Cromwell the political leader.[40] In his dealings with France, Cromwell grasped the uses to which diplomacy could be put. He never allowed foreign policy to operate in a political vacuum or to run itself. Diplomacy was consciously used to further the aims of the government. Cromwell did not repeat the ineptitude of James I or Charles I in this respect.

When Cromwell recognized that foreign affairs could be used to bolster his position at home, he formulated a policy to maximize the benefits. The manner in which he took England to war with a hated enemy not only disarmed many of his critics but had a lasting effect on Englishmen's views of themselves and the world. Cromwell had to replace traditional dynastic loyalties, and he substituted a sense of negative identification—his "subjects" were encouraged to see themselves as something different from members of foreign societies. Cromwell's policies led to a feeling of national identity and patriotism, or what Christopher Hill has aptly described as the "formation of a popular national consciousness."[41]

Hill has also pointed out that most commentators on the seventeenth century have missed the tremendous scope of Cromwell's foreign policy.[42] At the same time, Hill, in his attempt to describe the policy in terms of the expansion of trade and the creation of "foreign and imperial policies [that] were part of a single grand design," has overlooked the immediate impact Cromwell wanted his policy to have—the survival of the regime. A more important failing on the part of other historians has been their willingness to assert that Cromwell's policies were merely a reversion to the Elizabethan past. Certainly he could not free himself of Elizabethan prejudices, but the way in which he implemented his policies was based on his own situation. If Cromwell was a throwback to any specific policies, it was less to Elizabeth than to her grandfather. The use of alliances and diplomacy to insure the survival of a new regime was a course of action with which Henry Tudor was thoroughly familiar.

One need not view Cromwell as the founder of a worldwide strategy for England to recognize his interest in expanding its influence. Much of his policy foreshadowed measures taken by William III. The sources of power were different for both men, but they shared the fear of a dominant power in Europe, a sense of mission, a deeply Calvinistic view of fate, and the insecurities inherent in a revolutionary regime. Both of them had the feeling that they must maintain their positions in England to implement the higher goals for which they took power. When William III and Cromwell brought England into the Continental wars, they did not do it for mere plunder or glory but as a conscious attempt to fulfill their concepts of mission. Even though Cromwell never enunciated the precise nature of his mission, many of his goals can be inferred from the policies developed to implement them. Long-range goals had to be subordinated to the conviction that none of them could be achieved if he did not secure his position. Only as the acknowledged leader of a strong state could he play out his role as the representative of his uniquely English and religious conscience on the broader stage of his God's world.

Notes

INTRODUCTION

1. For a persuasively argued modification of this view about Cromwell, see Christopher Hill, *God's Englishman*. I do not think, however, that Hill explains how Cromwell developed his insights into international politics and on what he based his interpretations of foreign affairs.

2. Most studies dealing with Cromwell's foreign policy have tried to isolate it from other events. The monumental works of Samuel Rawson Gardiner and Sir Charles Harding Firth do consider it as part of political life, and Wilbur Cortez Abbott, *The Writings and Speeches of Oliver Cromwell*, paid special attention to the opinions of foreign diplomats about Cromwell and politics in England. Sir John R. Seeley, *The Growth of British Policy*, is an important example of the Victorian imperialist idea of Cromwell, his foreign policy, and his role in English history. More recent works that are valuable to any study of England's foreign relations in the mid-seventeenth century include: F. J. Routledge, *England and the Treaty of the Pyrenees*; and "Charles II and Cardinal de Retz"; Charles Wilson, *Profit and Power*; Christopher Hill, *God's Englishman*; J. R. Jones, *Britain and Europe in the Seventeenth Century*; Michael Roberts, "Cromwell and the Baltic"; Philip A. Knachel, *England and the Fronde*; Michael F. Foley, "John Thurloe and the Foreign Policy of the Protectorate, 1654-1658"; and J. F. Battick, "Cromwell's Navy and the Foreign Policy of the Protectorate, 1653-1658."

* Except where otherwise noted, all dates conform with the Gregorian, or New Style, calendar that was used on the Continent. I have adopted this method because most of the diplomatic correspondence and letters of intelligence were dated according to the New Style, and I wanted to make the chronology of events as easily understood as possible. The only exception to this system is the retention of the familiar dates, 30 January and 3 September, for the deaths of Charles I and Oliver Cromwell, respectively, although in the former case 1 January is used to mark the start of the new year.

214 *Notes*

CHAPTER 1

1. Christopher Hill, "The English Revolution and the Brotherhood of Man," in *Puritanism and Revolution*, pp. 123-152.

2. J. H. Elliott, *Imperial Spain, 1469-1716* (London), p. 346. For a provocative and valuable study of the revolt and its implications, see J. H. Elliott, *Revolt of the Catalans* (London, 1963).

3. John Lynch, *Spain under the Habsburgs*, 2:115-125.

4. Elliott, *Imperial Spain*, 347. G. Livet, "International Relations and the Role of France, 1648-1660."

5. The Sentence of the High Court of Justice upon the King, 27 January 1649, reprinted in Samuel Rawson Gardiner, *The Constitutional Documents of the Puritan Revolution* (Oxford, 1906), pp. 377-380.

6. *Calendar of State Papers, Domestic Series, 1649*, pp. 131, 135. Bulstrode Whitelocke, *Memorials of the English Affairs from the Beginning of the Reign of Charles the First to the Happy Restoration of King Charles the Second*, 3:30.

7. *A Declaration of the Most Christian King, Louis the XIV, King of France and Navarre Declaring the Reasons wherefore his Majesty Hath prohibited all Trade with England also that He hath given Commission to raise an Army for the Assistance of the King of England.*

8. Two examples of this feeling were: the Nineteen Propositions that were sent to Charles I on 2 June 1642, and a speech delivered by Cromwell on 10 November 1644. The former demanded an alliance with the United Provinces and other Protestant states "against all designs of the Pope and his adherents," quoted in Gardiner, *The Constitutional Documents of the Puritan Revolution*, pp. 253-254. In his speech, Cromwell issued a warning that Parliament would have to defeat Charles quickly; otherwise he would get massive aid from France, which would change the course of the struggle. Wilbur Cortez Abbott, *The Writings and Speeches of Oliver Cromwell*, 1:299 (hereafter cited as Abbott, *Writings and Speeches*).

9. *An Act Prohibiting the Importing of Any Wines, Wool, or Silk from the Kingdom of France into the Commonwealth of England or Ireland or Any of the Dominions Thereunto Belonging.*

10. Strickland to Cromwell, 14 January 1650, quoted in John Nickolls, ed., *Original Letters and Papers of State Addressed to Oliver Cromwell*, p. 51. Strickland asserted that France was "now willing to receive any [proposal] from this Commonwealth, in the same condition they did those sent from the King." All the materials in this collection are from the papers of John Milton.

11. Rene, Comte de Jarze to Mazarin, 7 April 1650, *Report of the Historical Manuscripts Commission on Morrison MSS*, Ninth Report (London, 1884), part 2, p. 441.

12. Prince of Orange to d'Estrades, 2 September 1650, Stowe MSS 85, f. 41b.

13. Mazarin to d'Estrades, 15 September 1650, *ibid.*, f. 42.

14. Projected treaty made between Prince of Orange and d'Estrades (September, 1650), *ibid.*, ff. 42b-43b. The provisions of the treaty were:

1. By 1 May, the King would have 6,000 foot and 6,000 horse ready to attack Bruges.

2. By 1 May, the Prince would break relations with Spain and would attack Antwerp with 6,000 foot and 4,000 horse.

3. By 1 May, Louis and the Prince would move against Cromwell and do all they could to reestablish Charles.

4. Neither side would make any accommodation with Spain without the consent of the other.

Secret articles appended to the treaty were:

1. Antwerp will be invested by the Prince, and France will aid the Prince in an attack on Brussels.

2. Concessions will be made by France on the structure of the joint military command.

3. The Prince promised to have a fleet ready in the Channel by 1 May, supplied to stay in those waters until the end of the year. It would operate against either Spain or the English rebels.

15. Philip A. Knachel, *England and the Fronde*, pp. 14-17. For an excellent discussion of the uprising in France, see E. H. Kossmann, *La Fronde* (Leiden, 1954).

16. Knachel, *England and the Fronde*, pp. 110-123.

CHAPTER 2

1. Morosini (Venetian ambassador to France) to the Senate, 3 January 1651, *Calendar of State Papers . . . Venice*, 28:168.

2. Croulle to Mazarin, 19 January 1651, P.R.O. Transcript 31/3/90, f. 420.

3. Dispatch of Richard Browne (Royalist ambassador in France), 21 January 1651, B.M. Add MSS 12186, f. 22lb.

4. Blake to the Governor of Cartegena, 15 November 1650, Portland MSS, *Report of the Historical Manuscripts Commission*, 13th Report (London, 1892), Appendix 1, pp. 539-540.

5. Blake to the King of Spain, 17 November 1650, *ibid.*, p. 540.

6. King of Spain to the Governor of Cartagena, 24 November 1650, *ibid.*, pp. 541-542.

7. Blake to the King of Spain, 15 December 1650, *ibid.*, p. 545.

8. King of Spain to Parliament, 2 December 1650, *ibid.*, p. 544. The letter also included an offer to aid the English fleet in its operations on the coast of Spain and in the Mediterranean.

9. Parliament to the King of Spain, 22 January 1651, *ibid.*, pp. 554-555.

10. Pietro Basadonna (Venetian ambassador to Spain) to the Senate, 8 February 1651, *Calendar of State Papers . . . Venice*, 28:169.

11. Basadonna also noted that the King of Spain was annoyed with Blake because the Englishman, after being well received at Cádiz, had

made a speech about destroying tyrannies and establishing republics everywhere. *ibid.*, pp. 169-170.

12. *Ibid.*, p. 170.

13. *Ibid.*, pp. 194-195.

14. *Ibid.*, p. 195. Basadonna stated that Cardenas thought some of the leaders in England believed the only way the Commonwealth could be secure was by establishing republics in other states.

15. *Ibid.*, pp. 191-193. A resolution was made by the Senate to instruct its representative in London to send the regards of the Senate to the new government in England. Despite the threat of the Commonwealth's fleet, this mild resolution passed by a vote of only thirty-two to twenty-three.

16. Memorandum of Servien concerning England (January, 1651), P.R.O. Transcript 31/3/90, ff. 430-435.

17. *Ibid.*, ff. 431-433. The "extreme peril" that Servien described was an alliance between England and Spain.

18. *Ibid.*, f. 434.

19. *Ibid.*, f. 435.

20. Dispatch of Richard Browne, 1 April 1651, B.M. Add MSS 12186, f. 241.

21. Instructions to Gentillot, 20 January 1651, P.R.O. Transcript 31/3/90, f. 423.

22. *Ibid.*, ff. 426b-427.

23. Strickland to Cromwell, 14 January 1650, John Nickolls, ed., *Original Letters and Papers of State Addressed to Oliver Cromwell*, p. 51.

24. Statement by Sexby to the council, in support of his claim for monies due him "for back wages and expenses," [9 May] 1654, *Calendar of State Papers, Domestic Series, 1654*, 7:160.

25. Philip A. Knachel, *England and the Fronde*, pp. 195-208.

26. Nicholas to Ormonde, 25 February 1651, Carte MSS 1, f. 407.

27. Dispatch of Richard Browne, 1 April 1651, B.M. Add MSS 12186, f. 241.

28. Memorial from Thomas Elyott to John IV of Portugal, 19 March 1650, B.M. Add MSS 38847, f. 40.

29. Letter of intelligence from Frankfurt, 31 May 1650, B.M. Add MSS 37047, f. 72.

30. Taaf's relations of his meeting with the Duke of Lorraine, written to Inchiquin, 18 March 1651, B.M. Add MSS 15856, f. 40.

31. I have seen no evidence that would suggest that the failure of these negotiations was attributable in any way to Charles's actions or lack of desire for success.

32. Anti-Catholic feelings in England would have been raised even more if part of Lorraine's plans had become known. He told Taaf that the Duke intended to ask the pope to confirm his divorce by saying that the war in Ireland is "for the defense of the Catholic religion there." Taaf to Inchiquin, 18 March 1651, *ibid.*

CHAPTER 3

1. Inchiquin to Ormonde, 6 August 1651, *Report of the Historical Manuscripts Commission . . . Ormonde*, New Series, (London, 1902), 1:180-181.

2. Ormonde to Inchiquin, 15 August 1651, *ibid.*, pp. 184-185.

3. Basadonna to the Senate, 30 August 1651, *Calendar of State Papers . . . Venice*, 28196.

4. Letter of intelligence from M. M. in Paris, 19 August 1651, State Papers, France (P.R.O.), f. 6.

5. Letter of intelligence from M. M. in Paris, 2 September 1651, *ibid.*, f. 10b.

6. "Declaration of the Army of England upon Their March into Scotland," 19 July 1650, *Calendar of State Papers, Domestic Series, 1650*, 1:242-247.

7. Lord Taaf to Ormonde, 30 September 1651, *Report of the Historical Manuscripts Commission . . . Ormonde*, New Series, 1:213.

8. John ap Griffith to Sir Richard Browne, 19 September 1651, *Memorials of the Civil War: The Fairfax Correspondence*, 2:125-126.

9. Nicholas to Hyde, 2 November 1651, B.M. Add MSS 31954, f. 52.

10. This issue is fully discussed in George A. Lanyi, "Oliver Cromwell and his age: A study in Nationalism," See also J. A. W. Gunn, "Interest Will Not Lie: 17th-Century Political Maxim."

11. Charles Wilson, *Profit and Power*, pp. 49-53.

12. Christopher Hill, *God's Englishman*, pp. 130-132.

13. H. R. Trevor-Roper, *Religion, the Reformation, and Social Change*, pp. 359-362.

14. *Ibid.*, p. 360.

15. Morosini to the Senate, 24 October 1651, *Calendar of State Papers . . . Venice*, 28:258.

16. Cardinal de Retz, *Oeuvres de Cardinal de Retz*, 3:115-15; Samuel Rawson Gardiner, *History of the Commonwealth and Protectorate*, 2:155.

17. Gentillot to Servien, 23 February 1652, P.R.O. Transcript 31/3/90, v. 458.

18. *Ibid.*, f. 458b.

19. [Colonel Edward Popham to the Governor of Dunkirk], [17 May 1651] *Report of the Historical Manuscripts Commission on the Leybourne-Popham MSS*, 100.

20. Samuel Rawson Gardiner, "Cromwell and Mazarin in 1652 "

21. Comte d'Estrades to Mazarin, 5 February 1652, Stowe MSS 85, ff. 38b-39.

22. Mazarin to Comte d'Estrades, 3 March 1652, *ibid.*, f. 39b.

23. Comte d'Estrades to [Colonel John Fitz-James], 12 March 1652, B.M. Add MSS 32093, f. 283. In this letter, Fitz-James was described as "Cromwell's agent."

24. Gardiner, "Cromwell and Mazarin in 1652."

25. Nicholas to Hyde, 18 April 1652, B.M. Add MSS 31954, f. 62.

26. Sagredo to the Senate, 24 September 1652, *Calendar of State Papers . . . Venice*, 28:665.

27. Sagredo to the Senate, 24 September 1652, *ibid.*, p. 666.

28. Letter to Hyde from The Hague (probably from Nicholas), 19 September 1652, B.M. Add MSS 4180, f. 73.

29. Philip A. Knachel, *England and the Fronde*, pp. 177-178.

30. Sagredo to the Senate, 22 October 1652, *Calendar of State Papers . . . Venice*, 28:679.

31. Palucci to Sagredo, 8 November 1652, *ibid.*, p. 685.

32. Nicholas to Hyde, 17 October 1652, B.M. Add MSS 31954, f. 77.

33. Knachel, *England and the Fronde*, 179ff.

34. Henrietta Maria to the Duke of York, 15 December 1652, P.R.O. Transcript 31/3/90, f. 27. Hyde and Nicholas had hoped to gain support from France, but by October, 1652, the latter expressed the view "that juggling Cardinal will not suffer the King of France to do any good for the King, and I may tell you, I very much apprehend, that the designe of the Cardinal is (and I pray God some in the Louvre do not concur in it) to keep the King still a pensioner of France." 1 October 1652, B.M. Add MSS 31954, f. 77.

35. B.M. Add MSS 29546, f. 89; B.M. Add MSS 32093, f. 281.

36. B.M. Add MSS 32093, f. 281b.

37. M. Augier was the Parliament's agent in Paris. He served in that capacity from November, 1644 to December 1650. *Calendar of State Papers, Domestic Series, 1651*, 3:209.

38. "Brief Information," B.M. Add MSS 29546, f. 89; B.M. Add MSS 32093, f. 281. It also cautioned that Mazarin would replace de Davignon if the Count did not get support from England.

39. B.M. Add MSS 32093, f. 281.

40. Sagredo to the Senate, 22 October, 1652, *Calendar of State Papers . . . Venice*, 28:679.

41. Livet, "International Relations and the Role of France, 1648-1660," p. 422.

42. Lynch, *Spain under the Habsburgs*, p. 121.

CHAPTER 4

1. Instructions to Bordeaux, 2 December 1652, P.R.O. Transcript 31/3/90 f. 522. J. J. Jusserand, ed., *Recueil des instructions donnees aux ambassadeurs et ministres de France . . . Angleterre, 1648-1665*, 1:152-157 (hereafter cited as Jusserand, *Recueil des instructions*).

2. Jusserand, *Recueil des instructions*, 1:154; P.R.O. Transcript 31/3/90, f. 523, 523b.

3. Sagredo to the Senate, 10 December 1652, *Calendar of State Papers . . . Venice*, 28:704.

4. Henrietta Maria to the Duke of York, 15 December 1652, P.R.O. Transcript 31/3/90, f. 527.

5. *Ibid.*, f. 527b.

6. Sagredo to the Senate, 10 December 1652, *Calendar of State Papers . . . Venice*, 28:704.

7. Nicholas to Hyde, 9 May 1652, B.M. Add MSS 31954, f. 65.

8. *A Great Victory obtained by the King of France against the Prince of Condé . . . His [Charles Stuart] granting forth new commissions to make war with England.*

9. Nicholas to Hyde, 17 October 1652, B.M. Add MSS 31954, f. 77.

10. Hyde to the Marquis of Newcastle, 14 December 1652, *Clarendon State Papers*, 2:161.

11. Bordeaux received help from the Portuguese ambassador in making contacts with Parliament. Bordeaux to Brienne, 22 December 1652, P.R.O. Transcript 31/3/90, f. 528.

12. Speech of Bordeaux at his audience, 21 December 1652. *Journal of the House of Commons*, 7:233. The speech had a distinct "neo-Elizabethan" flavor: an appeal to the glories of Drake and the militant Protestantism that motivated many Englishmen to aid the Dutch and Henry of Navarre in their struggles against the Habsburgs.

13. *Ibid.*

14. Bordeaux to Brienne, 6 January 1653, P.R.O. Transcript 31/3/90, f. 531.

15. Bordeaux to Brienne, 9 January 1653, *ibid.*, f. 549f.

16. Bordeaux to Brienne, 30 December 1652, *ibid.*, ff. 535b.

17. Bordeaux to Brienne, 30 December 1652, *ibid.*, ff. 536, 536b.

18. Ivan Roots, *The Great Rebellion, 1642-1660*, pp. 163-164; Robert S. Paul, *The Lord Protector*, p. 258.

19. Bordeaux to Brienne, 6 January 1654, P.R.O. Transcript 31/3/90, f. 531. Bordeaux said that since Parliament would not allow the army to rule the country, the army was treating England "as Spain does the Indies."

20. Paul, *The Lord Protector*, 265.

21. Bordeaux to Brienne, 10 February 1653, P.R.O. Transcript 31/3/90, f. 591. Bordeaux noted that representatives of the Commonwealth had displayed a marked coldness toward him in the past few days—something he attributed to the favorable treatment recently accorded to the Duke of York at the French court.

22. The best discussion of the Commonwealth's actions toward the city of Bordeaux is in Philip A. Knachel, *England and the Fronde*, pp. 164 ff.

23. Barrière to Condé, 7 March 1653, B.M. Add MSS 35252, f. 16.

24. Palucci to Sagredo, 8 March 1653, *Calendar of State Papers . . . Venice*, 29:52.

25. Bordeaux to Brienne, 10 March 1653, P.R.O. Transcript 31/3/90, f. 616b.

26. Bordeaux to Brienne, 6 February 1653, *ibid.*, f. 588.
27. Bordeaux to Servien, 20 February 1653, *ibid.*, f. 605.
28. *Ibid.*, ff. 605-605b.
29. Bordeaux to Brienne, 16 January 1653, *ibid.*, f. 558b.
30. Bordeaux to Brienne, 30 December 1652, *ibid.*, f. 536.
31. Bordeaux to Brienne, 27 February 1653, *ibid.*, f. 609b. Communication by J. T. [John Thurloe], 3 March 1653, B.M. Add MSS 4156, f. 42.
32. Bordeaux to Brienne, 13 March 1653, P.R.O. Transcript 31/3/90, f. 620.
33. Bordeaux to Brienne, 20 March 1653, *ibid.*, f. 624b.
34. Palucci to Sagredo, 22 March 1653, *Calendar of State Papers . . . Venice*, 29:62.
35. Major General Massey to the Duke of Ormonde, 13 March 1653, *Report of Historical Manuscripts Commission . . . Ormonde*, new series, 1:272.
36. Bordeaux to Brienne, 4 March 1653, P.R.O. Transcript 31/3/90, ff. 612-612b.
37. Barrière to Condé, 4 April 1653, B.M. Add MSS 35252, f. 24.
38. Barrière to Condé, 11 April 1653, *ibid.*, f. 31.
39. *Ibid.*
40. Barrière to Condé, 11 April 1653, *ibid.*
41. Bordeaux to Brienne, 10 April 1653, P.R.O. Transcript 31/3/90, f. 678.
42. Barrière to Condé, 18 April 1653, B.M. Add MSS 35252, f. 34.
43. Bordeaux to Brienne, 24 April 1653, Jules de Cosnac, *Souvenirs du regne de Louis XIV*, vol. 7.
44. Barrière presented the most grandiose view of Cromwell's position, stating he was the most powerful man in Europe since he had 100,000 men and 200 ships of war at his disposal. Barrière to Condé, 23 May 1653, B.M. Add MSS 35252, f. 43.

CHAPTER 5

1. Bordeaux to Mazarin, 9 May 1653, quoted in Francois P. G. Guizot, *History of Oliver Cromwell and the Commonwealth*, 2:426.
2. Nicholas to Hyde, 8 May 1653, B.M. Add MSS 31954, f. 93b.
3. Bordeaux to Mazarin, 9 May 1653, quoted in Guizot, *History of Oliver Cromwell and the Commonwealth*, 2:426. Bordeaux described his first priority as convincing Cromwell that Louis and Mazarin "will learn with joy the news of the happy success with which God favors his [Cromwell] enterprise."
4. Barrière believed that there was little sentiment in England to help the city, and that it would probably be lost, although negotiations were progressing which might establish a league between England, Spain, and Condé. Barrière to Condé (23 May 1653), B.M. Add MSS 35252, f.

43. M. Bordeaux also thought it unlikely that England would aid the city of Bordeaux, but that the Commonwealth might send an escort with merchant vessels heading for the city. Bordeaux to Brienne, 2 June 1653, P.R.O. Transcript 31/3/91, f. 1. M. Bordeaux paid close attention to the situation, because there was much apprehension at the court in France about the possibility of English help for the city. Letter of intelligence from Paris, 17 May 1653, John Thurloe, *A Collection of the State Papers of John Thurloe*, 2:189. Hereafter cited as *Thurloe Papers*.

5. Palucci to Sagredo, 23 May 1653, *Calendar of State Papers . . . Venice*, 29:108.

6. Bordeaux to Brienne, 5 June 1653, P.R.O. Transcript 31/3/91, f. 4.

7. Bordeaux to Brienne, 2 June 1653, *ibid.*, f. 3.

8. Bordeaux to Brienne, 12 June 1653, *ibid.*, f. 6.

9. Speech of Bordeaux at his first audience, 21 December 1652, *Journal of the House of Commons*, 7:233.

10. Bordeaux to Brienne, 16 June 1653, P.R.O. Transcript 31/3/91, f. 8b.

11. Nicholas to Hyde, 16 January 1653 and 30 January 1653, B.M. Add MSS 31954, f. 85b.

12. Francis Wentworth to Ormonde, 16 April 1653, *Report of the Historical Manuscripts Commission . . . Ormonde*, new series 1:283.

13. Francis Wentworth to Ormonde, 23 April 1653, *ibid.*

14. Letter to Hyde, from Amsterdam, 17 April 1653, B.M. Add MSS 4180 f. 86b.

15. *The Daily Proceedings, of the Army by Sea and Land under the Command of His Excellancy, the Lord General Cromwell.* A report in *The Daily Proceedings* stated that it was general knowledge in Amsterdam that "we have prayers here commonly used by the King of Scots party for the good success of the Dutch against the English, which is strangly looked upon by many, that people should pray against their own country. Sure they will make but ill government say some." For a more complete discussion of the growth of English "nationalism" during the Interregnum, see George A. Lanyi, "Oliver Cromwell and his age: a study in Nationalism."

16. Lady Hatton to Madam, 29 April 1653, B.M. Add MSS 29550, f. 185.

17. Palucci to Sagredo, 9 May 1653, *Calendar of State Papers . . . Venice*, 29:97.

18. Palucci to Sagredo, 23 May 1653, *ibid.*, p. 108.

19. Bordeaux to Brienne, 2 June 1653, P.R.O. Transcript, 31/3/91, f. 1.

20. The most representative statements of these interpretations are in: C. H. Firth, *Oliver Cromwell and the Rule of the Puritans in England* (reprint, London, 1958); Christopher Hill, *God's Englishman*; and H. R. Trevor-Roper, "Cromwell and his Parliaments" in *Religion, the Reformation and Social Change*, pp. 345-391.

21. Robert S. Paul, *The Lord Protector*, pp. 262-263.

22. *Thurloe Papers*, 1:255-256.

23. Memorial written by Brienne for Bordeaux, 10 July 1653, P.R.O. Transcript, 31/3/91, ff. 35b, 36b. Bordeaux was told to inform the English that "His Majesty views the reestablishment of a good intelligence between France and England useful to the two states and necessary for attaining the conclusion and strengthening of a general peace in Christendom." The phrase "general peace" was not defined, and various uses of the term led to difficulties in future negotiations.

24. *Mercurius Politicus*, 28 July 1653.

25. Letter of intelligence, 21 June 1653, *Thurloe Papers*, 1:285-288.

26. Cromwell to Mazarin, 19 June 1653, P.R.O. Transcript 31/3/91, f. 13.

27. Memorial of Mazarin for Bordeaux, 10 July 1653, *ibid.*, f. 33.

28. *Ibid.*

29. Palucci to Sagredo, 9 August 1653, *Calendar of State Papers . . . Venice*, 29:140.

30. *Ibid.*

31. Sexby was not the only agent who was used to gather information about conditions in France. Joachim Hane, a military engineer, also carried out an important intelligence mission for Cromwell at this time. See Joachim Hane, *Journal*.

32. Tract written by Sexby to the Protector, Rawlinson MSS A60, ff. 126-129.

33. Philip A. Knachel, *England and the Fronde*, pp. 210-214.

34. Bordeaux to Brienne, 4 August 1653, P.R.O. Transcript 31/3/91, f. 62.

35. Bordeaux to Brienne, 7 August 1653, *ibid.*, ff. 64b, 65.

36. Bordeaux to Brienne, 11 August 1653, *ibid.*, f. 68.

37. Bordeaux to Brienne, 14 August 1653, *ibid.*, f. 70.

38. *Ibid.*, f. 70b.

39. Hill, *God's Englishman*, pp. 138-145.

40. Trevor-Roper, "Cromwell and his Parliaments," pp. 363-370. For important and differing views of the Barebones Parliament, see: Austin Woolrych, "The Calling of the Barebones Parliament"; and Tai Lui, "The Calling of the Barebones Parliament Reconsidered."

41. P.R.O. Transcript, 31/3/91, f. 72.

42. Bordeaux to Brienne, 18 August 1653, *ibid.*, f. 76.

43. Nicholas to Hyde, 21 August 1653, B.M. Add MSS 4180, f. 101.

44. Bordeaux to Mazarin, 28 August 1653, P.R.O. Transcript 31/3/91, f. 81.

45. Boreel predicted that Anglo-French negotiations would be broken and Bordeaux recalled to make sure that England did not learn that M. Bordeaux's true mission had been to stop England from assisting the city of Bordeaux. Boreel's views presented an inaccurate, but logical interpretation of French diplomacy. The reasonableness of the assumptions helped to explain the coolness, noted by Bordeaux, in the English

attitude toward France. Boreel to the States General, 22 August 1653, *Thurloe Papers*, 1:436. Council of State to Captain Willoughby Hannum of the *Katherine*, 6 September 1653, *Calendar of State Papers, Domestic Series, 1653*, 6:131.

46. Commission by the keepers of Liberty of England to Edward Marston, letter of marque, 9 September 1653, *Calendar of State Papers, Domestic Series, 1653-1654*, 6:139.

47. For a further discussion of England's relations with Spain and Portugal, two recent unpublished Ph.D. dissertations should be consulted: A. MacFadyan, Anglo-Spanish Relations, 1625-1660, Liverpool University, and T. Bently Duncan, The English Commonwealth and Portugal, University of Chicago.

48. Barrière's and Condé's attachment to Spain was not so strong that they would not consider abandoning the King of Spain in return for assistance from Cromwell.

49. Charles Longland to the Admiralty Commissioners, 21 July and 25 July 1653. *Calendar of State Papers, Domestic Series, 1653-1654*, 42-63, 48.

50. Charles Longland to the Admiralty Commissioners, *ibid.*, pp. 81-82.

51. Barrière to Condé [August, 1653] B.M. Add MSS 35252, f. 73.

52. Letter of intelligence from The Hague, 28 July 1653, *Thurloe Papers*, 1:360.

53. Letter of intelligence from The Hague, 9 August 1653, *ibid.*, p. 389.

CHAPTER 6

1. For an excellent summary of the Dutch war, see Charles Wilson, *Profit and Power*, pp. 1-77.

2. There were various reports of the interview between van Beverningh and Cromwell. One of the most complete, including comments supposedly made by Nieupoort, was contained in a letter of intelligence received by Thurloe from The Hague, 5 September 1653, *Thurloe Papers*, 1:438-439.

3. Letter of intelligence from Holland to Thurloe, 12 September 1653, *ibid.*, p. 450.

4. Mazarin to Bordeaux, 13 September 1653, P.R.O. Transcript 31/ff/91, f. 83 and 17 November 1653, *ibid.*, ff. 17-20.

5. Resolutions of the Assembly of Zutphen, 20 September and 4 October 1653, *Thurloe Papers*, 1:469, 509. Reports of the plans of the Orangist agents in The Hague and the resolutions taken by the states of Gelderland and Zeeland were contained in letters of intelligence tha Thurloe received, dated 27 and 28 September, *ibid.*, pp. 487, 488-489. According to at least three different sources of intelligence from The Hague (who, incidentally, disagreed on other issues as important as the plans of the King of Denmark to declare war on England), Holland was campaigning actively for peace with England and for repudiation of both Stuart and Orange, and would oppose any opposing ideas set forth by other states. See *ibid.*, pp. 450, 460-461, 551.

6. Letter of intelligence from The ague, 28 November 1653, *ibid.*, pp. 593-594.

7. Bordeaux's attempts to foster greater harmony between England and France were not helped by some of the reports Thurloe received from Paris. One of the English informants admitted that Mazarin did not want to join the Dutch in a league against England, but "ouer envoy there mr. Bordeaux will not at all be removed, but all things there suffered to stand as they are till the issue of what is above sayd [peace between England and the Dutch which would include France] be knowne. In suma you may be assured that France does not but delude your Commonwealth." Rawlinson MSS A8, f. 212.

8. Bordeaux to Brienne, 1 December 1653, P.R.O. Transcript 31/3/92, f. 42.

9. Bordeaux to Brienne, 11 December 1653, *ibid.*, f. 62b. Although Bordeaux realized that there was no possibility of France's inclusion in the peace treaty, other interested observers, such as Barrière, were misled completely. On 12 December 1653, Barrière wrote to Lenet that peace between the United Provinces and England was assured and that "Denmark and France will be able to enter it . . . and Holland will mediate between them." B.M. Add MSS 35252, f. 116. Barrière had a tendency to be overly optimistic or pessimistic, but he was a shrewd observer and was not often fooled. His totally inaccurate report in this case showed some of the problems that diplomats faced in trying to anticipate England's policies.

10. Letter of intelligence from Paris to Thurloe, 1 December 1653, Rawlinson MSS A9, f. 87.

11. Speech of the ambassador from France to the States General of the United Provinces, 24 February 1654, *Thurloe Papers*, 2:87-88.

12. Letter from The Hague to Thurloe, 27 February 1654, *ibid.*, p. 98. On 16 January 1654, the Cardinal had written Cromwell a solicitous letter reminding him that Bordeaux had come to an agreement with the Commonwealth in September 1653. Mazarin said that the minor problems that had arisen in the treaty since that time should have been worked out between Bordeaux and the English commissioners. Once the treaty was concluded, Mazarin wanted to propose means "to more strictly confirme the same which I am confident will prove of mutuall conveience to both nations." Stowe MSS 185, ff. 59-60.

13. This statement of the Cardinal was quoted in a dispatch from Boreel, the Dutch ambassador to France, to the States General, 22 March 1654, *Thurloe Papers*, 2:160-161.

14. B.M. Add MSS 40795, f. 8; Stowe MSS 133, f. 307. Jean Dumont, *Corps universel diplomatique de droit des gens*, vol. 6, part 2, pp. 88-92.

15. *Thurloe Papers*, 2:238. Samuel Rawson Gardiner, *History of the Commonwealth and Protectorate*, 3:67-70.

16. Both Gardiner and Abbott put special emphasis on Cromwell's objections to fighting the other great Protestant power in Europe, the Dutch. For a more complete discussion of religious motivations in

Cromwell's actions, see Robert S. Paul, *The Lord Protector: Religion and Politics in the Life of Oliver Cromwell,* especially pp. 322-349.

17. Palucci was convinced that England would attack France as soon as preparations could be made. Palucci to Sagredo, 3 April 1654, *Calendar of State Papers . . . Venice,* 30:237.

18. Christopher Hill, *God's Englishman,* pp. 143-145; and Paul, *The Lord Protector,* pp. 296-301. For a discussion of the role played by the army officers, see also Maurice Ashley, *Cromwell's Generals,* pp. 99-113.

19. Bordeaux to Brienne, 8 September 1653, P.R.O. Transcript 31/3/91, f. 87b. Bordeaux reportedly told the commissioners that the reason England should ally with France was "the defense of the religion against the House of Austria."

20. Barrière to Condé, 12 December 1653, B.M. Add MSS 35252, f. 111.

21. Barrière to Condé, 20 February 1654, *ibid.,* f. 135.

22. White to Servien, 27 April 1654, P.R.O. Transcript 31/3/94, f. 93.

23. Letter of intelligence from the city of Marseilles to Barrière, 28 April 1654, B.M. Add MSS 35252, f. 150. The informant in this letter was probably Jean Baptiste Stouppe, minister of the Huguenot congregation in London. He was used by Cromwell as an agent to European Protestant communities. I have found no evidence that Cromwell made the statement to which the letter referred.

24. Letter of intelligence from Paris to Thurloe, 17 June 1654, *Thurloe Papers,* 2:351. This letter also stated that the French clergy were stirring up the people against the Huguenots. In these terms, Mazarin also became a protector of the embattled Huguenots.

25. Nicholas to Hyde, 2 October 1653, B.M. Add MSS 31954, f. 108b.

26. Barrière to M. Lenet, 24 October 1653, B.M. Add MSS 35252, f. 90.

27. Bordeaux to Brienne, 29 September 1653, P.R.O. Transcript 31/3/91, f. 100. Bordeaux to Brienne, 3 November 1653, P.R.O. Transcript 31/3/92, f. 1b.

28. Bordeaux to Servien, 17 November 1653, P.R.O. Transcript 31/3/92, f. 12.

29. Barrière to M. Lenet, 21 November 1653, B.M. Add MSS 35252, f. 104.

30. Mazarin to Bordeaux, 17 November 1653, P.R.O. Transcript 31/3/92, f. 18.

31. *Ibid.,* f. 20.

32. Letter of intelligence to Mazarin, 24 November 1653, B.M. Add MSS 4156, f. 29.

33. Bordeaux to Brienne, 25 December 1653, P.R.O. Transcript 31/3/92, f. 97. It appeared as though France could not avoid the stigma of being supporters of the Stuarts even when discussing a question like the Anglo-Dutch peace. Bordeaux told Brienne that there was a good chance of reaching a treaty with England, based on the Anglo-Dutch agreement, "if France can convince England it will not work against the regime in England' 15 December 1653, *ibid.,* f. 74.

34. Bordeaux to Mazarin, 18 December 1653, *ibid.*, f. 85.

35. Bordeaux to Mazarin, 5 January 1654, *ibid.*, f. 121b.

36. Bordeaux to Brienne, 5 February 1654, *ibid.*, f. 130.

37. De Baas to Mazarin, 13 January 1654, *ibid.*, f. 128. De Baas carried with him a message that Mazarin was willing to expel Charles Stuart from France if that would improve the chances for a treaty with Cromwell.

38. Palucci to Sagredo, 14 February 1654, *Calendar of State Papers . . . Venice*, 30:221.

39. Sagredo to the Senate, 17 February 1654, *ibid.*

40. Louis XIV to Bordeaux, 21 February 1654, P.R.O. Transcript 31/3/93, f. 34, Jusserand, *Recueil des instructions*, vol. 1, *1648-1665*, p. 173.

41. Bordeaux to Mazarin, 23 February 1654, P.R.O. Transcript 31/3/93, f. 46.

42. Thurloe to Whitelocke, 3 March 1654, *Thurloe Papers*, 2:135-136. B.M. Add MSS 32093, f. 326.

43. Letter of intelligence from Paris to Thurloe, 25 February 1654, *Thurloe Papers*, 2:88.

44. Bordeaux to Brienne, 2 March 1654, P.R.O. Transcript 31/3/93, f. 58. A Venetian ambassador thought that de Baas's second mission meant that Mazarin had "sacrificed formality to Political expediency." Sagredo to the Senate, 3 March 1654, *Calendar of State Papers . . . Venice*, 30:226.

45. Bordeaux to Mazarin, 28 February 1654, P.R.O. Transcript 31/3/93, f. 56.

46. Sagredo to the Senate, 3 March 1654, *Calendar of State Papers . . . Venice*, 30:226.

47. Bordeaux to Brienne, 5 March 1654, P.R.O. Transcript 31/3/93, f. 60.

CHAPTER 7

1. Letter of intelligence from Paris to Thurloe, 21 March 1654, *Thurloe Papers*, 2:159. The widely held attitude in England toward Mazarin was expressed in a tract written in London shortly after his death. "That France had run into the same distractions as us, had she lost a Mazarin, by the same violence we lost a Strafford. . . .I neither believe him to be . . . either friend or enemy to any Prince or Country, any further than as it stood with the interest of France, whose faithful minister of state he was and whose interest he pursued, according indeed to his duty, without respect either to Alliance or Consanguinity." *An Impartial Character of that famous Politician and late admired Minister of State, Cardinal Mazarine.* The tract was not only an appraisal of Mazarin but an interesting study of the post-Restoration view of the Protectorate.

2. Letter of intelligence from Paris to Thurloe, 21 March 1654, *Thurloe Papers*, 2:159. This letter also stated that Mazarin was holding serious

discussions with his advisers about a general peace.

3. Bordeaux to Servien, 25 March 1654, P.R.O. Transcript 31/3/93, f. 104. A few days earlier, Bordeaux had analyzed the situation in different terms, "the policy of the Protector is to promise to all the world, in order to put himself in a position to choose his party." Bordeaux to Mazarin, 19 March 1654, *ibid.*, f. 89b. Despite Bordeaux's accurate analysis, neither he nor Mazarin thought that France could afford to stop pursuing an alliance with Cromwell.

4. Letter of intelligence from The Hague to Thurloe 20 March 1654, *Thurloe Papers*, 2:152-153.

5. Bordeaux to Brienne, 19 March 1654, P.R.O. Transcript 31/3/93, f. 78b.

6. De Baas to Mazarin, 23 March 1654, *ibid.*, f. 92.

7. Samuel Rawson Gardiner, *History of the Commonwealth and Protectorate*, 3:118.

8. Anonymous letter from Brussels to Mazarin, 26 March 1654, P.R.O. Transcript 31/3/93, f. 113.

9. Mazarin to de Baas, 27 March 1654, *ibid.*, ff. 118, 119. Mazarin told de Baas to remind Cromwell how Spain had been unable to help the Duke of Lorraine, Condé, or the Duke of Savoy. The examples that Mazarin chose were, conveniently, men who were identified with either militant Catholicism or the Stuarts.

10. "More soldiers were boarding the ships than usual and assuredly the Protector has some design, and that seemingly would be against France, and it is said, to the Isle of Rhe." Bordeaux to Brienne, 30 March 1654, *ibid.*, f. 120b.

11. Bordeaux to Brienne, 2 April 1654, P.R.O. Transcript 31/3/94, f. 2b.

12. Mazarin to de Baas, 3 April 1654, *ibid.*, f. 8.

13. Godfrey Davies, "English Political Sermons," described the preaching in 1620s, with the purpose of persuading James I to go to war against the Habsburgs, and the opposition to the Spanish match as the "first definite example of an attempt to marshall public opinion in opposition to the foreign policy of a government in England.

14. Gage's comments on the West Indies. *Thurloe Papers*, 3:59-61. Thurloe dated Gage's appearance in December, 1654, but that must have been in error, because both Gage and the council ignored important events concerning the Indies which had occurred before then. Gage had published his views earlier in a book entitled *The English American ... or a New Survey of the West Indies*. Abbott, *Writings and Speeches*, 3:340-341.

15. *Thurloe Papers*, 3:59-61.

16. For a more complete discussion of this aspect of Puritanism, see: Michael Walzer, *The Revolution of the Saints*; Christopher Hill, "The Preaching of the Word," *Society and Puritanism in Pre-Revolutionary England* pp. 30-39; and H. R. Trevor-Roper, "The Fast Sermons of the Long Parliament," in *Religion, the Reformation, and Social Change*, pp. 294-344.

17. Although I do not agree with his interpretation of Cromwell's foreign policy, I found in Trevor-Roper's articles—"Three Foreigners: The Philosophy of the Puritan Revolution," "The Fast Sermons of the Long Parliament," and "Oliver Cromwell and his Parliaments"—a valuable discussion about the political divisions and philosophies that operated during the Protectorate. The articles have been reprinted in *Religion, the Reformation, and Social Change.*

18. Christopher Hill, *Oliver Cromwell.* See also Hill's excellent discussion of the "importance of the doer" in his chapter, "Providence and Oliver Cromwell," in *God's Englishman,* pp. 227-238.

19. There is a discussion of Gage and his influence in William Maltby's *The Black Legend in England,* pp. 94-97, 120-124. Maltby's study of the growth of the Black Legend provides the foundation for his analysis of its impact on Cromwell's plans for the Western Design. I found the work extremely helpful, but I am in disagreement with part of Maltby's conclusions about the Western Design. "There was little to be gained from an attack on the West Indies and much to be lost.... Anyone of Cromwell's undoubted ability would have realized this had he not been blinded by irrational hatred and a welter of misleading information" (pp. 120-121). I think that the policy had much to recommend it, and that it was Cromwell's ability to detach himself from the emotional aspects of the question that enabled him to see this. On the other hand, I support Maltby's position that the slipshod manner in which the Western Design was conducted shows that "the trouble with unfavorable national stereotypes is that they lead one to underestimate the enemy." pp. 121-122.

J. F. Battick, "Cromwell's Navy and the Foreign Policy of the Protectorate, 1653-1658," has a good description of the Western Design (pp. 139-168, 186-198). Battick's work was helpful to me in understanding the role played by the navy and the way in which Cromwell saw it could be used. I do not agree with most of Battick's conclusions about the motives behind Cromwell's policies or the success of his overall foreign policy. This disagreement in no way negates the value of Battick's study to my own work.

20. Pickering had already been asked by Bordeaux to intercede in behalf of French ships that had been seized by England. De Baas also thought that although Pickering showed good inclinations toward France, he was "completely faithful to the Protector." De Baas to Mazarin, 14 April 1654, P.R.O. Transcript 31/3/94, f. 49.

21. Mazarin to de Baas and Bordeaux, 25 March 1654, *ibid.,* f. 94b. Mazarin warned them that he had learned that Pickering was in close contact with Barrière and Spanish officials in Brussels.

22. Mazarin to Bordeaux, 25 March 1654, *ibid.,* f. 95. By this time, Mazarin was changing his view of Thurloe, and thought that the secretary might have deceived Spain into thinking he supported its cause. Mazarin certainly did not think it was hopeless to attempt to work through Thurloe's good offices.

23. White to Servien, 7 April 1654, *ibid.*, f. 20.

24. De Baas to Mazarin, 7 April 1654, *ibid.*, f. 12b. De Baas was convinced that one of the biggest obstacles to his negotiations was the pro-Spanish feelings of Thurloe.

25. De Baas to Mazarin, 14 April 1654, *ibid.*, f. 49b.

26. Bordeaux to Mazarin, 13 April 1654, *ibid.*, ff. 42-44. Bordeaux stated that the Protector kept saying how friendly he was toward France but that negotiations had not improved. Bordeaux blamed this on two factors at that time—rumors that Mazarin was persecuting the Huguenots, and the hostility of Thurloe, who "is very close the Spanish ambassador."

Barrière might have had a more accurate explanation for Bodeaux's difficulties. Barrière said that the King of France was committed to so many princes that he could not stretch his resources any further. He would have to end some commitments before he could make a satisfactory offer to Cromwell. Barrière to Condé, 17 April 1654, B.M. Add MSS 35252, f. 141. Bordeaux to Brienne, 16 April 1654, P.R.O. Transcript 31/3/94, f. 50b.

27. A detailed account of the meeting, based on the notes taken by Edward Montagu, is in *The Clarke Papers*, ed., C. H. Firth, vol 3, Appendix B., 203-206. There are two considerations about Montagu's account which must be kept in mind—it was based on an ex post facto compilation of his notes, and the debate was based on the premise of an attack against Spain. There was also a fear expressed that enthusiasm in Parliament might end if the invasion was not started soon. Battick has pointed out that there is no record in the *Calendar of State Papers, Domestic* of a meeting of the council for 20 April, and that no orders were calendared under that date. The meeting that Montagu described probably took place on 18 or 21 April ("Cromwell's Navy and the Foreign Policy of the Protectorate," p. 97, n. 40). To avoid confusion in future references, I shall use Montagu's dating when discussing the first meeting at which the Western Design was debated.

28. *Clarke Papers*, vol 3, Appendix B, pp. 203-206.

29. *Ibid.*, p. 207-208.

30. Barrière to Condé, 24 April 1654, B.M. Add MSS 35252, ff. 147-148.

CHAPTER 8

1. Bordeaux to Mazarin, 27 April 1654, P.R.O. Transcript 31/3/94, f. 91b.

2. Bordeaux to Mazarin, 13 April 1654, *ibid.*, f. 44.

3. Palucci to Sagrego, 8 May 1654, *Calendar of State Papers ... Venice*, 30:250.

4. Barrière to Condé, 15 May 1654, B.M. Add MSS 35252, ff. 160-161.

5. Bordeaux to Mazarin, 16 April 1654, P.R.O. Transcript 31/3/94, f. 53.

6. Montagu's account of the meeting of the council demonstrates that

Bordeaux was correct in his assumption that Lambert was pressing for England to go to war, probably against France. *Clarke Papers*, vol 3, Appendix B, pp. 206-207.

7. De Baas to Mazarin, 24 April 1654, P.R.O. Transcript 31/3/94, f. 81b.

8. Bordeaux to Brienne, 23 April 1654, *ibid.*, ff. 76-77.

9. Bordeaux to Brienne, 27 April 1654, *ibid.*, f. 88b.

10. Mazarin asserted that he had learned that "Some of the other principal figures in the present regime are using all their efforts to engage him in a break with France." Mazarin to Bordeaux, 29 April 1654, *ibid.*, f. 99. Thurloe's intelligence from M. Augier quoted Mazarin as saying, "I see M. Cromwell is not for us." Intelligence from Augier's secretary, 2 May 1654, *Thurloe Papers*, 2:246.

11. De Baas to Mazarin, 24 April 1654, P.R.O. Transcript 31/3/94, f. 82.

12. Barrière to Lenet, 1 May 1654, B.M. Add MSS 35252, f. 155.

13. Maurice Ashley, *The Greatness of Oliver Cromwell*, (London, 1958), pp. 276-278 and Ashley, *Cromwell's Generals*, pp. 99-113.

14. Ashley, *Cromwell's Generals*, p. 112.

15 *Clarke Papers*, 3:207-208. Lambert had not been present at the 20 April meeting.

16. Bordeaux to Brienne, 2 March 1654, *Thurloe Papers*, 2:106.

17. Bordeaux to Mazarin, 1 June 1654, P.R.O. Transcript 31/3/95, ff. 1-1b.

18. Intelligence from Paris to Thurloe, 26 May 1654, *Thurloe Papers*, 2:295.

19. For complete descriptions of the plot, see: David Underdown, *Royalist Conspiracy in England, 1649-1660*; Samuel Rawson Gardiner, *History of the Commonwealth and Protectorate*, 3:136-152, Abbott, *Writings and Speeches*, 3:301-304, 320-327.

20. Bordeaux to Brienne, 1 June 1654, P.R.O. Transcript 31/3/95, f. 10b.

21. Bordeaux to Mazarin, 4 June 1654, *ibid.*, f. 12.

22. De Baas to Mazarin, 1 June 1654, *ibid.*, ff. 4-6.

23. De Baas to Mazarin, 8 June 1654, *ibid.*, ff. 16-16b.

24. Bordeaux to Brienne, 8 June 1654, *ibid.*, ff. 18, 19.

25. Abbott, *Writings and Speeches*, 3:320-323. It should be noted that de Baas had already received his passport before the news of the conspiracy.

26. Bordeaux to Brienne, 25 June 1654, in Francois P. G. Guizot, *History of Oliver Cromwell and the English Commonwealth*, vol. 2, Appendix 2, pp. 55-57.

27. *Ibid.*, 52-58. Bordeaux also noted that there were many rumors reaching England from France which supported the accusations against de Baas. Bordeaux felt it was important for him to counteract these rumors and for Brienne and Mazarin to cut them off at their sources.

28. *Ibid.*, 59.

29. Abbott, *Writings and Speeches*, 3:324.

30. Mazarin to Bordeaux, 17 June 1654, P.R.O. Transcript 31/3/95, ff. 45-6. Mazarin cautioned Bordeaux against making any moves that might endanger the negotiations.

CHAPTER 9

1. Barrière to Condé, 17 July 1654, B.M. Add MSS 35252, f. 188.

2. Barrière to Condé, 24 July 1654, *ibid.*, f. 192.

3. Barrière to Condé, 17 July 1654, *ibid.*, f. 188.

4. Samuel Rawson Gardiner, *History of the Commonwealth and Protectorate*, 3:152-53.

5. Barrière to Condé, 26 June 1654, B.M. Add MSS 35252, ff. 178-179.

6. Intelligence from Brussels, 4 July 1654, *Thurloe Papers*, 2:397. This view was supported by intelligence received from captured Royalist letters.

7. Palucci to Sagredo, 26 June 1654, *Calendar of State Papers ... Venice*, 30:278.

8. Quirini to the Senate, 17 June 1654, *ibid.*, p. 273.

9. *Thurloe Papers*, 1:706.

10. F. J. Routledge, *England and the Treaty of the Pyrenees*, presents an excellent discussion of the dynastic considerations involved in the conclusion of the war as well as their effect on the English Restoration. The English commissioners asserted that the treaty of 1630 between England and Spain stated that there should be amity between the two states everywhere. Despite that statement, they complained that English merchants were treated as enemies by Spain when they tried to trade in the Indies. The commissioners also complained that English merchants and travelers were subject to the Inquisition and were not allowed to use English Bibles for their personal worship. The commissioners were not reluctant to rely on the treaties of Charles I when they served the purposes of the new regime. In this respect, the Protectorate was more like to establish links with the government of the Stuarts than the Commonwealth had been. *Thurloe Papers*, 1:706.

11. Intelligence from Spain to Thurloe, June 1654, *Thurloe Papers*, 2:338-340. Thurloe's informant stated that "their [Spain's] quarrel with France is almost irreconcilable. . . . They can make but a defensive war or campaign."

12. Montagu's account of the meeting of the council, 20 April 1654, *Clarke Papers*, vol. 3, Appendix B, p. 207.

13. *Ibid.*, p. 208.

14. "Instructions to General Penn . . . for managing the Southerne Expedition," 18 August 1654 [Old Style], B.M. Stowe MSS 185, f. 83.

15. H. R. Trevor-Roper, "Cromwell and His Parliaments," pp. 363-385.

16. Quirini to the Senate, 28 July 1654, *Calendar of State Papers . . . Venice*, 30:295.

17. Palucci to Sagredo, 31 July 1654, *ibid.*, p. 296.

18. Barrière to Condé, 24 July 1654, B.M. Add MSS 35252, f. 192.

19. Sagredo to the Senate of Vencie, 7 July 1654, *Calendar of State Papers . . . Venice*, 30:285.

20. Intelligence from Paris to Thurloe, 1 July 1654, *Thurloe Papers*, 2:388.

21. Intelligence from Paris to Thurloe 4 July 1654, *ibid.*, p. 398.

22. Sagredo to the Senate of Venice, 14 July 1654, *Calendar of State Papers . . . Venice*, 30:288. Although some diplomats assumed that the Cardinal had expelled Charles, Bordeaux made no attempt to use the departure in his negotiations.

23. Intelligence from Paris to Thurloe, 4 July 1654, *Thurloe Papers*, 2:398-399.

24. Intelligence from Paris to Thurloe, 4 July 1654, *ibid.*, pp. 442-443.

25. *Ibid.*, p. 443-444.

26. Bordeaux to Chanut, 31 July 1654, *ibid.*, pp. 482.

27. Bordeaux to Charost, 6 August 1654, *ibid.*, p. 491.

28. Bordeaux to Chanut, 7 August 1654, *ibid.*, p. 492. Bordeaux also admitted to Chanut that one "can not really tell what is in the minds of the English."

29. Bordeaux to Chanut, 14 August 1654, *ibid.*, p. 523.

30. Letter of Intelligence from Augier's secretary, 26 August 1654, *ibid.*, 544-.

31. Bordeaux to Chanut, 28 August 1654, *ibid.*, pp. 549-550.

32. Abbott, *Writing and Speeches*, 3:259.

33. Stouppe to the Prince of Tarante, 25 August 1654. Nicholas also thought the defeat at Arras might force Cromwell to support Spain. On 1 September, Nicholas wrote, "The Spanish infinite loss before Arras had brought the Crown so low in forces and reputation, that if their friend Cromwell do not help them, France will soon overrun Flanders" *Calendar of State Papers, Domestic Series, 1654* 7:324.

34. Nicholas to Mr. Jane, 1 September 1654, *Thurloe Papers*, 2:324.

35. Stouppe to the Prince of Tarante, 7 August 1654, *ibid.*, p. 498.

36. Letter from Stouppe, August 1654, Rawl MSS A17, f. 72.

37. Intelligence from The Hague, 14 August 1654, *Thurloe Papers*, 2:519.

38. Letter from Stouppe, August, 1654, Rawl MSS A17, f. 77. Intelligence from Bologna to Thurloe, 28 August 1654, *ibid.*, 2:546.

39. Bordeaux to Mazarin, 3 September 1654, *ibid.*, p. 559.

40. Abbott, *Writings and Speeches*, 3:434-437.

41. *Ibid.*, pp. 438-439.

42. *Ibid.*, pp. 440-441.

43. Bordeaux to Brienne, 14 September 1654, *Thurloe Papers*, 2:587-588. Bordeaux stated that Cromwell had said nothing about Spain, but Bordeaux had learned that the Protector had asked Cardenas for liberty of conscience and trade for Protestant Englishmen in Spain.

44. Abbott, *Writings and Speeches*, 3:451-462.

45. Barrière to Condé, 9 October 1654, B.M. Add MSS 35252, f. 215.

Barrière stated that Bordeaux's negotiations were "in a very bad state" at that time.

46. Intelligence from Brussels to Thurloe, 2 September 1654, *Thurloe Papers*, 2:557. De Lede did not arrive in England until April, 1655.

47. Quirini to the Doge, 2 September 1654, *Calendar of State Papers . . . Venice*, 30:311.

48. Thurloe's account of "Cromwell's negotiations with France and Spain," written after the Restoration, *Thurloe Papers, 1:761*.

49. Cromwell to Speaker Lenthall, 22 September 1654, Tanner MSS 52, f. 130; also Abbott, *Writings and Speeches, 3:468*.

50. Brienne to Bordeaux, September 1654, *Thurloe Papers*, 2:731.

51. Abbott, *Writings and Speeches*, 3:494.

52. Gardiner, *History of the Commonwealth and Protectorate*, 3:214; Abbott, *Writings and Speeches*, 3:493.

53. Palucci to Sagredo, 12 October 1654, *Calendar of State Papers . . . Venice*, 30:324.

CHAPTER 10

1. "Instructions to General Penn . . . for Managing the Southerne Expedition," 18 August 1654 [Old Style], Stowe MSS 185, f. 83.

2. Abbott, *Writings and Speeches*, 3:483-486; Samuel Rawson Gardiner, *History of the Commonwealth and Protectorate*, 3:214-217. See especially n. 2, p. 216, in which Gardiner discussed the possibility that Penn was a Royalist or had Royalist sympathies. Some foreign diplomats viewed the unrest in the fleet as a sign of the inherent weakness of the Protectorate. Palucci to Sagredo, 1 December and 6 December 1654, *Calendar of State Papers . . . Venice, 30:343, 346*.

3. Palucci to Sagredo, 7 November 1654, *Calendar of State Papers . . . Venice*, 30:337. Palucci thought that Bordeaux had delayed the sailing of the fleet (whose mission Palucci thought was against France) for many weeks while Cromwell considered proposals from France.

4. Palucci to Sagredo, 22 December 1654, *ibid.*, p. 355.

5. Intelligence from The Hague for Thurloe, 18 December 1654, *Thurlow Papers*, 3:14.

6. Intelligence from Paris for Thurloe, 14 November 1654, *ibid.*, 2:711-712.

7. Intelligence from Paris, January, 1655, Rawl MSS A22, f. 487.

8. Bordeaux to Brienne, 23 October 1654, *Thurloe Papers*, 2:668.

9. Bordeaux to Brienne, 14 December 1654, *ibid.*, 3:6.

10. *Ibid.*, p. 7. Also Bordeaux to Mazarin, 14 December 1654, *ibid.*, p. 8.

11. Bordeaux to Chanut, 21 December 1654, *ibid.*, p. 18.

12. Bordeaux to his father [December, 1654] *ibid.*, pp. 57-58. Bordeaux also showed that he had not fully grasped that Cromwell and the council—not Parliament—were making the decisions. Bordeaux thought

that Cromwell had asked Parliament's advice before sending any instructions to the fleet.

13. Bordeaux also told Mazarin that they had either to convince Cromwell that France would make no more concessions or to reconcile themselves to facing more demands from him. Bordeaux to Mazarin, 3 September 1654, *ibid.*, 2:565.

14. Brienne to Bordeaux [September, 1654], *ibid.*, p. 731.

15. Prince of Tarante to Stouppe, 1 October 1654, Rawl MSS A18, f. 282. Palucci said that the treaty was near completion, but that the English had lodged additional demands for the total exclusion of the Stuarts from France and new power for the Huguenots. Palucci to Sagredo, 4 October 1654, *Calendar of State Papers Papers . . . Venice*, 30:322.

16. Bordeaux to Brienne, 27 November 1654, *Thurloe Papers*, 2:729.

17. Bordeaux (senior) to his son, the ambassador, 5 December 1654, *ibid.*, p. 737.

18. Letter of intelligence from M. Augier to Thurloe, 28 November 1654, *ibid.*, p. 741. Bordeaux (senior) to his son, 5 December 1654, *ibid.*, p. 738.

19. Intelligence that Thurloe received from Paris warned him that France was prepared to break off negotiations unless the treaty was concluded soon. 9 December 1654, *ibid.*, p. 743. Thurloe also intercepted letters to Bordeaux from Brienne and the ambassador's father which stated that the Cardinal wanted to do everything within reason to avoid breaking off the negotiations.

20. Thurloe's informant in Rome wrote, "Cardinal de Retz . . . gets along quite well in the College despite Mazarin's cabals." Intelligence from Rome, 14 December 1654, *ibid.*, 3:29.

21. Palucci to Sagredo, 22 December 1654, *Calendar of State Papers . . . Venice*, 30:355.

22. Louis to Cromwell, 18 December 1654, B.M. Add MSS 4156, f. 103.

23. Bordeaux to Mazarin, 31 December 1654, *Thurloe Papers*, 3:34.

24. Intelligence from Paris, 16 January 1655, Rawl MSS A22, f. 133.

25. Chanut to Bordeaux, 15 January 1655, *Thurloe Papers*, 3:81.

26. Bordeaux to Chanut, 22 January 1655, *ibid.*, p. 103. Bordeaux told Chanut that everything had been done in London, to put the desires of the French court into effect. Bordeaux "needed [Chanut] and other witnesses to prove it."

27. Bordeaux to Chanut, 5 February 1655, *ibid.*, pp. 128-129.

29. "I had hoped, that this letter would have signified unto you the signing of the treaty." Bordeaux to Brienne, 11 February 1655, *ibid.*, p. 135.

30. Chanut to Bordeaux, 5 March 1655, *ibid.*, p. 168.

31. Bordeaux to his father, 11 February 1655, *ibid.*, p. 137.

32. Letter from Paris, Lands MSS 745, f. 63b.

33. Bordeaux to his father, 19 March 1655, *Thurloe Papers*, 3:185.

34. Bordeaux to Mazarin, 22 March 1655, *ibid.*, p. 221.

35. "His Highness' Speech to Parliament in the Painted Chamber, at their dissolution, upon Monday, the 22nd of January [Old Style] 1655," Abbott, *Writings and Speeches*, 579-593.

36. *Ibid.*, p. 654, see: also pp. 593ff. For a discussion of the uprising as well, Paul Hardacre, *The Royalists during the Puritan Revolution*; and David Underdown, *Royalist Conspiracy in England, 1649-1660*.

37. Abbott, *Writings and Speeches*, 3:593ff.

38. Chanut also stated that "the lord Protector hath as much interest as we have, not to leave any hope to those, who henceforth should frame new revolts under new pretences." Chanut to Bordeaux, 9 April 1655, *Thurloe Papers*, 3:322.

39. The embargo, which operated in Dieppe and Rouen, led to serious doubts in England about Mazarin's policies. One report in the *Mercurius Politicus* said that Mazarin's doubts about the stability of the Protectorate had convinced him that he should not make an alliance with Cromwell. The embargo was supposedly the outward manifestation of this new policy. Another report from Paris stated, "This news [the embargo] filled the whole court with extraordinary rejoycings and if any man doubted of it, he was lookt on as an enemy, so that they all reckoned the Protector a lost man." *Mercurius Politicus*, 29 March to 5 April 1655.

40. *London Newsletter,* 20 March 1655, Clarke MSS 37, reprinted in *Clarke Papers*, 3:29.

41. Bordeaux to Mazarin, 8 April 1655, *Thurloe Papers*, 3:311.

42. Bordeaux to his father, 8 April 1655, *ibid.*, p. 312.

43. Bordeaux (senior) to his son, the ambassador, 17 April 1655, *ibid.*, p. 351.

44. Mazarin to Bordeaux, 10 April 1655, *ibid.*, p. 327. Brienne told Bordeaux that the embargo had been an error, caused by the independent actions of provincial officials. The embargo illustrated the lack of centralized controls in France. Brienne to Bordeaux [10 April 1655], *ibid.*, pp. 328-329.

45. Bordeaux (senior) to his son, the ambassador, 21 April 1655, *ibid.*, p. 363.

46. H. Bennett to Charles II, 16 April 1655, Ormonde MSS *Report of the Historical Manuscripts Commission*, 14th Report, Appendix 7.

47. Note to Bordeaux, from Paris, 27 May 1655, Rawl MSS A26, f. 184.

CHAPTER 11

1. George Drake, "The Ideology of Oliver Cromwell," *Church History*, p. 260.

2. Much of Drake's argument is based on this type of evidence. A more convincing case for Cromwell's attempts to use religious passions for political purposes is presented by George A. Lanyi, "Oliver Cromwell and his age: A study in Nationalism."

3. Thurloe's account of Cromwell's negotiations with France and Spain, *Thurloe Papers*, 1:760.

4. A full discussion of the Puritan feelings toward Spain is in Marvin A. Breslow, *A Mirror of England*, pp. 45-73.

5. Father P [eter] T [albot] to the King, 28 July 1655, *Clarendon State Papers*, 3:144.

6. "Memorial presented by Marquis de Lede and Don Alonso de Cardenas to Cromwell," *Thurloe Papers*, 3:147. For the reactions of Cardenas and de Lede to Cromwell's failure to answer the memorial, see "Letter from the Ambassador of Spain to the Protector." 7 March 1655, *ibid.*, p. 154.

7. Chanut to Bordeaux, 5 March 1655, *ibid.*, p. 168. Chanut also thought that Cromwell would come to an agreement with Spain.

8. A. H. Woolrych, *Penruddock's Rising*, 1655, pp. 23-24.

9. Letter from Mr. Harris, in Madrid, to Thurloe, 13 July 1655, *Thurloe Papers*, 3:609-610.

10. Hyde to Sir H. De Vic, 2 July 1655, *Clarendon State Papers*, 3:128.

11. Fr. Peter Talbot to the King, 16 August 1655, *ibid.*, p. 151.

12. Hyde to Don Luis de Haro, 31 August 1655, *ibid.*, p. 154.

13. Brienne to Bordeaux, 22 September 1655, *Thurloe Papers*, 4:27.

14. "Letter of English merchants Whoe trade in Malaga or Spain, written from Malaga to the Protector," 21 September 1655, *ibid.*, pp. 24-25; also "Petition of Merchants trading in Spain," 30 September 1655, *ibid.*, p. 44.

15. Brienne informed Bordeaux that the seizure of English goods "is a declaration of war between his crown [Spain] and the Commonwealth of England." Brienne either misread the feelings of the King of Spain and the Protector, or he was engaged in a bit of wishful thinking. Brienne to Bordeaux, 22 September 1655, *ibid.*, p. 27.

16. Thurloe to H. Cromwell [19 October 1655], *ibid.*, p. 75.

17. Thurloe to H. Cromwell [2 November 1655], *ibid.*, p. 107.

18. Thurloe to H. Cromwell [19 October 1655], *ibid.*, p. 75.

19. Intelligence from Henry Nillowerve (in Brussels) to Thurloe, 30 October 1655, *ibid.*, p. 99.

20. "The Humble remonstrance of the merchants trading for Spain and its territory to the lord Protector," [November], 1655, *ibid.*, pp. 135-137.

21. Nieupoort to the States General, 5 November 1655, *ibid.*, p. 115.

22. John Bruce, "Memoir on the Diplomatic History of Great Britain . . . from Original Documents preserved in his Majesty's State Papers Office," London, 12 September 1820, B.M. Add MSS 38779.

23. Penn's instructions to Captain William Goodson, commander of the English fleet, remaining in the West Indies, 5 July 1655, *Thurloe Papers*, 3:582-583.

24. *Ibid.*, p. 584.

25. Until the middle of December, Thurloe continued to receive reports that although the King of Spain was angry at Cromwell, he would send

a new ambassador to England. Intercepted letter from Brussels, 11 November 1655, *ibid.*, 4:443; intelligence from Spain 17 December 1655, *ibid.*, p. 292; and letter from Brussels, 18 December 1655, *ibid.*, p. 298.

For accounts of the attack on Hispaniola and its aftermath see C. H. Firth, (ed.) *The Narrative of General Venables*; Granville Penn, ed., *The Memorials of the Professional Life and Times of Sir William Penn*, vol 2; I. A. Wright, ed., *Spanish Narratives of the English Attack on Santo Domingo 1655*; and Frank Strong, "The Causes of Cromwell's West Indian Expedition."

26. Even though Cromwell had attacked the Indies without warning, English merchants in Spain complained that the King had not given them six months' notice (as required by the treaty of 1630 and concessions they had purchased in 1645) before seizing their goods. "Remonstrance on behalf of Spanish merchants, and of the commonwealth in general," *Thurloe Papers*, 4:44-45 The procrastination of the King did not surprise many of Thurloe's agents. Intelligence from Rotterdam, 10 December 1655, *ibid.*, p. 269: and Intelligence from Spain, 17 December 1655, *ibid.*, p. 292. It was also reported to Thurloe that many of Charles's supporters "are beginning to wonder if there will be any help from Spain that will be of use to them."

27. Letter from Spain to Thurloe, 26 January 1656, *ibid.*, p. 419.

28. Letter from Mr. John Johnson [in Spain] 4 February 1656, *ibid.*, p. 461.

29. Boreel to the States General, 4 March 1656, *ibid.*, p. 553.

CHAPTER 12

1. Bordeaux to Brienne, 3 June 1655, *Thurloe Papers*, 3:470.

2. Bordeaux to his father, 3 June 1655, *ibid.*, p. 468.

3. *Ibid.*, p. 469.

4. For further discussion of the relationship between Cromwell's religious feelings and his policies, see Michael F. Foley, "John Thurloe and the Foreign Policy of the Protectorate, 1654-1658." I am in complete agreement with Foley's statement (p. 114): "Religion was a tactic, an ideal to be hoped for . . . but not one to endanger Cromwell's more vital objectives . . . the political circumstances of the Protectorate never allowed Cromwell the luxury of a religious crusade against a foreign enemy. For all of his devotion, Cromwell never allowed his religious ideal to compromise his diplomatic position." For another view, see, Robert S. Paul, *The Lord Protector*, pp. 333-349.

Barrière thought that France had rejected a treaty with Cromwell because he wanted too much control over the fate of the Huguenots. Barrière to Condé, 25 December 1654, B.M. Add MSS 35252, f. 227.

5. Bordeaux was certainly not convinced of the depth of the Protector's concern for his fellow Protestants. The ambassador wrote to Brienne: "I know not now to what I shall attribute the proceeding [the delay

in the negotiations] so contrary to all expectations. The zeal of religion certainly is not able to shake the designs of the lord protector." Bordeaux to Brienne, 3 June 1655, *Thurloe Papers*, 3:470.

6. Abbott, *Writings and Speeches*, 3:233-235.

7. Pell to Thurloe, 30 December 1654, Lands MSS 745, f. 40.

8. Pell to Thurlow, 6 January 1655, *ibid.*, f. 42.

9. Pell to Thurloe, 20 January 1655, *ibid.*, f. 48

10. Pell discounted the influence of the papacy in bringing about peace between France and Spain. Pell to Thurloe, 3 June 1655, *ibid.*, f. 94.

11. Pell to Hugh Peter, 21 April 1655, *ibid.*, f. 77.

12. Abbott, *Writings and Speeches,* 3:707. He has a brief explanation of the confusion about the dates when the news of the "massacre" of the Vaudois reached London.

13. Copy of a letter to Stouppe from Mr. Leger, born in the Piedmont and a divinity reader in Geneva [February 1655], B.M. Add MSS 4l56, f. 144.

14. "Collection of Papers Sent to His Highness the Lord Protector . . . concerning . . . Massacres . . . in Valley of Piedmont."

15. Pell to Thurloe, 8 April 1655 and 27 April 1655, printed in Robert Vaughn, ed., *The Protectorate of Oliver Cromwell* 2:164, 167-169, 171.

16. Thurloe to Pell, 8 May 1655, Vaughn, *The Protectorate of Oliver Cromwell,* 2:175, 177. Thurloe asked Pell to gather information on two important questions: the situation of the surviving Vaudois, and the role played by troops from France in the "massacre."

17. Thurloe to Pell, 25 May 1655, Vaughn, *The Protectorate of Oliver Cromwell,* 2:185. For Cromwell's message to the Duke of Savoy, the Kings of France, Sweden, and Denmark, and the States General, see Abbott, *Writings and Speeches* 3:726-732. Cromwell's actions were described in "The Perfect Diurnall."

18. Pell to Thurloe, 3 June 1655, Lands MSS 745, f. 94. Even Pell, who was in Switzerland, heard reports that the treaty with France was delayed because of the Vaudois, and that Spain was making a new effort for closer ties with Cromwell.

19. Pell to Thurloe, 3 June 1655, *ibid.*, f. 94b.

20. Mr. Leger to Stouppe, 6 June 1655, *Thurloe Papers*, 3:460.

21. Pell to Thurloe, 9 June 1655, Lands MSS 745, f. 101b.

22. Chanut to Bordeaux, 11 June 1655, *Thurloe Papers.* 3:498. Intelligence from Brussels to Thurloe 12 June 1655, *ibid.*, p. 502. Intelligence from Paris to Thurloe, 16 June 1655, *ibid.*, p. 520. These reports agreed on the strong reaction against the Duke of Savoy in Protestant (and some Catholic) countries. The intelligence from France also discussed the responsibility of France. "I do believe the King is innocent . . . as of many other fould acts executed by the commands of Cardinal Mazarin, who, to ingratiate himself to the new pope, and show a great zeal, is likely to have given orders to the French regiment, that were in Savoy, to do as they have done."

23. Intelligence from Paris to Thurloe, 16 June 1655, *ibid.*, p. 520.

520. Mazarin to Bordeaux, 19 June 1655, *ibid.*, p. 536.

24. Pell to Thurloe, 23 June 1655, and Thurloe to Pell, 12 July 1655, Vaughn, *The Protectorate of Oliver Cromwell*, 2:204, 219.

25. Copy of amnesty proposed by French ambassador, to the Protestants of the Vallies of Piedmont, *Thurloe Papers*, 3:626-627.

26. Letter from the Piedmont to Thurloe, 27 July 1655, *ibid.*, p. 654. Morland was taken on a tour of the Piedmont by French officials. They tried to convince him to tell Cromwell that France intended to protect the religious liberties of the Vaudois. Servien was annoyed at councillors of Savoy for replying to Morland "that those, who govern at present in England, ought to think it so much the less ill, in regard they have banisht and ill used the Catholics of Ireland, England and Scotland, to the prejudice of the concessions, which their legal kings had granted them." Pell reported that Swiss Protestants were waiting to see what Servien and France would do for the Vaudois. Pell to Thurloe, 14 August 1655, Lands MSS 745, f. 129.

27. Pell to Thurloe, 14 August 1655, Lands MSS 745, f. 129.

28. Servien, one of Mazarin's envoys to the Duke of Savoy, wanted a treaty concluded to give the Vaudois some religious liberties, but he made it clear that he had little regard for them. He also told the Vaudois that Louis had intervened in their behalf "to oblige the lord protector, who has taken this business to heart." Servien to Bordeaux, 21 August 1655, *Thurloe Papers*, 3:706. Brienne, in the same context, wrote to Bordeaux, "the chiefest reason, which did invite his majesty to interpose in this business, was his desire to make known to the protector . . . that he hath no aversion against those who make profession of the pretended protestant religion, and that it did displease him, that his troops had executed that which had been resolved by the Duke of Savoy." Brienne to Bordeaux, 3 September 1655, *ibid.*, p. 731.

29. Brienne to Bordeaux, 3 September 1655, *ibid.*, pp. 731-732.

30. *Mercurius Politicus* (6 September 1655 to 13 September 1655) printed a copy of the treaty and made "some observations on it." It was "alas a Peace far worse than the worst of war, forced on us [Vaudois] by the *minaces* of the *French Ambassador* and the falsehood of *others* entrusted . . . in the Treaty. The main grievances expressed in the *Mercurius Politicus* were: (1) The Protestants had to admit to being rebels against the Duke of Savoy. (2) Catholics could tell Protestants where to live. (3) Catholics had no restrictions placed on them. (4) There was no way to enforce the treaty on the Duke. In the next issue, the *Mercurius Politicus* printed a letter that supposedly originated in the Piedmont. It thanked the Protector for saving the Vaudois from destruction, but appealed to him to stop the treaty that Servien was forcing on the Vaudois.

Another letter summed up much of the correspondence concerning the reception of the treaty by Protestant leaders on the Continent, especially those in Savoy. "They accuse the French ambassador of the menacing part . . . and many of them do not believe that England showed warmth enough in this occasion." There were also questions raised concerning the disposition of the money that had been collected in England for the relief of the Vaudois. Mr. Longe to Colonel Bampfylde, 29 September 1655, *Thurloe Papers*, 4:43.

31. Bordeaux to Mazarin, 2 September 1655, B.M. Add MSS 4156, f. 203.

32. Brienne to Bordeaux, 15 July 1655, *Thurloe Papers*, 3:613.

CHAPTER 13

1. Bordeaux rejected the view held by other foreign observers that Cromwell and his advisers had been too shocked by the defeat at Hispaniola to react to Bordeaux's proposals. The ambassador reasoned that the provisions of the treaty had not changed much since October, 1654, and Cromwell had been able to study them since then.

2. Intelligence from Paris to Thurloe, 31 July 1655, *Thurloe Papers*, 3:679.

3. Intelligence from Paris to Thurloe, 31 July 1655, *ibid.*, p. 658. Another of Thurloe's informants reported that there was a belief in Paris that "Spain is so low; that if he not be assisted, he will be in danger to lose all he hath in the Low Countries," *ibid.*, p. 679.

4. Instructions from the King [Charles] to ambassador at Rome, June, 1655, *Clarendon State Papers*, 3:123.

5. Extract from a letter from Rome [to Hyde], 26 June 1655, *Thurloe Papers*, 3:124.

6. Newsletter from Paris, 11 July 1655, P.R.O. State Papers, France, f. 54b.

7. "News from Paris," 24 July 1655, *ibid.*, f. 58.

8. Report of the Swedish ambassador (in London) to home (trans. C. H. Firth) 23 August 1655, B.M. Add MSS 38100, f. 4b. Charles Longland, (England's representative at Leghorn) to Thurloe, 27 August 1655, *Thurloe Papers*, 3:720.

9. Letter to Downing, sent from Geneva, 2 September 1655, B.M. Add MSS 22919, f. 7. The author of the letter said that Downing had written him earlier, saying that it was not safe to see the King of France.

10. Downing to Thurloe, 4 September 1655, *Thurloe Papers*, 3:734-735.

11. Bordeaux (senior) to his son, the ambassador, 7 September 1655, *ibid.*, p. 740.

12. Chanut to Bordeaux, 30 September 1655, *ibid.*, p. 749.

13. Bordeaux (senior) to Mazarin, 12 September 1655, B.M. Add MSS 4156, f. 210. The letter made it clear that Bordeaux's son, the ambassador, wanted to stay in London long enough to complete the negotiations for the treaty.

14. Bordeaux (senior) to his son, 17 September 1655, *Thurloe Papers*, 4:12.

15. *Ibid.* Both the ambassador and his father feared that a new

ambassador to England would receive credit for making the treaty, even though Bordeaux had done the work.

16. *Ibid.* The ambassador was advised by his father, "I would either bring him [Cromwell] to a conclusion of the treaty, or a rupture, in a short time."

17. *Ibid.*

18. Bordeaux to his father, 4 October 1655, *ibid.*, p. 51.

19. Thurloe to H. Cromwell, 19 October 1655, *ibid.*, p. 75. Thurloe's statement makes Bordeaux's optimism (and his opposition to any attempt to replace him) more reasonable.

20. Thurloe to H. Cromwell, 2 November 1655, *ibid.*, p. 107.

21. Nieupoort to States General, 5 November 1655, *ibid.*, pp. 115-116.

22. "Articles of Peace, Friendship, and Entercourse Concluded and Agreed between England and France . . . the third of November, new stile, in the year of our Lord God, 1655 (London, Henry Hills and John Field, Printers to his Highness, 1655), B.M. Add MSS 40795, f. 22. Jean Dumont, *Corps universal diplomatique de droit des gens: depuis le regne de l'empereur Charlemagne jusquis a present: contenant un Recueil de Traitez,* vol. 6, part 2, pp. 121-124.

23. "List of people to be excluded from France," 3 November 1655, Egerton MSS 2542, f. 6. See also *Thurloe Papers,* 4:114.

24. "Treaty of 3 November 1655," State Papers 103 (P.R.O.), v. 12, ff. 52-66. Thurloe's comments on the treaty begin with f. 68.

25. Also Abbott, *Writings and Speeches,* 3:841.

26. Hyde to de Vic, 26 November 1655, *Clarendon State Papers,* 3:1851.

27. P[eter] T[albot] to the King, 9 December 1655, *ibid.*, pp. 191-192.

28. Hyde to Lord Norwich, 21 December 1655, *ibid.*, p. 200.

29. Intercepted letter, from Hyde, 23 November 1655, *Thurloe Papers,* 4:188.

30. Intercepted letter, from Brussels, 27 November 1655, *ibid.*, p. 210. See also George A. Lanyi, "Oliver Cromwell and his age: a Study in Nationalism."

31. Intelligence from Cologne to Thurloe, 9 November 1655, *Thurloe Papers,* 4:122. For a more complete account of James's position in France, see *The Memoirs of James II: His Campaigns as Duke of York 1652-1660, pp. 57-225.*

32. Henrietta Maria to Charles II, 26 November 1655, Lambeth MSS 645, Article 97, reprinted in *Letters of Henrietta Maria.*

33. Intelligence from Cologne to Thurloe, 9 November 1655, *Thurloe Papers,* 4:122.

34. Mazarin to Bordeaux, 9 November 1655, *ibid.*, p. 121.

35. Papers of Colonel Bampfylde (one of Thurloe's most important informants, who had worked his way into the confidence of many of the leading Royalists) [10 December] 1655, *ibid.*, p. 268.

36. Longland to Thurloe, 31 December 1655, *ibid.*, p. 331.

37. Chanut to Bordeaux, 12 November 1655, *ibid.*, p. 146.

38. Intelligence from The Hague to Thurloe, 19 November 1655, *ibid.*,

p. 174. The role of the Protectorate in the Baltic has been brilliantly discussed by Michael Roberts, "Cromwell and the Baltic."

39. Intelligence form The Hague to Thurloe, 20 November 1655, *Thurloe Papers*, 4:200.

40. Intelligence from The Hague to Thurloe, 25 November 1655, *ibid.*, p. 201.

41. Intelligence from the Hague to Thurloe, 26 November 1655, *ibid.*, p. 202.

42. *Ibid.*, p. 203. Also letter from The Hague, 16 December 1655, *ibid.*, p. 285.

43. Intelligence from The Hgue to Thurloe, 17 December 1655, *ibid.*, p. 289.

44. Pell to [Thurloe] 14 November 1655, Lands MSS 746, f. 41b.

45. Report of the Swedish ambassador (trans. C. H. Firth), 11 January 1656, B.M. Add MSS 38100, f. 10.

46. Report of Swedish ambassador, 11 January 1656, *ibid.*

47. Longland to Thurloe, 18 December 1655, *Thurloe Papers*, 4:295.

CHAPTER 14

1. Mazarin to Bordeaux, 9 November 1655, *Thurloe Papers*, 4:120.

2. Kelsey to Thurloe, 9 December 1655, *ibid.*, p. 293. See also Abbott, *Writings and Speeches*, 4:38.

3. Cromwell to Louis XIV, 4 December 1655, *ibid.*, pp. 38-40.

4. Bordeaux to M. de la Bastide, 15 January 1656, *Thurloe Papers*, 4:392.

5. M. Augier to the Protector, 12 January 1656, *ibid.*, p. 375.

6. Cromwell, while complaining about Mazarin's conduct, was not prompt in implementing the secret articles in England. He allowed Barrière to remain in England until 1 April 1656, Condé to Fiesque, B.M. Add MSS 35252, f. 239. The break between Barrière and Cromwell was accomplished with a minimum of bitterness, and Barrière and Condé retained hopes that Cromwell would change his mind and help them at a later time. Condé to Barrière, 25 March 1656, *Thurloe Papers*, 4:618. Barrière to the Protector 29 April 1656, *Thurloe Papers*, 4:748.

7. Boreel, one of the best informed of the diplomatic observers, wrote the States General "that the lord protector was very earnest for a league offensive and defense [with France], not as a general business against all, but Spain alone, with whom both kingdoms were ready to engage in an open war." Boreel to the States General, 7 February 1656, *Thurloe Papers*, 4:470.

8. Mazarin thought that Cromwell's main reason for sending an ambassador to France was the rumor that France was engaged in secret peace talks with Spain. Mazarin told Bordeaux to convince Cromwell that the rumor was false. The Cardinal also instructed Bordeaux, "You will do well to persuade my lord protector, if you can, not to send an

ambassador to this court." Mazarin to Bordeaux, 26 April 1656, *ibid.*, p. 703.

9. The council gave Lockhart his orders to proceed to France and bills of exchange on 19 April 1656, *Thurloe Papers*, p. 688.

10. Instructions to Lockhart, P.R.O. State Papers, France, f. 84b.

11. *Ibid.*, f. 85b.

12. See *Dictionary of National Biography* article for summary of Morrell's activities.

13. Lockhart was also instructed to "use all possible endeavours by such proper medium as you shall see fitt to hinder and obstruct the aforesaid peace [between France and Spain]." Lockhart was also to keep in communication with Pell and other English representatives in the Protestant communities. He was told to "try to influence France in favour of the Protestant cantons" and remind France of its obligations to the Vaudois. Instructions to Lockhart, April 1656, P.R.O. State Papers, France, f. 86.

14. Lockhart to Thurloe, 6 May 1656 (written from Dieppe), *Thurloe Papers*, 4:739.

15. Lockhart to Thurloe (received in London, 14 May 1656), B.M. Add MSS 4157, ff. 58-59.

16. Lockhart to Thurloe, 24 May 1656, *Thurloe Papers*, 5:21.

17. Lockhart to Thurloe, 2 June 1656, *ibid.*, pp. 52-54.

18. This suggestion by Cromwell was intended to serve two purposes: to pay his army, and to counter Mazarin's apology that France's forces were too weak to do much at that time.

19. The Protector to Lockhart, 3 June 1656, *ibid.*, p. 41.

20. Lockhart to Thurloe, 28 June 1656, *ibid.*, p. 131.

21. Lockhart to Thurloe, 30 June 1656, *ibid.*, pp. 142-143.

22. Lockhart to Thurloe, 10 July 1656, *ibid.*, p. 172.

23. Lockhart to Thurloe, 20 July 1656, *ibid.*, p. 202. Lockhart also complained to Henry Cromwell that nothing had happened in France since the start of the embassy. Lockhart to Henry Cromwell, 30 July 1656, Lands MSS 821, f. 210.

24. Letters of intelligence from Paris, 19 July 1656, *Thurloe Papers*, 5:198.

25. Letter of William Swft to Thurloe, 26 July 1656, B.M. Add MSS 32093, f. 343.

26. Letter of intelligence from Sir G. Ratliffe, in Paris, 19 August 1656, *Thurloe Papers*, 5:294.

27. Lockhart to Thurloe, 24 July 1656, *ibid.*, p. 210.

28. *Ibid.*

29. Lockhart to Thurloe, 26 July 1656, *ibid.*, p. 217.

30. Lockhart to Thurloe, 26 July 1656, *ibid.*, p. 218.

31. *Ibid.*

32. Lockhart to Thurloe, 8 August 1656, *ibid.*, p. 252.

33. *Ibid.*, p. 253.

34. Lockhart to Thurloe, 24 May 1656, *ibid.*, p. 21.

35. Lockhart to Thurloe, 9 June 1656, *ibid.*, p. 75.
36. Lockhart to Thurloe, 8 August 1656, *ibid.*, p. 253.
37. *Ibid.*

CHAPTER 15

1. Intelligence from Zurich, 1 June 1656, B.M. Lands MSS 747, f. 84b. This letter emphasized that the threat posed by raiders from Flanders was increased by the alliance between Charles Stuart and Spain.
2. In June, the "Dunkirkers" took twenty English ships that had sailed from Holland. Intelligence from Antwerp to the Venetian agent in London, 10 June 1656, *Thurloe Papers*, 5:78. The impact of the "Dunkirkers" was shown again when "The King [of Denmark] cannot send you [Cromwell] the horses which he promised the protector, by reason of the threat at sea by the Dunkirkers." Intelligence from Copenhagen to Petkum, 6 July 1656, *ibid.*, p. 160.
3. Cromwell to Blake and Montague, 19 June 1656, *ibid.*, p. 701.
4. Lockhart to Thurloe, 27 August 1656, *ibid.*, pp. 317-318, contained Lockhart's views about a campaign to capture Dunkirk.
5. Mazarin tried to convince Lockhart that the only reason for the delay of the treaty was written assurances from Cromwell that Lockhart had the power to contract it. Lockhart to Thurloe, 21 October 1656, *ibid.*, p. 488. After Lockhart resolved the complaint, the Cardinal began to quibble over the exact charges for Cromwell's troops. Lockhart to Thurloe, 8 November 1656, *ibid.*, pp. 532-533.
6. Lockhart to Thurloe, 8 October 1656, *ibid.*, p. 450. Lockhart was disturbed by the negotiations taking place between representatives of Condé and Mazarin. If there was an accommodation between them, Lockhart thought "that the Cardinal (whatever pretences he hath had to the contrary) intends a peace with Spain in good earnest. . . . the restoration of princes stuck more with him, than either the redelivery of towns, or the leaving of his allies to the Spanysh mercy." Lockhart to Thurloe, 3 October 1656, *ibid.*, p. 441.
7. Intelligence from Madrid to Thurloe, 23 September 1656, *ibid.*, p. 412.
8. Lockhart to Thurloe, 3 October 1656, *ibid.*, p. 441. Brienne assured Bordeaux, "Those reports in London which you hear about a peace between his majesty and the King of Spain, have little ground here." Brienne to Bordeaux, 11 November 1656, *ibid.*, p. 546.
9. Lockhart to Thurloe, 11 September 1656, *ibid.*, p. 368.
10. *Ibid.*, p. 369.
11. Intelligence from Bruges to Thurloe, 6 October 1656, *ibid.*, p. 447. Intelligence from Slys to Thurloe, 21 October 1656, *ibid.*, p. 489. The latter summed up the situation, "It is supposed that the French will next summer sweepe away the most parts of Flanders, especially if the English join with them."

12. Lockhart to Thurloe, 11 November 1656, *ibid.*, p. 574.

13. Lockhart to Thurloe, 25 November 1656, *ibid.*, p. 594.

14. Lockhart to Thurloe, 14 Februar 1657, *ibid.*, 6:39. Turenne visited Lockhart to make sure that differences of opinion concerning Dunkirk had not lessened the amity between Cromwell and Turenne.

15. Lockhart to Thurloe, 11 February 1656, *ibid.*, p. 32.

16. For the text of the treaty of 13 March 1657, see Abbott, *Writings and Speeches*, 4:911-915. The secret articles are on pages 911-915. Lockhart's comments about the final arrangements for the treaty, Lockhart to Thurloe, 10 March 1657, P.R.O. State Papers, France, f. 107.

17. Lockhart to Thurloe, 26 February 1657, *Thurloe Papers*, 6:63.

18. Lockhart to Thurloe, 17 February 1657, *ibid.*, p. 44.

19. For text of the secret article, see P.R.O. State Papers, 103, XXI, f. 80, or B.M. Add MSS 32093, ff. 377-378.

20. Longland to Thurloe, 2 September 1656, *Thurloe Papers*, 5:338. Longland asserted that Spain offered Dunkirk to the Dutch in return for an alliance against England.

21. Papers of Colonel Bampfylde [10 December 1655], *ibid.*, 4:268.

22. For an excellent discussion of feelings in England about the loss of Calais, see R. B. Wernham, *Before the Armada*, pp. 232-240, 265-267.

23. Major General Whalley to the Protector, 21 August 1656, *Thurloe Papers*, 5:299.

24. Cromwell's speech at the opening of Parliament, 17 September 1656, Abbott, *Writings and Speeches*, 4:26-79.

25. Bordeaux to Mazarin, 28 September 1656, *Thurloe Papers*, 5:427.

26. Thurloe to Henry Cromwell, 9 October 1656, *ibid.*, p. 454. In another letter, Thurloe stated, "the house expresses a good readiness [to support the war against Spain] . . . if any things can be done this way without taxinge the people too high." Thurloe also commented on the value of the war, "Successe against Spain hath somewhat discouraged our enemies [in Parliament and the country]." Thurloe to Henry Cromwell, 7 November 1656, *ibid.*, pp. 524-525.

27. Major General Boteler to Montagu, 9 January 1657, Carte MSS 73, f. 18. Bordeaux to M———, 11 January 1657, B.M. Add MSS 31953, f. 3.

28. Thurloe to Henry Cromwell, 7 November 1657, *Thurloe Papers*, 5:524.

29. Major General Boteler to Montagu, 9 January 1657, Carte MSS 73, f. 18. Examinations of John Toop and John Cecill by the council, 19 January 1657, *Thurloe Papers*, 5:774, 776. The fear expressed by army leaders was that Parliament was trying to gain control over the army.

30. Intelligence from Mr. Vincent Gookin, 13 February 1657, *Thurloe Papers*, 6:37.

31. Bordeaux to Mazarin, 26 February 1657, printed in Francois P. G. *History of . . . the English Commonwealth*, 2:Appendix.

32. Bordeaux to ———, 22 March 1657, *Thurloe Papers*, 6:76.

33. Bordeaux to ———, 29 March 1657, *ibid.*, 87.

34. Declaration of members of Parliament, lately dissolved by Cromwell [September, 1656], *ibid.*, 5:420. Despite grumblings against Cromwell, his position was still secure. The Venetian Giavarina well summed up the situation, "But unless there is some dissension among the troops who form the support of the Protector, he has nothing to fear." Giavarina to the Doge, 15 September 1656, *Calendar of State Papers . . . Venice*, 31:261.

35. Intelligence from Utrecht to Thurloe, 16 March 1657, *Thurloe Papers*, 6:99.

36. Brienne to Bordeaux, 11 November 1656, *ibid.*, 5:546.

37. Intelligence from The Hague to Thurloe, 17 November 1656, *ibid.*, p. 568.

38. Courtin to Bordeaux (written from The Hague) 24 November 1656, *ibid.*, p. 587.

39. Boreel to the States General, 14 December 1656, *ibid.*, p. 682.

40. Nieupoort to the States General, 20 December 1656, *ibid.*, p. 697.

41. Intelligence from Holland to Thurloe, 22 December 1656, *ibid.*, p. 701.

42 Commission of Admiralty to Admiral de Ruyter, 20 December 1656, *ibid.*, p. 696.

43. Intelligence from The Hague, 23 February 1657, *ibid.*, 6:60-61.

44. Christopher Hill, *God's Englishman*.

45. Letter of Intelligence from The Hague for Stouppe, 9 March 1657, *Thurloe Papers*, 6:82.

46. Sir Charles Harding Firth, *The Last Years of the Protectorate, 1656-1658*, 1:263.

47. Boreel to the States General, 30 March 1657, *Thurloe Papers*, 6:133.

48. Courtin to Bordeaux (from The Hague), 6 April 1657, *ibid.*, p. 147.

49. Letter from Boreel, 6 April 1657, *ibid.*, p. 148.

50. "Part of the resolution of the States General," 11 April 1657, *ibid.* p. 159.

51. Lockhart to Thurloe, 13 April 1657, *ibid.*, p. 164.

52. Lockhart to Thurloe, 7 April 1657, *ibid.*, p. 149.

53. Brienne to Bordeaux, 28 April 1657, *ibid.*, p. 214.

54. Courtin to Bordeaux, 20 April 1657, *ibid.*, p. 191.

55. Intelligence from The Hague, 2 June 1657, B.M. Add MSS 21233, f. 22. This letter supported the view that the Dutch were afraid to make peace with France because they feared the treachery of the Protector.

56. Lockhart to Thurloe, 31 May 1657, *Thurloe Papers*, 6:209.

57. Nieupoort to Ruysch, 1 June 1657, *ibid.*, p. 303.

58. Thurloe to Henry Cromwell, 5 June 1657, *ibid.*, p. 311.

59. Nieupoort to Ruysch, 22 June 1657, *ibid.*, p. 347.

60. Excerpt from de Thou's memoirs, 13 June 1657, B.M. Add MSS 21233, f. 25.

61. Section from the "register of the States General," 26 June 1657, *Thurloe Papers*, 6:350.

62. "Memoire pour . . . Deputies des Provinces," July, 1657, B.M. Add MSS 21233.

63. Nieupoort to Ruysch, 22 June 1657, *Thurloe Papers*, 6:347.

64. Nieupoort to Ruysch, 13 July 1657, B.M. Add MSS 21233, f. 102.

65. Nieupoort to Ruysch, 20 July 1657, *ibid.*, f. 103.

66. Boreel to Ruysch, 18 May 1657, *Thurloe Papers*, 6:273. Boreel said that the Protector had supposedly told Nieupoort that if the States General broke with France, "then the protector would remain no longer a friend of the United Provinces."

67. "Memoir for the Deputies of the Provinces," July, 1657, B.M. Add MSS 21233, f. 49.

68. Memorial of Downing to the States General, 28 January 1658, B.M. Add MSS 7677X, f. 13. Memorial of Downing to the States General, 13 March 1658, *ibid.*, f. 38b.

69. Lockhart to Thurloe, 25 April 1657, *Thurloe Papers*, 6:202.

70. *Calendar of State Papers, Domestic Series, 1656-1657*, 10:372-374.

71. Lockhart to Thurloe, 28 and 31 May 1657, *Thurloe Papers*, 6:290, 297.

72. Lockhart to Thurloe, 31 May 1657, *ibid.*, p. 295.

73. Lockhart to Thurloe, 1 June 1657, *ibid.*, p. 301. Lockhart also feared that the defeat at Cambrai might cause a break between Mazarin and Turenne. The ambassador wanted to prevent that. He regarded Turenne as the best general serving France, and had special regard for Turenne's religious situation.

74. Cromwell to Lockhart, 10 September 1657, *ibid.*, p. 489.

75. Lockhart to Thurloe, 14 August 1657, *ibid.*, p. 437.

76. Lockhart to Thurloe, 12 September 1657, *ibid.*, p. 495.

77. Thurloe to Lockhart, 25 February 1658, *ibid.*, p. 804.

78. Lockhart to Thurloe, 17 March 1658, *ibid.*, p. 853. Michael F. Foley, "John Thurloe and the Foreign Policy of the Protectorate," pp. 235ff.

79. Sir Charles Harding Firth, *The Last Years of the Protectorate*, 2:184-185, 190-200.

80. Clyde L. Grose, "England and Dunkirk", *American Historical Review*, 39 (1933), 1-27.

81. "The Delivery of Dunkirke to the English Defended from the Malise of Libellers and Enemyes by the Chancelour of France (P. Seguier)," B. M. Sloane MSS 3083. This tract was written shortly after Cromwell's troops took control of Dunkirk. It spelled out the complaints that had been made in France against Mazarin's action, and then defended him on the grounds that he had acted in the interests of France.

CHAPTER 16

1. Edward Gibbon, *Letters*, (New York, 1956), 3:286.

2. Speech of Oliver Cromwell to Parliament, 25 January 1658, Abbott, *Writings and Speeches*, 4:713.

3. *Ibid.*, p. 714.

4. See also Godfrey Davies, *The Restoration of Charles II*, 1658-1660, p. 174. This point was forcefully made by Cardinal de Retz, "who claimed that the alliance with England had doomed France to eternal war since Cromwell could not advance the general peace, the greatest block in the way of his fortune." The statement was made in one of de Retz's pamphlets condemning the ministry of Mazarin. *France no Friend to England*, p. 18.

5. Abbott, *Writings and Speeches*, 4:714.

6. The delays by the Protector, and Bordeaux's and Cardenas's responses to them, led to much mockery of the Kings of France and Spain. The most flagrant example of this was a picture for sale showing Cromwell "on a close-stool at his business and the King of Spain on one side and the King of France on the other, offering him paper to wipe his breech." Letter of intelligence to Thurloe, 28 July 1655, *Thurloe Papers*, 6:658.

7. Montagu's account of the debates in the Protector's council, 20 April 1654 and 20 July 1654, *Clarke Papers*, vol 3, Appendix B, pp. 203ff.

8. George Drake, "The Ideology of Oliver Cromwell," pp. 259-272.

9. Marvin A. Breslow, "English Puritan Views of Foreign Nations, 1618-1640," p. 500 A revision of this work was published in 1969 as *A Mirror of England*.

10. Breslow, "English Puritan Views of Foreign Nations," p. 125.

11. For a provocative interpretation of the economic considerations behind Cromwell's foreign policy, see Christopher Hill, *God's Englishman*, pp. 154-168.

12. "Concerning the Foreign Affairs in the Protector's Time"— "Belonging to H. Powle (Speaker of the Convention) who said the original was supposedly drawn up by Thurloe," B.M. Add MSS 35838, ff. 188-191. This manuscript does not contradict the printed version that was supplied to Hyde, but it contain's more pointed criticisms of the actions of Charles II.

13. *Ibid.*, f. 189.

14. *Ibid.*, f. 191.

15. "The Court Career, Death Shadowe'd to Life." Much of the post-Restoration literature dealing with Cromwell's foreign policy stressed the ability of Mazarin and the way in which he used Cromwell's desire for power to dupe him into acting as a tool of French ambition. For example, see Benjamin Priola, *The History of France under the Ministry of Cardinal Mazarin*.

16. Edward Hyde, Earl of Clarendon, *The History of the Rebellion and Civil Wars in England*, 6:94.

17. Slingsby Bethel, *The World's Mistake in Oliver Cromwell*. The phrase "interest" was widely used by both supporters and critics of Cromwell's policies toward France during the Interregnum as well as after the Restoration. Some very good examples of this controversy include: John Fell *The Interest of England stated*; John Harris, *Peace*

and not Warre: or the Moderator; Robert MacWard, *The English Ballance: weighing the Reasons of England's present Conjunction with France*; J. Heath, *Flagellum, or the Life and death, birth and burial of Oliver Cromwell*; J. Heath, *Discourse upon the moderne affaires of Europe.*

18. "Thurloe's account of Cromwell's negotiations with France and Spain from the time of Oliver Cromwell's assuming power to the restoration." *Thurloe Papers*, 1:760.

19. *Ibid.*, pp. 761-763.

20. Michael F. Foley, "John Thurloe and the Foreign Policy of the Protectorate, 1654-1658," especially pp. 114-117.

21. Christopher Hill, *Oliver Cromwell*, p. 21.

22. Samuel Rawson Gardiner, *History of the Commonwealth and Protectorate*, 3:83.

23. *Clarke Papers*, 4:143-146.

24. Thurloe's memorandum also stressed the idea that England was protected from attack by the Channel. He viewed the invasion routes across the Channel as only a one-way passage.

25. See the discussion on Mary and Calais in R. B. Wernham, *Before the Armada*, pp. 232-240, 265-267. Seguier, *The Delivery of Dunkirke to the English*, B. M. Sloane MSS 3083, ff. 2b-4, stressed the point that Cromwell had played off France against Spain in order to get more concessions before allying with either. Seguier accepted the assertion (it also provided him with a convenient justification for Mazarin's policies) that Spain had offered Calais to England in exchange for an alliance, and that Cromwell had seriously considered accepting the offer.

26. "Breslow, English Puritan Views of Foreign Nations," p. 141.

27. Clarendon to Lockhart, 10 September 1657, *Thurloe Papers*, 6:489.

28. For the anti-Cromwell view, see Fell, *The Interest of England Stated*; Harris, *Peace and Not Warre*. For a favorable view of Cromwell's policy, see Michael Hawke, *Killing is Murder and no Murder*, which was a reply to: William Allen, *Killing, No Murder*; also see *Discourse upon the moderne affaires of Europe: The French Intrigues Discovered.*

29. "Concerning the Foreign Affairs in the Protector's Time," B.M. Add MSS 34838, f. 191. The memorandum also pointed out the advantages of forcing Charles to ally with Spain. If a combination of Spain and the Irish tried to restore Charles, "it was conceived [by the Protector and Thurloe] to be the likeliest Means of Uniting the Severall divided Interests of the Kingdome together in that Quarrell."

30. Much of the later support for Cromwell's policies was brought about by the feeling that Charles II was doing nothing to combat Louis XIV's attempt to achieve hegemony in Europe. Complaints against Charles often focused on his sale of Dunkirk. For some examples, see: *Discourse upon the modern affaires of Europe: The French Intrigues Discovered*; *The French Politician Found Out* (London, 1680). Even Slingsby Bethel warned that the policies of Charles II were endangering England's

interests. See: *The Interest of Princes and States*; and *An Account of the French Usurpation upon the trade of England*. The sale of Dunkirk was defended by: J. Howell, *Discourse of Dunkirk, with some Reflexes upon the late surrender thereof*; and Edward Hyde, the Earl of Clarendon, *The History of the Reign of Charles II*, pp. 428ff.

31. See Michael Roberts, "Cromwell and the Baltic," p. 175, for a discussion of Thurloe's realiability as a witness and historian. However, Thurloe's desire to justify the programs of the Protector does not negate the plausibility of his explanations. Even if the Protector's plans were not as far-reaching as Thurloe stated, they were still formulated within the context he described. For another explanation of Cromwell's policies, which parallels Thurloe's explanations for the reasons behind it but which does not justify Cromwell's actions, see *Discourse of the National Excellencies of England*.

32. Roberts, "Cromwell and the Baltic," p. 174.

33. For further discussion of the international aspects of the Revolution on France, see: Philip A. Knachel, *England and the Fronde*; and Christopher Hill, "The English Revolution and the Brotherhood of Man," in *Puritanism and Revolution*, pp. 123-152.

34. Christopher Hill, in his pamphlet *Oliver Cromwell*, pointed out the importance of the instability of the regime and the compromises the Protector had to make in order to retain his power. Hill also saw that something had to be done to give a mission to the army—an aim for which the alliances with France were well suited.

35. For a valuable discussion of the delayng tactics of Queen Elizabeth, see Charles Wilson, *Queen Elizabeth and the Revolt of the Netherlands*, especially pp. 122-136. In earlier chapters, Wilson presents an important set of criteria by which foreign policy should be evaluated.

36. An interesting English summary of Mazarin is presented in *An Impartial Character of that famous Politician and late admired Minister of State, Cardinal Mazarine*.

37. In the spring and summer of 1657, there was serious consideration given in England to the possibility of having to support Mazarin in order for him to retain his position in France. A letter of intelligence from one of Thurloe's informants, who had supplied him with valuable information in the past, discussed this problem in its most extreme form. The letter described Mazarin as "cursed up and downe Paris" for concluding an alliance with England. Despite its inaccurate predictions concerning Mazarin, the letter did point out the benefits that Cromwell and Mazarin gained from their cooperation, and described why both of them wanted to continue the alliance. The author also realized the dangers posed to England by a general peace, and tried to demonstrate why Mazarin wanted to avoid peace as long as it did not endanger his position in France. Rawl MSS A50, 1277.

38. For a more favorable view of Cromwell's policies, if not his motives, see Bethel, *The Interest of Princes and States*. Implied criticisms of Charles II's foreign policies were well articulated in Marchmont Nedham,

Christianissimus Christianandous or the Reason for the Reduction of France to a more Christian State in Europe; and *Discourse upon the moderne affaires of Europe: The French Intrigues Discovered.*

39. William Lamont, *Godly Rule*, esp. pp. 136-186.
40. Hill, *Oliver Cromwell*, 19.
41. Hill, *God's Englishman*, p. 257.
42. *Ibid.*, pp. 165-166.

Bibliography

Manuscripts Cited in the Text

British Museum
    Additional Manuscripts 4156, 4157, 4180, 12186, 15856, 15858, 17677X, 21233, 22919, 29550, 31953, 31954, 32093, 35252, 35838, 37047, 38100, 38779, 38847, 40795.
    Egerton Manuscripts 2542.
    Birch Manuscripts 4156, 4157.
    Landsdowne Manuscripts 745, 747, 821.
    Sloane Manuscripts 3083, 4188.
    Stowe Manuscripts 85, 132, 133, 142.

Bodleian Library
    Rawlinson Manuscripts A17, A22.
    Carte Manuscripts 1, 73, 119.

Public Records Office
    SP 78 (State Papers, France).
    SP 103 (Treaty Papers).
    Transcripts of Paris Archives, Nos. 31/3/90-31/3/96.

Worcester College, Oxford
    Coxe Manuscripts 27, 37.

Pamphlet Collections Cited In The Text

British Museum, Thomason Collection
E574 (2) *A Declaration of the Most Christian King, Louis the XIV, King of France and Navarre Declaring the Reasons wherefore his Majesty Hath prohibited all Trade with England also that He hath given Commission to raise an Army for the assistance of the King of England* (London, 2 September 1649).

253

E663 (5) *A Great Victory obtained by the King of France against the Prince of Condé . . . his [Charles Stuart] granting forth new commissions to make war with England* (London, 1652 [1 May]).

E701 (9) *The Daily Proceedings, of the Army by Sea and Land under the Command of his Excellency, the Lord General Cromwell.*

E708 (2) *Mercurius Politicus* (28 July 1653).

E831 (7) *Mercurius Politicus* (29 March to 5 April 1655).

E842 (1) "The Perfect Diurnall" (28 May to 4 June 1655).

E842 (11) "Collection of Papers sent to His Highness the Lord Protector . . . concerning . . . massacres . . . in Valley of Piedmont" (London, 1655).

E853 (22) *Mercurius Politicus* (6 September 1655 to 13 September 1655).

E1085 (4) *An Impartial Character of That Famous Politician and late admired Minister of State, Cardinal Mazarine* (London, 22 March 1660).

E1583 (2) "Discourse of the National Excellencies of England" (London, 21 Novmber 1657).

L699 f. 14 *An Act Prohibiting the Importing of any Wines, Wool, or Silk from the Kingdom of France into the Commonwealth of England or Ireland or any of the Dominions thereunto belonging* (London, 1649).

London Museum, Tangye Collection

136 "The Court Career, Death Shadowe'd to Life" (London, 1659).

Published Primary Sources

Abbott, Wilbur Cortez, *The Writings and Speeches of Oliver Cromwell*, 4 vols. (Cambridge, Mass., 1937-1947).

Allen, William [Edward Sexby], *Killing, No Murder* (London, 1657).

Bell, Robert, ed., *Memorials of the Civil War: The Fairfax Correspondence* (London, 1849).

Bethel, Slingsby, *An Account of the French Usurpation upon the Trade of England* (London, 1679).

———, *The Interest of Princes and States* (London, 1680).

———, *The World's Mistake in Oliver Cromwell* (London, 1668), reprinted in *Harleian Miscellany*, vol 1 (London, 1808).

Britain's Glory: being a relation (London, 1660).

Britain's Triumphs (London, 1656).

Burton, Thomas, *Diary of Thomas Burton, Esq., Member in the Parliaments of Oliver and Richard Cromwell, from 1656 to 1659*, ed. John T. Rutt, 4 vols. (London, 1828).

Calendar of State Papers, Domestic Series, 1649-1660, ed. M. A. E. Green, 13 vols. (London, 1875-1886).

Calendar of State Papers and Manuscripts, Relating to English Affairs,

Existing in the Archives and Collections of Venice, and in Other Libraries of Northern Italy, ed. Allen B. Hinds et al., 38 vols. (London, 1864-1947).

Carlyle, Thomas, and S. C. Lomas, *The Letters and Speeches of Oliver Cromwell*, new ed., 3 vols. (London, 1904).

Carte, Thomas, ed., *A Collection of Original Letters and Papers, concerning the Affairs of England, from the Year 1641 to 1660*, 2 vols. (London, 1739).

Cheruel, Pierre, and D'Avenel, G., ed., *Lettres du Cardinal Mazarin pendant son ministere. Collection de documents inedits sur l'histoire de France*, 9 vols. (Paris, 1872-1906).

Cosnac, Jules de, *Souvenirs du regne de Louis XIV*, 8 vols. (Paris, 1866-1882).

Court Career, Death Shadowe'd (London, 1660).

Discourse of the National Excellancies of England, Stated (London, 1655).

Discourse upon the moderne affaires of Europe: The French Intrigues Discovered (London, 1681).

Dumont, Jean, *Corps universal diplomatique de droit des gens: depuis le regne de l'empereur Charlemagne jusquis a present: contenant un recueil de traitez*, vol. 6 (Amsterdam, 1738).

Estrades, Comte d', *Lettres, memoires et negociations de M. le Comte d'Estrades*, vol. 1 (Paris, 1743).

―――, *Relation inedite de la defense de Dunkerque (1651-1652)*, ed. Phillipe Tamizey de Larroque (Paris, 1872).

Fell, John, *The Interest of England Stated*, (London, 1659).

Firth, Sir Charles Harding, ed., *The Clarke Papers, Camden Society Publications*, 4 vols. (London, 1891-1901).

―――, *The Narrative of General Venables, Camden Society Publications* (London, 1900).

France no Friend to England (London, 1659).

French Intelligencer.

The French Politician Found Out (London, 1680).

Great Britain, Historical Manuscripts Commission, *Calendar of Manuscripts of His Grace the Duke of Portland*, 10 vols. (Norwich and London, 1891-1931).

―――, *Calendar of the Manuscripts of the Marquess of Ormonde*, (London, 1893, 1902).

―――, *Calendar of the Leyborne-Popham Manuscripts* (London, 1899).

―――, *Calendar of the Manuscripts of the Marquis of Bath*, 3 vols. (London, 1904-1908).

―――, *Fifth Report* (London, 1876); *Sixth Report* (London, 1877); *Eighth Report* (London, 1878); *Ninth Report* (London, 1883); *Twelfth Report* (London, 1891); *Thirteenth Report* (London, 1898); *Fifteenth Report* (London, 1903); *Eighteenth Report* (London, 1917).

―――, *Report on Manuscripts in Various Collections*, vol. 2 (London, 1903).

Hane, Joachim, *Journal*, ed. C. H. Firth (Oxford, 1896).

Harris, John, *Peace and Not Warre: or the Moderator* (London, 1659).

Hawke, Michael, *Killing is Murder and No Murder* (London, 1657).

Heath, J., *Discourse upon the moderne affaires of Europe* (The Hague, 1680).

———, *Flagellum, or the life and death, birth and Burial of Oliver Cromwell* (London, 1669).

Henrietta Maria, *Letters of Henrietta Maria*, ed. Mary A. E. Green (London, 1858).

Howell, J., *Discourse of Dunkirk, with some Reflexes upon the late surrender thereof* (London, 1664).

Hyde, Edward, Earl of Clarendon, *Calendar of State Papers*, ed. W. Dunn Macray and F. J. Routledge, vols. 2-4 (Oxford, 1889-1932).

———, *The History of the Rebellion and Civil Wars in England*, ed. W. Dunn Macray (Oxford, 1888).

———, *The History of the Reign of Charles II* (London, 1672).

An Impartial Character of that famous Politician and late admired Minister of State, Cardinal Mazarine (London, 1660).

James II, *Memoirs of James II: His Campaigns as Duke of York 1652-1660*, trans. A Lytton Sells (Bloomington, Ind., 1962).

Jenkinson, Charles, First Earl of Liverpool, *A Collection of all the treaties of peace, alliance, and commerce between Great Britain and other powers*, vol. 1 (London, 1875).

Journals of the House of Commons, August 1651 to March 1659 (London, 1813).

Jusserand, J. J., *Recueil des instructions donnees aux ambassadeurs et ministres de France depuis les traites de Westphalie jusqu'a la revolution francaise, Angleterre*, vol. 1 (Paris, 1929).

Ludlow, Edmund, *Memoirs*, ed. C. H. Firth, vol. 1 (Oxford, 1894).

MacWard, Robert, *The English Balance: Weighing the Reasons of England's Present Conjunction with France* (London, 1672).

Mercurius Politicus, 1650-1656.

Milton, John, *The Works of John Milton*, Columbia University Edition, 18 vols. (New York, 1931-1938).

Morland, Samuel, *The History of the Evangelical Churches of the Valleys of the Piedmont* (London, 1658).

Nedham, Marchmont, *The Case of the Commonwealth Stated* (London, 1650).

———, *Christianissimus Christianandous or the Reason for the Reduction of France to a more Christian State in Europe* (London, 1678).

Nicholas, Edward, *The Nicholas Papers: Correspondence of Sir Edward Nicholas*, ed. George F. Warner, 4 vols. Camden Society Publications (London, 1886-1920).

Nickolls, John, ed., *Original Letters and Papers of State Addressed to Oliver Cromwell; Concerning the Affairs of Great Britain, 1649-1658* (London, 1743).

Penn, Granville, ed., *The Memorials of the Professional Life and Times of Sir William Penn*, 2 vols. (London, 1833).

Powell, J. R., ed., *The Letters of Robert Blake*, Navy Records Society (London, 1937).

Priola, Benjamin, *The History of France under the Ministry of Cardinal Mazarin* (London, 1671).

Retz, Cardinal de *France No Friend to England* (London, 1659).

———, *Oeuvres de Cardinal de Retz* vol. 3, (Paris, 1873).

St. John, Oliver, *The Case of Oliver St. John, Esq., Concerning His Actions during the Late Troubles* (London, 1660).

Somers, John, ed., *A Collection of Scarce and Valuable Tracts*, 15 Vols. (London, 1748-1751).

Steele, Robert, ed., *Tudor and Stuart Proclamations*, vol. 1 (Oxford, 1910).

Thurloe, John, *A Collection of the State Papers of John Thurloe, Esq., Secretary, First to the Council of State, and afterwards to the Two Protectors, Oliver and Richard Cromwell*, ed. Thomas Birch, 7 vols. (London, 1742).

Vaughn, Robert, ed., *The Protectorate of Oliver Cromwell, and the State of Europe during the Early Part of the Reign of Louis XIV*, 2 vols. (London, 1838).

Whitelocke, Bulstrode, *A Journal of the Swedish Embassy in the Years 1653 and 1654*, ed. Henry Reeve, new ed., 2 vols. (London, 1855).

———, *Memorials of the English Affairs from the Beginning of the Reign of Charles the First to the Happy Restoration of King Charles the Second*, new ed., 4 vols. (Oxford, 1853).

Wright, I. A., ed., *Spanish Narratives of the English Attack on Santo Domingo 1655* (London 1926).

Secondary Sources

Unpublished Works

Battick, J. F., "Cromwell's Navy and the Foreign Policy of the Protectorate, 1653-1658," Ph.D. dissertation, Boston University, 1967.

Breslow, Marvin A., "English Puritan views of Foreign Nations, 1618-1640," Ph.D. dissertation, Harvard University, 1963.

Bruce, John, "Memoir on the Diplomatic History of Great Britain . . . from Original Documents preserved in his Majesty's State Papers Office," B.M. Add MSS 38779.

Foley, Michael F., "John Thurloe and the Foreign Policy of the Protectorate, 1654-1658," Ph.D. dissertation, University of Illinois, 1968.

Hoffman, Wilson J., "Mr. Secretary Thurloe: His Role in the Domestic Affairs of Oliver Cromwell's Protectorate," Ph.D. dissertation, Western Reserve University, 1963.

Lanyi, George A., "Oliver Cromwell and His Age: A Study in Nationalism," Ph.D. dissertation, Harvard University, 1949.

Smith, H. J. "The English Republic and the Fronde," B. Phil. Thesis, Oxford University, 1958.

Wentworth, M., "The Paradox of Cromwell's French Alliance," M.A. Thesis, University of California-Berkeley, 1950.

Books

Albion, Robert G., *Forests and Sea Power* (Cambridge, Mass., 1926).

Ashley, Maurice, *Cromwell's Generals* (London, 1954).

——, *Financial and Commercial Policy under the Cromwellian Protectorate* (Reprint) (London, 1962).

Bastide, Charles, *The Anglo-French Entente in the XVIIth Century* (London, 1914).

Bigby, Dorothy A., *Anglo-French Relations, 1641 to 1649* (London, 1933).

Bowman, Jacob N., *The Protestant Interest in Cromwell's Foreign Relations* (Heidelberg, 1900).

Brailsford, H. N., *The Levellers and the English Revolution* (London, 1961).

Breslow, Marvin Arthur, *A Mirror of England* (Cambridge, Mass., 1969).

Carte, Thomas, *A History of the Life of James Duke of Ormonde, from His Birth in 1610, to his Death in 1668*, 2 vols. (London, 1736).

Cheruel, Pierre-Adolphe, *Histoire de France pendant la minorite de Louis XIV*, 4 vols. (Paris, 1879-1880).

——, *Histoire de France sous le ministere de Mazarin*, 3 vols. (Paris, 1882).

Cooper, J. P., ed., *The New Cambridge Modern History*, vol. 4, *The Decline of Spain and the Thirty Years War* (Cambridge, 1970).

Corbett, Julian S., *England in the Mediterranean: A Study of the Rise and Influence of British Power within the Straits, 1603-1712*, 2 vols. (London, 1904).

Davies, Godfrey, *The Restoration of Charles II, 1658-1660* (San Marino, Calif., 1955).

Dictionary of National Biography, ed. Sir Leslie Stephen and Sir Sidney Lee, new ed., 22 vols. (London, 1922).

Doolin, Paul R., *The Fronde* (Cambridge, Mass., 1935).

Elliott, J. H., *Imperial Spain* (London, 1963).

Feiling, Keith, *British Foreign Policy, 1660-1672* (London, 1930).

Firth, Sir Charles Harding, *The Last Years of the Protectorate, 1656-1658*, 2 vols. (London, 1909).

——, *Oliver Cromwell and the Rule of the Puritans in England*, reprint (London, 1958).

Gardiner, Samuel Rawson, *History of the Commonwealth and Protectorate*, 4 vols. (London, 1903).

——, *History of the Great Civil War, 1642-1649*, 4 vols. (London, 1898-1901).

Geyl, Pieter, *The Netherlands in the Seventeenth Century, Part Two, 1648-1715* (London, 1964).

Guizot, Francois P. G., *History of Oliver Cromwell and the English Commonwealth*, trans. A. R. Scoble, 2 vols. (London, 1854).

———, *History of Richard Cromwell and the Restoration of Charles II*, trans. A. R. Scoble, 2 vols. (London, 1856).

Hardacre, Paul, *The Royalists during the Puritan Revolution* (The Hague, 1956).

Hill, Christopher, *God's Englishman* (New York, 1970).

———, *Intellectual Origins of the English Revolution* (Oxford, 1965).

———, *Oliver Cromwell* (London, 1958).

———, *Puritanism and Revolution* (London, 1958).

———, *Society and Puritanism in Pre-Revolutionary England* (London, 1964).

Hinton, R. K., *The Eastland Trade and the Common Weal in the Seventeenth Century* (Cambridge, 1959).

Jones, Guernsey, *The Diplomatic Relations Between Cromwell and Charles Gustavus X of Sweden* (Lincoln, Neb., 1897).

Jones, J. R., *Britain and Europe in the Seventeenth Century* (London, 1966).

Knachel, Philip A., *England and the Fronde: The Impact of the English Civil War and Revolution on France* (Ithaca, N. Y., 1967).

Lachs, Phyllis S., *The Diplomatic Corps under Charles II and James II* (New Brunswick, N. J., 1965).

Lynch, John, *Spain under the Habburgs*, vol 2 (London, 1970).

Lamont, William, *Godly Rule* (New York, 1969).

Maltby, William S., *The Black Legend in England* (Durham, N. C., 1971).

Parry, R. H., ed., *The English Civil War and After* (Berkeley and Los Angeles, 1970).

Paul, Robert S., *The Lord Protector: Religion and Politics in the Life of Oliver Cromwell* (London, 195).

Payn, F. W., *Cromwell on Foreign Affairs* (London, 1901).

Prestage, Edgar, *The Diplomatic Relations of Portugal with France, England, and Holland from 1640 to 1668* (Watford, 1925).

Ranke, Leopold von, *A History of England—Principally in the Seventeenth Century*, vol. 3 (Oxford, 1875).

Roots, Ivan, *The Great Rebellion, 1642-1660* (London, 1966).

Routledge, F. J., *England and the Treaty of the Pyrenees* (Liverpool, 1953).

Seeley, Sir John R., *The Growth of British Policy*, 2 vols., (Cambridge, 1895).

Taylor, S. A. G., *The Western Design* (London, 1969).

Trevor-Roper, H. R., *Religion, the Reformation, and Social Change* (London, 1967).

Underdown, David, *Royalist Conspiracy in England, 1649-1660* (New Haven, 1960).

Walzer, Michael, *The Revolution of the Saints* (Cambridge, Mass., 1965).

Wernham, R. B., *Before the Armada* (London, 1966).

Wilson, Charles, *Profit and Power: A Study of England and the Dutch Wars* (London, 1957).

———, *Queen Elizabeth and the Revolt of the Netherlands* (Berkeley and Los Angeles, 1970).

Wolf, John B., *Louis XIV* (New York, 1968).

Woolrych, A. H., *Penruddock's Rising* (London, 1655).

Zeller, Gaston, *Histoire des relations internationales, les temps modernes, de Christophe Colomb à Cromwell* (Paris, 1953).

Articles

Barbour, Violet, "Dutch and English Merchant Shipping in the Seventeenth Century," *Economic History Review*, 2 (1929-1930), 261-290.

Barker, Ernest, "Puritanism and Christianity and Nationalism," *Church, State, and Study* (London, 1930).

Beer, George L., "Cromwell's Economic Policy," *Political Science Quarterly*, 16 (1901), 582-611; 17 (1902), 46-70.

Catterall, Ralph C. H., "Anglo-Dutch Relations, 1654-1660," in *Annual Report American Historical Association* (1910), (Washington, D.C., 1912).

Cunningham, W., "The Imperialism of Cromwell," in *The Wisdom of the Wise: Three Lectures on Free Trade Imperialism* (Cambridge, 1906).

Davies, Godfrey, "English Political Sermons," *Huntington Library Quarterly*, 3 (1939), 1-22.

Drake, George, "The Ideology of Oliver Cromwell," *Church History*, 35, no. 3. (Sept., 1966), 259-272.

Firth, Sir Charles Harding, "Cromwell and the Insurrection of 1655," *English Historical Review*, 3 (1888), 313-350; 4 (1889), 313-338, 525-535.

———, "Cromwell's Instructions to Colonel Lockhart in 1656," *English Historical Review*, 21 (1906), 742-746.

———, "Royalist and Cromwellian Armies in Flanders, 1657-1661," *Transactions of the Royal Historical Society*, n.s. 17 (1903), 69-119.

———, "Secretary Thurloe on the Relations of England and Holland," *English Historical Review*, 21 (1906), 319-327.

———, "The Study of British Foreign Policy," *Quarterly Review*, 226 (1916), 472.

———, "Thomas Scot's Account of His Actions during the Commonwealth," *English Historical Review*, 12 (1897), 116-126.

Gardiner, Samuel Rawson, "Cromwell and Mazarin in 1652," *English Historical Review*, 11 (1896), 479-509.

Grose, Clyde L., "England and Dunkirk," *American Historical Review*, 39 (1933-34), 1-27.

Gunn, J. A. W., "Interest will not lie: 17 Century Political Maxim," *The Journal of the History of Ideas*, 29, 4 (October-December, 1968), 551-564.

Jusserand, J. J., "Le Marechal d'Estrades et ces critiques," *Revue historique*, 158 (1928), 225-254.

Kohn, Hans, "The Genesis and Character of English Nationalism," *Journal of the History of Ideas*, 1 (1939), 79-93.

Livet, G., "International Relations and the Role of France, 1648-1660," in *New Cambridge Modern History*, 4 (Cambridge, 1970), 411-434.

Lockhart, R. M. "Sir William Lockhart, the Ambassador the Commonwealth and Government of France," *Westminster Review,* 148-150.

Lui, Tai, "The Calling of the Barebones Parliament Reconsidered," *Journal of Ecclesiastical History*, 22, no. 3 (July, 1971), 223-236.

Oppenheim, M. "The Navy of the Commonwealth," *English Historical Review*, 11 (1896), 20-81.

Prestwich, Menna, "Diplomacy and Trade in the Protectorate," *Journal of Modern History*, 22 (1950), 103-121.

Quainton, G. E., "Colonel Lockhart and the Peace of the Pyrenees," *Pacific Historical Review*, 4 (1935), 267-280.

Roberts, Michael, "Cromwell and the Baltic," in *Essays in Swedish History* (London, 1967), pp. 138-194.

Routh, E. M. G., "Attempts to establish a balance of power in Europe in the second half of the seventeenth century," *Transactions of the Royal Historical Society*, new ser. 18 (1904).

Routledge, F. J., "Charles II and Cardinal de Retz," *Transactions of the Royal Historical Society*, 5th ser. 6 (1956).

Strong, Frank, "The Causes of Cromwell's West Indian Expedition," *American Historical Review*, 4 (1898-1899), 228-245.

Swaine, S. A., "The English acquisition and loss of Dunkirk," *Transactions of the Royal Historical Society*, 1 (1884), 93-118.

Turner, E. R., "Parliament and foreign affairs, 1603-1760," *English Historical Review*, 34 (1919), 172-197.

Woolrych, A. H., "The Calling of the Barebones Parliament," *English Historical Review*, 80 (1965), 492-513.

———, "The Good Old Cause and the Fall of the Protectorate," *Cambridge Historical Journal*, 13 (1957), 133-161.

Index

263